CARIBBEAN CRICKETERS
from the Pioneers to Packer

Clayton Goodwin

Foreword by Colin Cowdrey

Harrap London

First published in Great Britain 1980
by GEORGE G. HARRAP & CO. LTD
182 High Holborn, London WC1V 7AX

© *Clayton Goodwin* 1980

All rights reserved. No part of this
publication may be reproduced in any
form or by any means without the prior
permission of George G. Harrap & Co. Ltd

ISBN 0 245 53458 X (boards)
ISBN 0 245 53590 X (paper)

Designed by Michael R. Carter

Filmset by Woolaston Parker Ltd, Leicester
Printed in Great Britain by offset lithography by
Billing and Sons Ltd, Guildford, London and Worcester

Contents

	Foreword	v
	Preface	ix
1	The Pioneers	1
2	Learie Constantine	13
3	George Headley	24
4	Frank Worrell	37
5	Weekes and Walcott	46
6	Rae and Stollmeyer	56
7	Ramadhin and Valentine	64
8	The Fifties	74
9	Professional Captaincy	86
10	Gary Sobers	98
11	Rohan Kanhai	107
12	Wesley Hall	116
13	Lance Gibbs	126
14	The Sixties	134
15	Years of Transition	146
16	Batsmen of the Seventies	157
17	The Return of Speed	168
18	Fredericks and Greenidge	177
19	Viv Richards	186
20	The Packer and Prudential Age	193
21	Recollection and Reflection	202
22	Towards the Future	213
	Statistical Appendix	216
	Index of Names	253

Illustrations

Line map of Caribbean page xii

Between pages 68 and 69

Nursery of Talent

Woods and Cumberbatch
Learie Constantine

1928 Team

George Headley

Clyde Walcott
Everton Weekes

Frank Worrell

Sonny Ramadhin
Alfred Valentine

Gary Sobers

Between pages 180 and 181

West Indian Spectators

Wesley Hall
Andy Roberts
Joel Garner

Michael Holding

Rohan Kanhai
Roy Fredericks

Clive Lloyd
Alvin Kallicharran

Viv Richards

Gordon Greenidge

Prudential Cup Winners

Foreword
by COLIN COWDREY

Clayton Goodwin has sought to trace the course of West Indian cricket from the early days, highlighting the special matches and spending time with all those personalities who have made a contribution to the game's development in that part of the world. Skilfully, he has succeeded in making it so much more than a catalogue of people and events. It is a highly entertaining story too—most perceptive, and providing much that will be new to most people.

In terms of date of publication he has timed it to perfection. For West Indies come to England in 1980, on top of the world, proven champions in Australia. At this moment of time they are more talented than any other side.

For me it has been an endless fascination wondering why those enchanting islands of the Caribbean have nurtured so many brilliant cricketers. Of course, under the warmth of a hot sun, day after day, we all feel younger and fitter. But the West Indian has the greater degree of suppleness, and, I suspect, a sharper eye, in the bright light. By nature, they bring a less studied approach, never happier than when throwing themselves into the fray with a glorious abandon. In adversity gloom can set in, yet even then never far away lies that infectious sense of fun and the captivating smile.

I have had the privilege of visiting the West Indies twice as an England cricketer with MCC teams and on several private cricket tours. They are the jewel of the cricket world. Every cricketer yearns to play in the West Indies and I have not met anyone who has come home disappointed.

Caribbean Cricketers

I have enjoyed Clayton Goodwin's account tracing the gradual development, especially as I have been given the opportunity of coming to know most of the leading figures—George Challenor apart, for he had died before I started. The Challenor Stand at the Kensington Oval has watched over the emergence of a unique succession of outstanding cricketers, for he was the first of the long line. But he was much more than that, of course, for it was his enthusiasm and example which contributed more than anyone else's to establishing cricket as a game for West Indians to take to their hearts. The explosive magnetism of that all-round genius Learie Constantine was to follow later, and the fast-bowling pair of Martindale and Herman Griffith. The remarkable skill of George Headley demonstrated—if indeed proof were needed—that it was just a matter of time and opportunity before a West Indies team might beat the best in a Test series away from home. Even so, no one could have anticipated that John Goddard's first team to England would have such a powerful triumvirate in the 'three W's', which ensured that the new-found spin twins of Ramadhin and Valentine were backed up by such formidable totals.

I did not meet them until some seven years later, but by that time some young and promising fast bowlers were making their mark—Gilchrist, Hall, Charlie Griffith and Watson. And so began two decades of 'pace like fire', for as these stalwarts tired Roberts, Holding, Garner and Croft have taken their place.

The leadership of Sir Frank Worrell in the sixties set the West Indians new horizons, and they are extraordinarily fortunate to have found Sir Garfield Sobers to take up the reins from Sir Frank, to be succeeded in turn by Clive Lloyd. Each has been a batsman of the highest pedigree, and a calm, shrewd leader, too.

There have been so many great names, wonderful cricketers and warm friends, that I have to mention a few for whom I have had especial admiration.

In my memory their best openers were Rae and Stollmeyer, both of whom are playing an invaluable administrative role in cricket's affairs today—and a special thought for Gerry Gomez. Having said that, I have particular memories of Conrad Hunte and Gordon Greenidge, supreme in different eras. Who will forget the charm of Collie Smith, who died prematurely and might have played as long as Sobers? No one could play with more panache than Rohan Kanhai, particularly in later years. Two Cambridge blues, Gerry

Foreword

Alexander and Deryck Murray, have had a monopoly behind the stumps and have proved themselves in the heat of battle. In Lance Gibbs the West Indies were lucky enough to unearth one of the best off-spinners there has ever been.

Those who saw him in his prime will say there will never be a better batsman to come out of the Caribbean than George Headley. I used to say the same thing about each of Walcott, Weekes and Worrell (I could argue a case for them all) until I saw Sobers. But then came Lloyd and, to cap it all, Vivian Richards, currently the best batsman in the world.

I just cannot believe my good fortune that I played alongside them—mostly against them, but sometimes with them. Whenever I see them in action it is not long before my mind wanders to those islands of their birth, surrounded by a warm sea and basking under cloudless skies. I picture cricket being played, Test Matches at Queen's Park or Kensington, Bourda or Sabina, cricket in the smaller islands—St Lucia and Antigua, Grenada, St Vincent—and many more. So many games of cricket on the savannah in Port of Spain, cricket on every cane clearing in Barbados, by the side of the road and on the beach everywhere. A primitive bat, any old ball, an uncertain pitch and, in Lord Harris's words, 'the classroom, God's air and sunshine'. Cricket from the West Indies, may it thrive a thousand years!

Preface

West Indian cricket is known throughout the world. Its players are household names, and this has been so for as long as anyone alive can remember. Sport in the Caribbean has a natural blend of excitement, skill and temperament, but it has been documented less than that in almost any other country.

Part of the reason is the approach of the West Indian players, and of the crowds themselves. The Caribbean attitude is consistently in tune with the requirements of the present. A flashing boundary and a sharp delivery is relished more than the statistical relevance of a tactical situation. A West Indian cricketer is only as good as his last match, and even that is often forgotten in the anticipation of present promise.

The manner in which the game developed in the islands has also not been conducive to the preparation of a comprehensive record. Until only a few years ago the principal loyalties were to the individual territory rather than to the West Indies, in spite of the need for regional unity in undertaking overseas tours and in playing against visiting teams. Apart from the cricket context, there is no such thing as a West Indian. Fans are nevertheless well aware of their former heroes, even if they do not keep talking about them or comparing them to the current side, in the manner of English supporters. In a sense they know them better, and in a more personal way. Old cricketers have their own place in the community, and are not mere names in the record books or known only to the specialist few.

There is no West Indian press as such. Each territory has its own newspapers, which concentrate on the achievements of the local heroes. Even Englishmen are aware of a certain regional feeling if more of the Test team are drawn from Surrey than Yorkshire, or vice versa, and that is in a country having newspapers with national distribution. There is no similar agency in the Caribbean to stimulate more than an insular conception of the sporting past.

Many books have been written already about West Indian cricketers, especially biographies of individuals with unusual talent. The outstanding player has been recognized as standing out from his environment. Other books have recorded in isolation the events of a particular tour or series. Former players have committed their thoughts and recollections to print, and these men are even more interesting outside the restricted conventions of writing, and where there is less need for brevity. Wives and children are also keen to promote their own memories and observations, and their detached view highlights incidents which may escape the professional historian.

This fragmented information has comprised the sole generally available record of West Indian cricket until the present decade. There was no overall pattern, no H. S. Altham or Johnny Moyes to bring the scattered threads together, but that approach is no longer enough. Whatever the political or social situation, the West Indies are an entity in world competition. As cricketers, they do have a distinctive style and their own history. The increase in the number of international matches, and the development of a professional career in county, commercial or League cricket, puts greater emphasis on identification as a West Indian than on being a native of any component territory.

For these reasons there have been more attempts of late to explain the origins and achievements of Caribbean cricket. The resulting books have filled an urgent need, yet events are moving so quickly that something more detailed is now required. *Caribbean Cricketers* sets out to define the comprehensive history of West Indian cricket, illustrated through the careers of the players themselves, and set in the relevant international context. Everyone who has played for the West Indies at the highest level is mentioned. For the days before official international competition, chief attention is given to games played by and against touring sides. The importance of the latter was to be superseded by the introduction of Test Matches, and every cricketer who has played for the West Indies in a Test Match is

Preface

included, usually in the text but invariably in the statistical appendix. There are also detailed references to those West Indians who made their career in the English county game, to their contemporaries overseas, and in passing to women's cricket. Such concentration leaves no room for unnecessary comment or controversy.

In addition to my own observations, I am indebted to reliable comment in newspapers and books, and to the helpful memories of players, their families and spectators. In particular, I have found great value in the writings of Sir Pelham Warner, Tony Cozier, 'Strebor' Roberts, Jack Anderson, C. L. R. James, Gordon Ross, Alan Ross, G. D. Martineau, Jack Fingleton, Johnny Moyes, Jim Swanton, Bruce Harris and S. Canynge Caple. *Wisden* has been invaluable for cross-checking facts and for correcting faults in my recollection.

This book is more than a reference to settle disputes and refresh memories, though hopefully it does that as well: it provides a comprehensive record, illustrated by the occasional anecdote, of Caribbean cricket from its earliest days to its present state. So much has happened between the time of the pioneers and the advent of Kerry Packer. Contemporary West Indian cricket has even less in common with the world of Aucher Warner than has present English first-class administration with that of his brother Pelham. Events have moved that much further and faster in the Caribbean, and not only in cricket. Nevertheless, while the outward appearance may be different, the soul is the same. Only the West Indians have the personality to remind the rest of us of what cricket was really like in its golden age, when the game was played for enjoyment: in their attitudes Gordon Greenidge and Viv Richards are the real descendants of the Edwardian batting aristocrats.

My thanks are due to many people in the planning, research and writing of this book—to the late Sir Frank Worrell for his initial inspiration, to Mr Colin Cowdrey for his kindness in writing a foreword, to my various editors for their encouragement, to my family and publishers for their understanding, to Miss Judith Fox for the drawing of the Caribbean, and to my wife for typing copy and deciphering my notes (even though she does not understand the game). Above all, I thank the cricketers themselves, without whose deeds on the field of play this book would not have been possible.

December 1979   C. J. G.

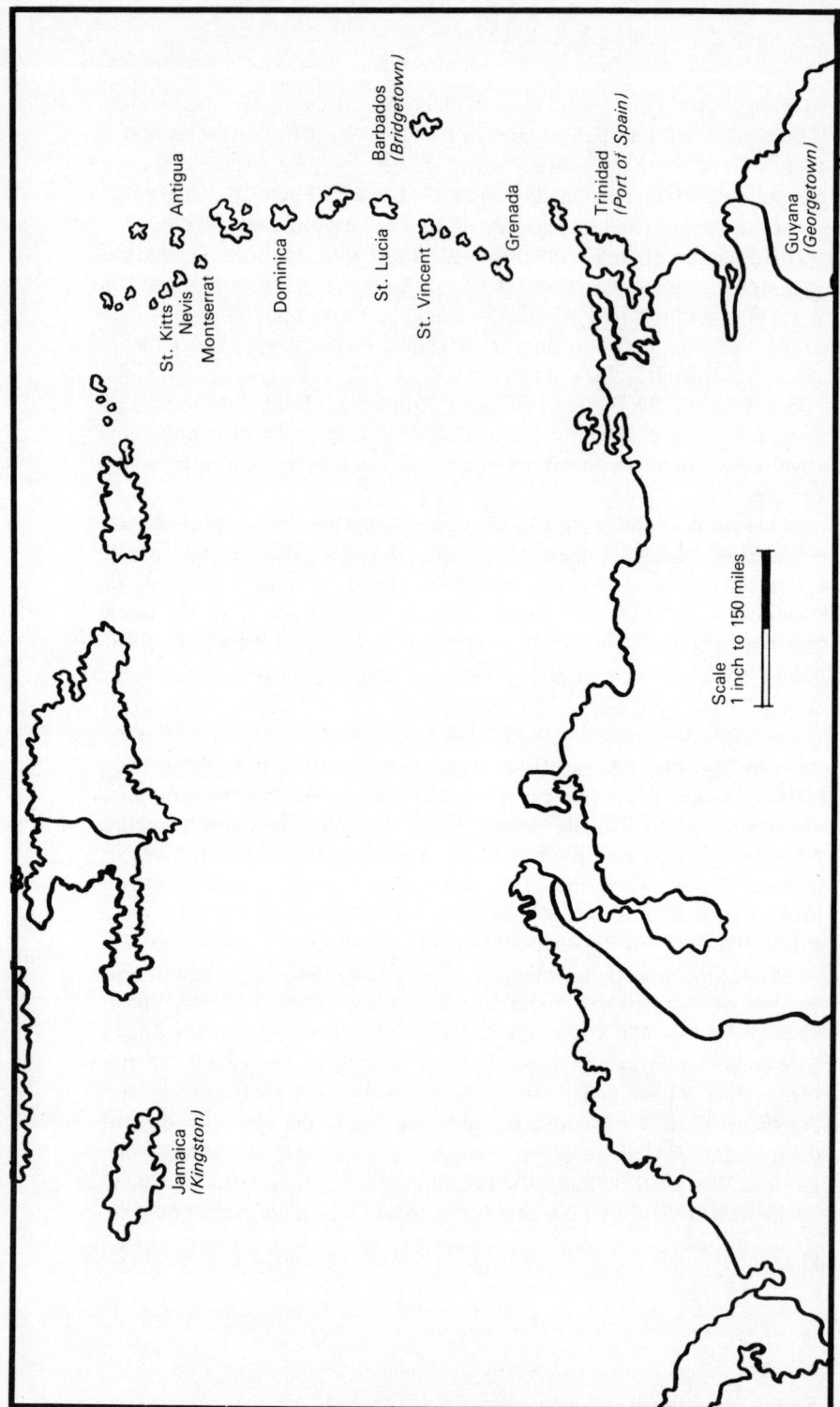

The Caribbean: the cricketing countries. *Bracketed names indicate Test venues*

CHAPTER ONE
The Pioneers

The distinctive character of West Indian cricket was not blended overnight. The scintillating stroke-play, the superlative fielding and the awe-inspiring fast bowling which have given it an individual flavour have been there in essence since the beginning. Yet these basic ingredients have had to be tempered with years of disappointment, frustration and the occasional bursts of indiscretion, and to be compounded with an irresistible will to win.

The first West Indian team toured England in 1900, when Queen Victoria was still alive, the Boer War was in progress, and the almost legendary Dr W. G. Grace was the game's outstanding personality. The tourists were outclassed, but gained much in experience. The same thing happened twenty-eight years later when they achieved official Test Match status. West Indian cricket has come a long way since then. The party of wide-eyed innocents abroad whose limitations were exposed so cruelly in those early days have become the most professional side in the world. The West Indies have proved their international superiority again only recently, in both the commercial and the conventional codes of cricket. Learning their skills at the grass-roots level of home-made bat and ball on the seashore or in the backyard, the West Indians have taken the Caribbean brand of the game triumphantly to England's industrial cities, the surf beaches of Australia, New Zealand's provincial grounds, and the many venues and pitches of India and Pakistan.

Each age has had its own representative heroes. In the early days George Headley symbolized the struggle for parity, when even the wickets and the climate seemed to be against them. Fast bowlers

Caribbean Cricketers

George Francis, Learie Constantine, Herman Griffith and Manny Martindale defied the elements and the batsmen of the established cricketing countries to take them anything but seriously. The great flowering of individual talent in the late 1940s and early 1950s gave rise to Frank Worrell's exquisite artistry, Everton Weekes's savage efficiency, the muscular power of Clyde Walcott, and the complementary first-wicket matching of Jeff Stollmeyer's gracefulness with Allan Rae's watchful defence. Sonny Ramadhin and Alfred Valentine brought their own natural talent to the bowling.

Gary Sobers, the complete all-rounder, heralded and typified the professional precision of the 1960s. Conrad Hunte was a sound technician, Rohan Kanhai matured into a master executioner of the opposing bowling and Basil Butcher allowed little scope for mistake. Pacemen Wesley Hall and Charlie Griffith wedded psychology to bowling ability, and off-spinner Lance Gibbs struck with the accuracy and certainty of a cobra. Clive Lloyd's side of the past decade brought together all the various strands of ability into a team whose names alone are bywords for all that is best in international cricket—Roy Fredericks hooking with erratic assurance, Gordon Greenidge's flashing bat, Viv Richards the unbowlable, Lloyd's feline talent for transforming almost any situation into victory, Alvin Kallicharran's cool composure under fire, the enigmatic genius of Lawrence Rowe, Deryck Murray's outstanding work behind the stumps, the combined thunderbolts and deadly grace of Andy Roberts, Michael Holding and Colin Croft, and Vanburn Holder's accurate persistence.

The roots of this achievement go back a very long way.

Club cricket had been established in the main territories of the Caribbean by the early years of the nineteenth century, or, if Mr Jingle of the *Pickwick Papers* is to be believed, perhaps considerably longer. Its overall popularity was stimulated by the increased military and commercial travel during and immediately after the Napoleonic wars, and the standard of play was not all that far behind its contemporary development in England. Competition between the West Indian territories was more difficult, due to the considerable time and inconvenience involved in crossing such extensive distances in those days before air travel. Barbados played Guyana in 1865, but though neighbouring Trinidad joined in shortly afterwards, as well as some of the smaller Windward and Leeward Islands, far-away Jamaica was isolated for another thirty-one years. In such cir-

The Pioneers

cumstances it was impossible for Caribbean cricket to develop a corporate identity.

Individual players achieved greater recognition overseas. Sam Morris, a Jamaican all-rounder, represented Australia against England in a Test Match in 1884, and he is said to have been a useful batsman, bowler and wicket-keeper without mastering any single art. Several West Indians, including Peter Jackson, the famous heavyweight boxer, made their homes in Australia at this time. Five years later G. Elliott scored 117 not out, the first century by a West Indian in England, in club competition against Tufnell Park. Commonwealth cricketers have been an integral part of the English sporting scene from such an early time. At home E. F. Wright made the first recorded inter-territorial hundred in the Caribbean with 123 for Guyana against Trinidad in 1882, and Harold Austin (who was later knighted) and G. B. Y. Cox of Barbados put on the first double-century stand at Trinidad's expense in 1897/98. A definite pattern was beginning to take shape.

International contests were initiated with a tour to Canada and the United States in 1886. It was just as well that the matches were not first-class, because when the Americans returned the visit just over a year later they routed a combined West Indian side for only 19 runs. The Philadelphians, the leading exponents of swing and swerve bowling, were much better players than is often realized, and they came to Jamaica as late as 1909 with H. V. Hordern, the great Australian googly bowler and dentist, in their party. The visits of various amateur sides in the closing decade of the century developed the link with English cricket. R. Slade Lucas led the first expedition in 1895, and there were two teams the following year, captained respectively by Lord Hawke and Arthur Priestley. The latter's otherwise modest side included the England opening batsman and captain A. E. Stoddart, who was the most famous cricketer to play in the Caribbean until that time, Sammy Woods and R. C. N. Palairet. Hawke's side had the better overall record, but were defeated twice by Trinidad. The horizons of world cricket were expanding rapidly following Australia's unexpected victory over England in 1882. Although social and business considerations prevented most of the leading players from leaving home, those enthusiastic amateurs who did go encouraged the embryonic game throughout the Commonwealth, and their styles were emulated by all who played against them or watched them.

Caribbean Cricketers

Aucher Warner brought the first team to England in 1900, but the matches are not now regarded as first-class. Although no representative games had been arranged, the West Indians were still hard put to beat any but the weakest county sides. Their initial programme was over-ambitious at a time when England was well established in its own 'Golden Age'. W. G. Grace set the tone of the summer by leading London County to victory by an innings and almost 200 runs in the opening engagement. The 52-year-old veteran scored 71 and took 5 wickets for 52 in the second innings. Later in the season Gilbert Jessop, one of history's greatest hitters, slammed 157 in an hour against them for Gloucestershire, and the West Indians fell about laughing at the ease with which he despatched their bowling to the boundary so frequently. The visitors contributed to their own discomfort that year by their understandable immaturity, especially in respect of running between the wickets. They learned quickly, and were able to hold their own before they went home. The team members were excellent ambassadors, who were popular wherever they played.

Charles Augustus Ollivierre from hitherto unfashionable Saint Vincent was the tour's outstanding batsman. He scored 883 runs for an average of 32·7 and the aggregate might well have been much higher if he had been assured of any support. Even so his overall average was only two runs less than that of the great Victor Trumper in England the previous year. Ollivierre played two particularly important innings. He scored 159 in a first-wicket partnership of 238 runs with Pelham Warner against Leicestershire, in which the tourists won comfortably by an innings, and later he made 94 out of the 208 runs put on with P. J. Cox against Surrey at the Oval. The county side included Tom Richardson, the world's top fast bowler of the 1890s.

Derbyshire invited Ollivierre to stay on after the tour to play for them in the county championship. In accepting he became the first of the many compatriots who have since made their professional home in England. In 1906 he emphasized his value by scoring 64 not out in helping his new county to defeat the next West Indian visiting team by 6 wickets. Although Ollivierre had made 167 against Warwickshire in his first season with Derbyshire, his greatest contribution was in the remarkable match against Essex at Chesterfield in 1904. P. A. Perrin, who could have played for England if his fielding ability had matched his batting, hit a record 68 boundaries in scoring 343 not out in the southern county's total of 597. The West Indian retaliated with 229

The Pioneers

in Derbyshire's 548 runs reply. Essex collapsed in their second innings, and were bowled out for 97. Ollivierre made another 92 not out as his side won from behind by 9 wickets. It was an unprecedented come-back after facing such a large score in the first innings of a three-day county match. Three years later Ollivierre retired from the first-class game through eye trouble. He played club cricket regularly in Yorkshire, where he lived in later life, and for sixteen years until the outbreak of the Second World War he coached schoolboys in the Netherlands. Even if nothing else had been achieved, his participation and development made the first West Indian tour worth while, and put Caribbean cricket on the map.

Aucher Warner, the captain from Trinidad, had little opportunity to perform with either the bat or the ball. He suffered ill-health for much of the summer, and handed over the captaincy to S. W. Sproston after a bout of malaria. Warner's place in history is certain, and a talent for cricket ran in his family. His brother, Pelham Warner, who had settled in England since coming to university, toured the Caribbean with Lord Hawke's party in 1896/97, and made his Test Match debut for his adopted country against South Africa two years later. At about this time the England team contained several other players born overseas, including Billy Murdoch and Jack Ferris of Australia and India's Prince Ranjitsinhji. Pelham Warner scored 113 against Leicestershire in his only game for the tourists in 1900. He led England to victory in Australia in 1903/4, and captained Middlesex successfully in the county championship. When his playing days were over Pelham served cricket even better as an administrator, for which he was knighted, and became associated with the *crème de la crème* of the game's Establishment. In particular he kept open the lines of communication to Lord's during the war years, and was instrumental in founding the *Cricketer* magazine.

In many ways the first touring team was not representative of Caribbean standards. Too many of the leading players were not available for selection. Harold Austin, allegedly the best batsman in the hemisphere, was fighting in the Boer War, and several bowlers—who derived generally from the less affluent parts of the community—could not take the time away from their work. Cox, who was second to Ollivierre in aggregate, included a memorable 142 against Surrey in his 755 runs. Percy Goodman did not fully live up to his reputation in spite of an undefeated century in the drawn game against Derbyshire. Lebrun Constantine scored 113 against the MCC, the nearest to a representative match, and kept wicket. The bowling was even less effective than the batting. In the absence of Cumberbatch, who had performed so well at home against visiting teams, too much depended on Woods and Burton. They responded well enough by taking 72 and 78 wickets respectively at an almost identical average of 21·5 runs. Nobody else managed more than thirty. These two bowlers had significant roles in each of the principal victories. They took 15 wickets between them against the Minor Counties at Northampton, the first West Indian win in England. Woods returned 5 wickets for 39 and Burton 4 wickets for 39 in skittling Leicestershire for a meagre 80 runs. The former took 7 wickets for 48 in an innings against Surrey, and the latter put out lowly Norfolk for only 32 runs with 8 wickets for 9.

After the maturing experience of visits by two more amateur English sides the second West Indian touring team in 1906 had greater all-round strength, even if it was not reflected immediately in the results. As a tribute to the tourists' popularity the two sporting autocrats, W. G. Grace and Lord Harris, were recalled from retirement to play against them. Harold Austin of Barbados led a nucleus of proven batting which included Constantine and Goodman from the previous visit. Newcomers Oliver Layne, Sidney Smith and George Challenor, as well as the captain himself, were already established on their own pitches. The bowling showed greater balance and improvement with R. C. Ollivierre, the brother of the earlier tourist, and all-rounder Smith most prominent. The greatest single weaknesses were the lack of a specialist wicket-keeper, now that Constantine had given up the gloves, and an inadequate technique for English conditions. Even so the counties paid them the compliment of selecting more of their front-line players than hitherto.

Sidney Gordon Smith of Trinidad dominated the batting and bowling in exceeding Ollivierre's achievements. His standard of performance has been equalled subsequently by only Learie Constantine and Gary Sobers. The left-handed Smith had first attracted attention by taking 16 wickets for 85 in the match against R. A. Bennett's side in 1902, and two years later he impressed in his island's victory by 5 wickets over Lord Brackley's team. In 1906 he scored 1107 runs and took 116 wickets, a fine double. His best innings were 100 against Hampshire at Southampton and 140 not out against South Wales at Cardiff. In the latter game Smith also

The Pioneers

routed the Welshmen for 122 runs with 5 wickets for 28, which led to a massive win by almost 300 runs. In the final fixture of the tour he took 12 wickets for 99 against Northamptonshire, who regarded his performance so highly that they asked him to play for them.

The county had been raised to first-class status only the year before, and Smith's example brought about such an immediate improvement that he was appointed captain shortly afterwards. Under his leadership Northamptonshire came second in the championship in 1912, an achievement which they have not bettered in the seventy years since then. The Trinidadian played several times for the Gentlemen against the Players at Lord's, which in an era of restricted international competition was equivalent to many Test Matches in our own time, and he returned to the Caribbean as a member of A. F. Somerset's touring party. He was chosen by Wisden as a 'cricketer of the year' for his performances in 1914. When war brought cricket to a halt almost everywhere Smith had been at his peak for almost a decade. On the resumption of peace he played for Auckland in New Zealand and represented that fledgling country against visiting English and Australian sides. His efforts went a long way towards achieving Test Match recognition for New Zealand in the late 1920s, by which time his own career was effectively over. Few other players, if any, have done as much to raise the standard of the game in three continents.

Although Lebrun Constantine did not reach a hundred in any one innings he made a thousand runs for the tour with 92 against Leicestershire and other half-centuries against Yorkshire, South Wales and London County. He was considered a possible candidate for a third tour in 1923, even though almost fifty years old, but his son did more than enough to maintain the family's reputation. Layne, who finished third in the bowling, fell away as a batsman after scoring a century against Essex in the first county game, and Goodman, who made a hundred in the historic win over Yorkshire, saved his best innings for the concluding match against Northamptonshire.

George Challenor, a teenager who finished just behind Smith and Constantine in aggregate, was the best young batsman. He improved considerably as the tour progressed. The young Barbadian scored 108 in a rain-affected match against Nottinghamshire, one of the most powerful sides in the country, and hit an entertaining 90 against

Scotland. He filled the vacancy left by Ollivierre, and his next visit was awaited with special interest. In the event he had to wait another seventeen years, but what he did then made all the waiting very much worth while.

The victory over Yorkshire by 262 runs at Harrogate was the highlight of the season. The county, which had beaten the famous 1902 Australians by bowling them out for 23, seemed almost invincible in English domestic cricket. The West Indians batted competently on the first day without any hint of the drama which was to come. Then R. C. Ollivierre and Smith bowling unchanged scuttled Yorkshire for only 50 runs, with the former taking 7 wickets for 23. The touring captain did not enforce the follow-on to keep his bowlers fresh for the second assault. David Denton scored 112 in a commendable fight-back, but the West Indians would not be denied the triumph which was within their grasp.

The First World War disrupted the development of West Indian cricket more than it did in any other country. England resumed their county-championship programme the summer after the armistice, and the Australian Imperial Forces' side was the forerunner of Warwick Armstrong's irresistible team in the early 1920s. On the other hand, the West Indians had to wait a whole generation between their second and third tours. With very little action at home to help him in the selection Harold Austin had to start again almost from scratch. Apart from Challenor and himself, all the members of the 1923 side were new to England. The tourists made up for any shortcomings in their batting by energetic fast bowling and lively fielding. They showed their potential in defeating Sussex by 26 runs in the second match of their schedule, and in surprising Surrey by ten wickets when Challenor set the pace with 155 not out and George Francis took 5 wickets in routing the county for 87 runs.

George Challenor was the success of the summer. He realized the full promise of his youth, and in fact had come into the tour on a record-breaking sequence in which he had become the first West Indian to score a double century and century in the same match. By making 1895 runs, including eight hundreds, in an entertaining manner the Barbadian became known as the best visiting batsman between Victor Trumper and Donald Bradman. In terms of charisma and national identification he ranked with Jack Hobbs (England), Charlie Macartney (Australia) and Herbie Taylor (South Africa) among his contemporaries. After a series of useful scores Challenor

The Pioneers

made his first century in the tightly fought game against Oxford University in which the West Indians came back to win by 2 wickets. The following fixture against Essex was equally close, with Challenor's 101 swaying the balance in a narrow victory by 3 wickets. Thereafter he reached a degree of consistency which was rarely shaken, and, like Trumper before him, he achieved these feats without recourse to any mammoth innings just for the sake of scoring runs. Against Nottinghamshire he shared an unbroken partnership of 219 with Tarilton which almost brought about an unexpected victory.

Shortly afterwards he carried his bat for 111 against Gloucestershire in a prelude to his most prolific period of the entire season. In addition to his undefeated hundred in the first innings against Surrey, Challenor made another 66 not out in knocking off the winning runs. He followed with a lone 110 amid defeat at Cardiff, and scored 79 in the convincing victory over Somerset. His value to the side could hardly be overstated. As he continued this success with 124 for Barbados against the next MCC touring side Challenor's batting was one of the most important factors in achieving Test Match recognition.

The support batting was disappointing. Tarilton, the first West Indian to score a triple century in first-class cricket, made 109 not out on a featherbed pitch at Nottingham, but generally he and the left-handed Harry Ince could not produce their excellent home form. Fernandes had a sound innings of 110 against Leicestershire and little else, while the underrated and consistent Joe Small was second in the run aggregates. Austin, who was nearing fifty years of age, played more for his expertise than for any expectations with the bat. He was far from well, and often handed over the captaincy to Karl Nunes.

Fast bowlers George John, a Trinidad stalwart of several years, and newcomer George Francis ripped through the English county batting, which was just recovering from similar humiliation by Australia's Ted McDonald and Jack Gregory in 1921. Francis took 96 wickets at 15·32 runs each, and his partner had 90 wickets at 14·68. Francis produced the more spectacular innings analyses with 10 wickets in the match against Sussex and 6 wickets for 34 in an innings against Middlesex, as well as spearheading the successful bowling blitz against Surrey and H. D. G. Leveson-Gower's XI, but John, who had the better reputation at the time, matched him in deed and effect. He was unfortunate in that his best years coincided with the international cricketing lull immediately after the war. Cyril 'Snuffy'

Browne, the third string in the seam attack and a vigorous lower-order batsman, took 91 wickets, including 6 wickets for 66 against Somerset and 4 wickets for 41 in the defeat of Surrey. Victor Pascall, who dismissed 77 opponents, was the only slow bowler to compete with this battery of pace. His nephew, Learie Constantine, showed precocious all-round skill and exuberance. In spite of his limited opportunities, especially in bowling, the youngster displayed the enthusiasm which distinguished his later career, and his fielding at cover-point was exemplary in even this very good fielding side. Constantine took 48 wickets as first or second change bowler and played two noteworthy innings in his own highly personalized style. He scored 77 against Oxford University, and 60 out of a 97 runs total in the rain-ruined draw with Derbyshire.

The final moments of the last match of the season against H. D. G. Leveson-Gower's XI at Scarborough have become one of cricket's legends. The selectors did not patronize the tourists by choosing a weakened side. The powerful batting (which included Jack Hobbs, Ernest Tyldesley, Percy Chapman, Johnny Douglas, Wilfred Rhodes and Percy Fender) needed to score only 28 runs in their second innings to win. Francis dismissed Hobbs almost immediately as he and John attacked with such fury and accuracy that 6 wickets were down for only 19 runs. It seemed that the form-book might be turned upside down, but the Englishmen edged home by 4 wickets. They did not forget that fright easily. Francis took 4 wickets for 12 in a session of play which more than any other made the public and administrators take notice of West Indian cricket.

In 1925/26 Freddie Calthorpe brought out the strongest English team to date to tour the Caribbean. Their purpose was to test whether or not the West Indians were ready yet for official Test Matches. The party included Walter Hammond and Percy Holmes, both of whom made double centuries; Lionel Tennyson, a previous captain of England who had stood up to the Australian fast bowlers with a broken arm; all-rounders Ewart Astill and Roy Kilner; and fast bowler Fred Root. Even the bad weather which hampered most of the games could not take away from the importance of the occasion.

The tourists were unlucky not to win the first representative match at Bridgetown. Hammond, who scored 238, led the way to a commanding first-innings total of 597–8 dec. In spite of both opening batsmen, Challenor and Tarilton, reaching 50 the home side had to follow on 450 runs behind. Root followed his first-innings 4

The Pioneers

wickets for 37 with another 4 wickets for 9 as the batsmen plunged to 21–6. The rain which caused the conditions to deteriorate throughout the game relented at last and washed out all further play. All the same, the West Indians could not have been too happy about their ability to perform well against high-quality fast bowling.

The second representative match at Port of Spain lacked outstanding personal achievement and was determined more on mistakes than merits. The West Indians began badly in losing Challenor before he had scored. His partner, George Dewhurst, steadied the innings, but the best batting came from 'Snuffy' Browne in partnership with veteran Harold Austin. The MCC gained a narrow lead by virtue of their more consistent batting. Austin scored 69 as his team struggled to keep their opponents at bay. Though losing some early wickets, the tourists won comfortably with only five men out.

The West Indians learned from this experience, and staged a fighting recovery at Georgetown. Challenor and Dewhurst got away well with over a hundred for the first wicket. After Wilton St Hill had built on their sound start Browne—who suffered an injury to his head—hit an undefeated century in a substantial stand with Claude Wight. The Englishmen had to follow on 198 runs behind. With 6 further wickets going down for 96, Tennyson held the side together with 57 not out until rain flooded the ground. Honours had been more or less shared over the three-match series.

The depth of talent in each of the main territories was even more encouraging than the performances in the representative games. The tour opened with some outstanding fast bowling by George Francis and Herman Griffith in Barbados. With 9 wickets each they overwhelmed the MCC for scores of 151 and 65 in winning by 73 runs. It was the only defeat the tourists suffered. Francis took another 7 wickets in the first innings of the drawn second match against Barbados, which the island came very close to winning. Challenor had already made a hundred to show that there was nothing wrong with the conditions.

The two encounters with Trinidad were both drawn. Walter Hammond's bowling was quite devastating on each occasion. His batting triumphs in the next decade have obscured the memory of the all-round success of his younger years. Although the home bowlers drew little life from the matting wickets, the batsmen fared much better, with Wilton St Hill and Cipriani hitting hundreds. The former was very much a folk hero. Learie Constantine has told the story of young Wilton arriving for an important club match with all the appearance of a casual country boy and then knocking the great George John out of sight. Perhaps he was too much of an individual to succeed in the higher reaches of the game. The fixtures in Guyana—or British Guiana, as it was then known—were ruined for competitive interest by excessively high scoring. Maurice Fernandes scored 120 after another century by Hammond.

Jamaica, which was then almost cut off from the other cricket centres in the Eastern Caribbean, was given three matches to make up for the absence of any representative fixture. The first game was the most interesting. Jamaica had the better of the initial exchanges with some sound batting by Frank Martin, E. A. Rae and Morales. A sudden collapse against Kilner (who took 7 wickets) let the MCC back into the game, and with Holmes scoring his second half-century of the match the visitors won by 5 wickets, after being 96 runs behind on the first innings. The other two games were drawn, with some very high scoring. Karl Nunes, the most successful Jamaican batsman and the future West Indian captain, made 140 not out. Percy Holmes, who scored 224, and Astill closed the tour with a stand of 330 runs.

The West Indies were granted Test Match standing along with India and New Zealand, and they commenced the next chapter of their development with a series against England in 1928. Caribbean cricket had already made great strides forward since Aucher Warner's tentative enterprise. Charles Ollivierre, Pelham Warner, Sidney Smith, George Challenor, the two Constantines, George Francis, George John and 'Snuffy' Browne had a pedigree comparable to that of any other country at this point in their history. It remained to be seen whether that individual talent could be welded into an effective team. Only time would tell.

CHAPTER TWO
Learie Constantine

The sight of an athletic young man approaching the wicket at increasing velocity and releasing a delivery of explosive speed has always excited spectators with apprehension and enthusiasm. The West Indians satisfy this expectation in abundance. Apart from the 1950s (when there was an inexplicable dearth in the art) fast bowling has always been the cornerstone of their attack. Pace also provided the decisive thrust in each of the four Tests which they won before the Second World War. The fast bowlers were almost irresistible in the Caribbean, where only Patsy Hendren's run of high scores kept England in the contest, and they would have brought greater success overseas if the fragile batting had given them more substantial totals to bowl against.

Learie Constantine was the first West Indian cricketer to be universally recognized by the public. Whereas Ollivierre, Smith and Challenor were known only to the comparatively few people who saw them play, Constantine's achievements were brought home to a much larger public by the improved communications media. He personified the spirit of Caribbean cricket to the outside world. His infectious enthusiasm and natural skill are remembered longer than some other performances which are written larger in the record books.

Constantine came closer than anyone else to the cricket ideal of the third Duke of Dorset, who played for Kent and Hambledon a century and a half before the Trinidadian's time. Even so, the following words could have been written about him as well.

Caribbean Cricketers

Equalled by few he plays with glee
Nor peevish seeks for victory . . .
And far unlike the modern way
Of blocking every ball at play
He firmly stands with bat upright
And strikes with his athletic might
Sends forth the ball across the mead
And scores six notches for the deed.

There was something about Learie's whole approach which echoed the sentiments of that earlier age when cricket was still a game for peasants and patrons.

Constantine's family had been closely involved with cricket in Trinidad for as long as people could remember. Learie learned much of his attitudes and application from Victor Pascall, his mother's brother, and from asking passers-by to give him a few minutes of their time for a knockabout with a home-made bat and an orange for a ball. Unlike his father, who was essentially a batsman, the younger Constantine was primarily a bowler, at international level at least, with an unusual variety of pace. Although his batting could change the tempo of any game, it tended to be short-lived, if spectacular. He scored only four half-centuries in five series, but his bowling was more consistent.

While George Francis, Herman Griffith and Manny Martindale fell away after their early triumphs Constantine was the one permanent fixture in the new-ball attack and was just as effective in his last match in 1939 as he had been in his youth. Even if he had not bowled a ball or hit a run, Learie Constantine would have been invaluable for his outstanding catching and ground fielding. Spectators came just to see him field. In later life he attributed his amazing anticipation to a careful study of the bowler from the start of his run-up and his exceptional catching ability to the family's habit of throwing the crockery to each other while washing up. It didn't pay for anything to get broken. His lightning reflexes could snap up even half a chance coming at him from any angle. Frederick Spofforth, the Australian 'demon' bowler of the 1880s, similarly explained his own sharp fielding with a childhood story. He claimed that other youngsters flushed the sparrows from the hedgerows for him to catch as they flew by. At least the Constantines really did have family practice; the father, 'Old Cons', insisted on it.

Learie Constantine

The Trinidadian took the first wicket to fall to a West Indian in a Test Match. He had Charlie Hallows—batting in place of the injured Jack Hobbs—caught by Griffith in the opening session at Lord's in 1928. Then he bowled Walter Hammond, and finished the innings by bowling wicket-keeper Smith and 'Tich' Freeman in his 4 wickets for 82. Even those batsmen who made runs proceeded cautiously against his accurate deliveries. Hobbs, who came into the side later in the series, said that Constantine's first few overs were as fast as anything he faced in his entire career, and he played against McDonald and Gregory in their prime.

Constantine seemed to be everywhere on that first day. In addition to his bowling he caught out the three leading run-scorers, Ernest Tyldesley, Percy Chapman and Herbert Sutcliffe. By watching the ball from the bowler's hand onto the bat he was already moving in the direction of the catch. On this form he was clearly the all-rounder of his generation, but he could not maintain the momentum throughout the rubber. Constantine's general performance in Test Matches, considerable though it was, did not reflect his achievements in other first-class cricket. This was most obvious on the 1930/31 tour to Australia. He failed completely in the international games, in spite of beating Queensland almost single-handed and overrunning other state sides.

In 1928 he was irrepressible against the counties, and turned the matches against Middlesex and Northamptonshire into near-solo exhibitions. Although he scored 86 he could not stop Middlesex from leading by 122 runs on the first innings. Then Constantine sent back six county batsmen for only 11 runs, five of them bowled, and finished with 7 wickets for 57. When the tourists struggled at their second attempt he hit a quick-tempo century in an hour to turn apparent defeat into victory. Later in the summer he broke the back of the Northamptonshire batting with some very fast bowling. He followed that by scoring 107 in less than even time, and performed a second-innings 'hat-trick' in winning the game and bringing his match aggregate to 13 wickets. That was the Learie Constantine style which the public adored and still remember.

Constantine bowled well in each of the three matches he played in 1929/30. With Francis missing the first two fixtures, he opened the bowling with Griffith. It was not their fault that the rubber was not won. He started the series on the right foot at Bridgetown by dismissing Leslie Ames, Andy Sandham and Freddie Calthorpe without the help of any fieldsman, and he held three catches. He hit the top score of 58 in the lost second Test at Port of Spain, where the two fast bowlers sent down seventy-eight overs in the last session when nobody else did more than twenty.

Then came the long-awaited victory at Georgetown. The initial assault of Constantine and Francis sealed the tourists' fate on the first day. The Trinidadian dismissed Bob Wyatt before he had scored, and broke through the top of the batting in his 4 wickets for 35. His captain, Fernandes, gave the bowlers a rest by not enforcing the follow-on. Learie frightened the Englishmen again early in the second innings by catching Sandham off his own bowling and by dismissing Wyatt. He shattered the middle batting and rounded off a great triumph for himself and his team with 5 wickets for 87.

Learie Constantine was also the first West Indian to captivate the northern League crowds. He developed a good relationship with his Lancashire club, Nelson, which enhanced his reputation and boosted his popularity with the English public. Because of his skill in so many aspects of the game Constantine was an ideal League player at a time when, prior to the relaxation of the county residential qualifications in the late 1960s, this code of cricket gave the West Indians their one and only chance of regular competition. Over the next few years Learie came to represent all that was best about Saturday afternoon cricket. When raised to the peerage later in life he took the names of Nelson in Lancashire and Maraval in Trinidad into his title.

Because of his League commitments Constantine played only at Manchester in 1933. Significantly this was the one match in which the tourists held their own. Martindale and Constantine replied to 'Nobby' Clark's attempted body-line by giving the English batsmen a torrid time around the leg-stump. To his credit Douglas Jardine, the captain who had initiated these tactics on the recent controversial tour of Australia, stood up to the battering well and scored a hundred, but some of his colleagues were less than convincing. Constantine also hit the top score of 64 in the second innings of this drawn game.

There are many stories about Learie's sense of humour on the field. 'Father' Marriott, who took 11 wickets in the third Test at the Oval, was not picked again for England because his fielding and his batting were far below that expected of an international cricketer. While batting in a county match at Canterbury, Constantine sent up a high catch off a misdirected hook and started to walk away from the

Learie Constantine

wicket immediately. He knew that he was out, or would have been if anybody other than Marriott had attempted to catch him. The fielder positioned himself perfectly, and still dropped the ball. Constantine's good-natured laugh reverberated around the ground.

The 1934/35 series was probably the pinnacle of his career. Learie missed the first Test Match on the notorious quagmire at Bridgetown, where his presence might have helped Martindale tip the scales against England. However, he played an important part in squaring the rubber in the next game at Port of Spain. Constantine struck a sparkling 90, and dismissed D. C. H. Townsend and Maurice Leyland as the visitors tumbled to 28–5 in their first innings. He took another 3 wickets in the second as the West Indies won by 217 runs. Everything was set for the deciding showdown at Kingston. The tired Englishmen, who laboured in the field as George Headley scored 270 not out, were ill prepared for the ordeal which they had to endure. Constantine and Martindale forced them to follow on 264 runs behind. The former took over the captaincy while Jackie Grant was temporarily out of action and wrapped up victory by catching Hendren and dismissing three more. The West Indies won the match by an innings and 161 runs, and with it the series. The balance of world cricket would never be the same again.

The clouds of war which rolled over Europe in 1939 brought the first age of great West Indian fast bowling to a close. The curtain came down after another zestful performance by Learie Constantine, the one man who had been there from the beginning. He mixed spin with pace in order to conserve his strength, but he was still capable of bowling the occasional delivery with great speed. During this tour he specialized in slip fielding. With the rest of the bowling breaking down at Lord's, the only game to be decided, the Trinidadian all-rounder took 4 wickets in England's second innings at Manchester. He successfully put a brake on the home batsmen's attempt to score quick runs for an early declaration which would trap the West Indians on a rain-affected pitch. Inspired by this success, he took 5 wickets for 75 at the Oval, and went out of Test Match cricket on a blaze of stroke-play. The tourists were already ahead with one century and three fifties when Constantine began his innings. He responded by throwing the bat at the ball as if it were just another county game, and sprayed the outfield with boundaries. Finally he miscued at 79 and was caught by wicket-keeper Arthur Wood scurrying backwards to hold a skier. Although he played regularly in the wartime Dominions side, Constantine was too old for international competition when cricket resumed eight years later.

When Learie Constantine retired from cricket he found similar success and perhaps more widespread fame in politics. He was awarded a cabinet post in his native Trinidad (which became independent from Britain in 1962) and a knighthood and eventual peerage. I am not certain that political life really suited his talents. Lord Constantine was respected for his work in improving the opportunities of many of his fellow West Indians and for his campaign against racial injustice. Until the end of his days he remembered the pain and indignity of being refused a hotel room just because he was black, but his manner of expression tended to become prickly and impatient. The last time I saw him was at a reception for Norman Manley, the former Prime Minister of Jamaica, at the Porchester Hall, Paddington, in 1965. Constantine was annoyed that the attendants had flocked into the hall after the politician and had left him and the other dignitaries waiting in the foyer. Learie Constantine's greatest achievements were on the cricket field where the action was so much more straightforward, and where he did as much to raise the status and reputation of the black man as did Joe Louis in professional boxing.

If George Francis is overshadowed by Constantine in current recollection his contribution was considered just as effective at the time. The Barbadian's success in 1923, and against Freddie Calthorpe's first side, jerked the West Indies into the first division of cricketing countries. As a result he was invariably asked to open the bowling, irrespective of who else was in the side. George bowled fast and straight in a basic and uncomplicated style. His approach to the wicket ended with a leap in the air which disconcerted the opposing batsman as much as the delivery itself, and it was fitting that he sent down the first ball by a West Indian in a Test Match.

Francis did not repeat his previous form in 1928 because he sacrificed accuracy for speed, and he took some time to get into the series. At Lord's his first international victim was Herbert Sutcliffe—no mean feat in itself—and he dismissed Ernest Tyldesley, the first man to score a century against the West Indies. After Hobbs and Sutcliffe had begun the third Test at the Oval with over 100 runs for the first wicket Francis bowled the latter and then had the master caught for 159, prising open the innings for Griffith to take 5 quick wickets against the middle batting.

Learie Constantine

As he could not take too much time off work, George Francis played only at Georgetown in 1929/30, and was immediately successful. With the advantage of high scoring by Clifford Roach and George Headley the fast bowlers could afford to go flat out for victory. Francis forced fifty-year-old George Gunn to hit his own wicket in taking 4 wickets for 40 as he routed the tourists with Constantine for a paltry 145. England fought more tenaciously in their second innings, but Francis had Gunn taken at the wicket, and sealed the victory by dismissing Bill Voce.

The West Indians broke new ground by touring Australia in 1930/31. The administrative task was so difficult for a young country that it was not repeated for another twenty years. The Australian batting was unusually strong, with Don Bradman, who held the records for the highest individual scores in Test Match and all first-class cricket, experienced openers Billy Woodfull and Bill Ponsford, Archie Jackson who died so tragically young, Stan McCabe and Alan Kippax. On pitches which did not have nearly as much pace as was expected the West Indian fast bowlers were soundly caned, and could not contain the Australians to less than 300 runs in any of the first four matches, which were lost by one-sided margins. There was little reason to suspect that the fifth Test Match at Sydney would end any differently.

Instead of testing new players in a series which was already decided the home selectors chose their strongest side in an attempt to win all five games. The tourists were given an unexpected boost by centuries from Frank Martin and George Headley. The fast bowlers, working effectively together for the first time on the tour, recovered their fire for a final effort. As the batsmen encountered rare pace in the pitch Francis took 4 wickets and Australia trailed by 126 runs. By declaring his second innings closed at the perilously insecure score of 124-5 Jackie Grant, the West Indian captain, gambled everything on his fast bowlers. They rose to the occasion admirably. Francis and Griffith bowled the tourists home by 30 runs. As they had declared twice the victory, though narrow, was conclusive.

Herman Griffith, who was included in the party as a first-change bowler, finished top of the averages in 1928. His best achievement was in the third Test Match at the Oval. The West Indian fast bowlers almost clawed back England's early grip on the game. In his second spell the persevering Griffith struck a good length to dismiss Tyldesley, Hammond, Leyland, Hendren and Chapman in one explosive burst. Nobody could maintain the pressure when he was rested, and the lower-order batsmen regained much of the lost ground. Griffith closed the innings at 438 by dismissing Freeman, his sixth wicket for 103. Poor batting and missed catches frittered away the advantage he had provided.

Griffith was similarly frustrated at Port of Spain in 1929/30, where he put his side in sight of what should have been their first Test Match victory. He started the day well by bowling Sandham for a duck, and came back later to finish with 5 wickets for 63. Batting unevenly, the West Indies went ahead by only 46 runs. Even that seemed enough as Herman again bowled Sandham cheaply and dismissed Greville Stevens. Yet again nobody could take over from him, as Patsy Hendren with 205 not out and wicket-keeper Leslie Ames pulled England out of danger. The West Indians were so demoralized at coming so near and yet so far that they offered scant resistance to left-arm seamer Bill Voce (who took 7 wickets) and they lost by 167 runs. Ironically, Griffith did not play at Georgetown where that elusive victory was achieved.

Having borne the brunt of Bradman's double century at Brisbane in 1930/31, Herman Griffith had a surprise revenge in the final fixture at Sydney. When Grant's declaration caused them to bat last on a rain-damaged pitch the Barbadian fast bowler shocked the Australians by bowling Bradman for his first duck in a Test Match. The West Indians seized the initiative from the bemused batsmen before Alan Fairfax, a much underrated all-rounder, organized some semblance of resistance. Griffith took four second-innings wickets in that historic win. Age was catching up on them, and neither he nor Francis were as effective again.

Manny Martindale, yet another in the outstanding tradition of Barbadian fast bowlers, made such an impressive debut against England in 1933 that his presence in Australia might have shortened the odds. He was the first fast bowler to develop exclusively since Test Match status had been granted, and for three years he could have been the greatest of them all. Martindale gave the attack a cutting edge just when it seemed that the earlier impact would be lost. Throughout his six-year international career he played in only ten Test Matches, no more than most present-day bowlers play in a single year. The restricted scope of competition gave him no chance to keep match-fit, and prevented him from reaching the same statistical records as those who came after.

Learie Constantine

Martindale and Griffith bowled creditably against a powerful batting side at Lord's and shared 7 wickets. With Francis clearly out of touch Martindale dismissed the two opening batsmen, the dependable Sutcliffe and attractive stylist Cyril Walters. He finished with 4 wickets for 85 in putting England under pressure right from the start of the series. Within a short time this prospect of victory was turned into the reality of defeat. The batsmen were put out for 97 and, following on, lost by an innings and 27 runs. It was the old story of lost opportunity. For the rest of the summer Martindale carried the bowling as much as Headley did the batting.

The batsmen excelled themselves for once at Manchester by scoring 375. Whatever happened after that, the game could not be lost. Sutcliffe's rare run-out gave the bowlers an unlooked-for breakthrough. Then Martindale and Constantine subjected England to leg-theory for the first time. The Barbadian dismissed Walters and Wyatt, and caught Hammond off Constantine's bowling. Jardine and Ames restored their side's fortunes for a while, but both batsmen were caught off Martindale, who bowled Clark for the West Indies to lead by one run on the first innings. There was not enough time for either side to force victory after that.

A further innings defeat at the Oval dashed the West Indian hopes of drawing level. Once again they started only too well. Martindale had Walters caught before the proceedings were hardly under way. The other batsmen continued to struggle while Alfred Bakewell, the new opening batsman in place of Sutcliffe, scored a commendable century. Martindale dismissed three middle-order batsmen before Charlie Barnett, batting unusually low, and Stan Nichols brought about a minor recovery. Manny closed the innings by bowling Marriott, to end with 5 wickets for 93. He had taken 14 wickets in the only three innings available to him, a feat equal to almost any fast-bowling performance in the next fifty years. The dismal pattern of the Lord's match was repeated with Martindale, in final irony, not out in each innings.

The 1934/35 series began on a rain-ruined pitch at Bridgetown with falling wickets almost as numerous as runs. The West Indies began badly by scoring just 102 runs, with only two batsmen reaching double figures, but the Englishmen fared even worse. Martindale and Leslie Hylton exploited the treacherous conditions so well that 7 wickets were down for 81, including 43 by Walter Hammond, when Wyatt declared. Jackie Grant shared the mistrust of the pitch, reversed the batting order and declared only 72 runs ahead. Sensible cricket was obviously impossible. Wyatt's like ploy of sending in lower-order batsmen until the pitch improved failed when Martindale sent back George Paine, Errol Holmes, Jim Smith, Maurice Leyland and Patsy Hendren at a personal cost of only 22 runs. If he had been supported the match might have ended there and then. As it was Hammond chanced his arm with 29 not out in bringing England home by 4 wickets.

The fast bowlers made inroads into the English batting for most of the season. Although the final Test Match at Kingston began with both teams equal at a victory apiece, the West Indians had the psychological advantage of improving while their opponents had deteriorated. Headley's double century on his home ground had the tourists reeling, and then came Martindale. He brought a lightning delivery in from outside the off-stump and broke Wyatt's jaw. The English captain had such a tough time with injuries that he thought he was under a curse. Immediately afterwards Manny had Townsend caught by wicket-keeper Cyril Christiani, and dismissed Paine and Errol Holmes before either had scored. Martindale took another 4 wickets in the second innings, including Hammond's valued scalp, in winding up the victory.

Leslie Hylton, a well-built Jamaican, shaped up for a time as Martindale's partner, and even his eventual successor. He bowled well enough at Bridgetown without the experience to bring victory out of adversity, and took 3 wickets in the final stages of the win by 217 runs at Port of Spain. When he returned 4 wickets for 27 in the evenly contested draw at Georgetown his future seemed certain. The public thought so too, because they subscribed for Hylton to be taken to England in 1939 after he had been left out of the original selection, but he failed to do himself justice and was not heard of again as a cricketer. Later he was hanged for his wife's murder.

Spin bowling had no regular part in pre-war play. Left-arm spinner Ellis 'Puss' Achong won the respect of friends and opponents alike without taking the wickets he deserved in Test Matches. His style so confused the English team in 1934/35 that one famous batsman who failed to read which way the ball would turn blamed his failure on the 'chinaman', and a new term passed into cricket terminology.

Jamaican spinner Tommy Scott took 9 wickets for 374 runs in 105.2 overs during the almost timeless Test Match at Kingston in

1929/30. Although he was punished heavily by batsmen for whom the placid pitch had no worries, it was the only time before the Second World War that a slow bowler fared appreciably better than the faster men. Andy Sandham, the Surrey opener who played so long in the shadow of Jack Hobbs, scored 325, then the highest individual score in a Test Match until Don Bradman beat it three months later. Scott slowed down the tourists' rate of scoring in the second innings before a tropical downpour, and the departure of the visitors' ship home caused the game to be given up as a draw after ten days. Scott bowled tidily later in Australia, especially at Adelaide where he took three wickets for no runs in one spell, and Sydney, but did not do as well as expected in England.

Leg-spinner Bertie Clarke was possibly the best West Indian slow bowler sent to England in the 1930s. He performed well in 1939, when he was still too young. The war ended his international career. Clarke played in county and club cricket afterwards, and was regarded as one of the best exponents of his style in the country. In the late 1960s Bertie wrote for the same publication as myself, and we judged some beauty contests together.

CHAPTER THREE
George Headley

Brittle, though frequently brilliant, batting was the main weakness in West Indian cricket between 1928 and 1939. Only too often reckless or negative stroke-play threw away a winning chance set up by the bowlers. Even George Headley's genius could not compensate entirely for such inconsistency. The difference between performances at home and those overseas showed up a fundamental defect in technique. Free scoring on firm ground where the ball hurried straight through and at an even height permitted cavalier and enjoyable cricket. Rain-dampened tracks on which the ball spun, turned and deviated were more unsettling. West Indian batsmen who could play Larwood, Voce and Farnes with no apparent difficulty came unstuck against almost anybody spinning the ball. They tended to hit across the line of flight, stepping back in front of their stumps.

Initially the West Indians lacked the necessary application to build an innings, and they tried to score their runs too quickly. As a result the exciting exhibitions of free hitting which made them so popular wherever they went were doomed to summary failure. Their cross-bat strokes in defence and lofting the ball into the outfield always gave the bowlers a chance. Maybe they were cheated by time. The Edwardian 'Golden Age', revelling in individual enterprise almost irrespective of the result, took Victor Trumper, Clem Hill and Prince Ranjitsinhji to its heart. The West Indies, however, made their entry into official international cricket in the more clinical and methodical era of Don Bradman and Billy Woodfull. The prevailing attitudes, not the Caribbean, could have been the more out of touch with the game's basic spirit. In the circumstances the West Indians adapted

George Headley

their approach and techniques to the general mood quickly, and without losing any of the charm which still makes their seasons so appealing to all but the most partisan opponents.

The pattern of play and team composition was considerably influenced by the social and geographical environment. The cost of administration, match-promotion and transport between the islands was prohibitive, especially as rain could wipe out all chance of recouping the investment at the 'gate'. There was no recourse to commercial sponsorship, advertisement or broadcasting revenue. Inter-territorial competition was scarce, and for Jamaica almost non-existent. As a result the West Indies could not field their best team at any given time. Availability and past performance had to count for more than current form. Although there was a core of regular bowlers, too many batting places were filled by gifted amateurs on an occasional basis. Team-selection changed drastically from game to game. Even into the late 1950s experience of an English university was valued more than proven ability against international opposition. The rival interests of the different islands had to be taken into account as well, an attitude which applied also to the captaincy. The captain of each home territory—four different leaders in all—alternated in office during the 1929/30 series, and something similar almost happened in 1947/48. Maurice Fernandes, under whom the first Test Match victory was won, did not play outside Guyana.

Following the batting débâcle which led to three heavy defeats in 1928 George Headley emerged as the batting star of the first home series, the decade and the era. In his first year he scored one double century and three other hundreds. Headley stood head and shoulders above his colleagues in batting ability, and in statistical terms alone he bears comparison with Grace and Bradman. More than that, he scored his runs in an attractive way and in circumstances which made his career unique. Without this slightly built Jamaican the character of West Indian cricket would have been very different.

Headley was the master of back play, and his driving on either side of the wicket stemmed more from his technique and timing than from any physical power. He watched the ball right on to the bat, and could cut, drive or pull with equal ability. George chose where to put the ball, and he did it accurately. Opposing bowlers argued that he might have been more vulnerable on the front foot, but 'the blighter wouldn't come forward unless he was sure of hitting us through the covers'. In this respect his achievements in England, and to some extent Australia as well, were even more remarkable. Several visiting batsmen, including more than a few West Indians, have been surprised on the back foot by a late variation in spin or by the ball cutting back. Headley had the eyesight, the footwork, the timing and the natural ability to counter any such late movement.

During his first tour to England in 1933 he was described as the best bad-wicket batsman since Victor Trumper, and few others have come forward to rival him since then. His best innings in England, Australia and the Caribbean were all played in difficult conditions with the bowlers apparently on top. 'King George', as he was affectionately known, scored briskly and ran swiftly between the wickets, though his scurrying up the pitch led quite frequently to his own run-out. His whole approach was refreshing to a public which had become disillusioned with cricket as entertainment by the tight and (especially during 1932/33) bad-tempered battles of attrition between England and Australia. Headley did as much with the bat as Constantine in the field to improve the image of West Indian cricket.

Jamaica's first national hero—with respect to Paul Bogle and Marcus Garvey—was not born in the island but in Panama. He rose rapidly through local club and regional cricket, and his overall international record would have been even better in a later age. Apart from his first Test Match series, Headley came into bat almost invariably on the loss of an early wicket with the shine still on the ball. Because there was no adequate opening partnership, he did not have time to adjust himself to the pitch. Wickets fell steadily at the other end. On the few occasions anybody stayed with him for a length of time—as at Manchester in 1933 and Sydney—the game took on an entirely new dimension. Clyde Walcott, Everton Weekes and Frank Worrell had each other, as did Gary Sobers and Rohan Kanhai, or Clive Lloyd and Viv Richards. George was alone.

While he was still in his teens Headley made 211 runs against Lionel Tennyson's unofficial touring team of Jamaica in 1928. He shared an unbroken world record stand of 487 with Clarence Passailaigue against his lordship's second side three years later, of which his own share was 344 not out. Perhaps he was lucky to miss selection for the first demoralizing tour of England. By the time he was called on for his international debut at Bridgetown in January 1930 he was twenty-one years old, hungry for runs and capable of getting them.

George Headley

The West Indies started their second innings 98 runs behind, and soon lost Teddy Hoad for a duck. They ended by forcing the tourists to hold on for a draw. The difference was Headley's own 176 and his huge partnerships with Clifford Roach and Frank De Caires. It was the first time that two West Indian batsmen had hit form together. The exultant English bowlers were stopped in their tracks, and not for the last time.

Roach was then considered to be Challenor's natural successor. When he failed to score in either innings at Port of Spain young Headley seemed the better prospect. Both of them came good in the third Test at Georgetown. Aided by fielding lapses, Roach and Errol Hunte put on 144 runs for the first wicket, and Headley joined the former in a punishing stand of 196 runs for the second. Headley, who scored 114 in this run feast on the first day, became the first West Indian to hit two separate centuries in the same Test Match by making another 112. His second innings was more restrained than usual, due perhaps to the inability of the other batsmen to push the score along with him. When 'Snuffy' Browne came in and laid about him for 70 not out there was no doubt that the West Indies had the time as well as the determination to win their first Test Match.

Visiting captain Freddie Calthorpe set the near-impossible task of scoring 836 runs to win the fourth Test at Kingston. Although England led by 563 runs on the first innings, he did not enforce the follow-on, probably because his elderly fieldsmen (who included fifty year-olds George Gunn and Wilfred Rhodes) were tired. As there was no regular time limit on the game, England were strong favourites to win, especially as their opponents had shown some earlier signs of indiscretion and indecision. That did not take account of George Headley. He stayed at the crease for six and a half hours in scoring 223, an outstanding demonstration of concentration and application. Rain finally washed out play with the West Indies at 408–5 and the issue still far from settled.

It was April 1930, and the Englishmen returned for their first home meeting with young Donald Bradman the following month. The Australian's sequence of high scores compiled in the spotlight of full press coverage distracted international attention from Headley's batting in distant Jamaica, but the world did not have to wait long to hear of him.

The West Indian batsmen hoped to do well in Australia. The opposing bowlers were supposedly less formidable than their batsmen. Admittedly Clarrie Grimmett was the top spinner of his day, and the tourists had already shown their vulnerability to the turning ball. On the other hand, the firmer Australian pitches were expected to be faster and more in keeping with those in the Caribbean. It was their misfortune to run into cheerless weather with enough rain to affect the wickets sufficiently for Grimmett to bowl at his deadliest, supported by several good though hardly exceptional medium-paced and slow bowlers. The batting did not reach 200 in any of six consecutive innings in mid-season, and passed 300 only in the final match. The lesson in the ways of the world was painful.

George Headley began the tour and the series as badly as the others. Runs were hard to come by on the slower pitches, and he had a problem with his grip. In working out a solution he showed clearly that his batting success was based as much on acquired know-how as natural talent. The West Indians gave a good account of themselves at Adelaide, but lost faith after having the worst of a brutish wicket at Sydney. On going to Brisbane they were not helped by a long chase in the field, as Bradman made a double century and Ponsford a single hundred. Headley, however, hit back with a superb 102 not out. He was now back to his brilliant best, but nobody stayed with him, and the innings closed at 193. The second total was even lower, and Australia won by an innings and 217 runs.

The fifth Test Match at Sydney promised to be little more than a further humiliation, a final purgatory before the journey home. Once again Headley went for his strokes, and this time, surprisingly, somebody stuck it out at the other end. Fellow-Jamaican Frank Martin was as steady as a rock while they handled the bowling as if the previous four games had not happened. The Australians now were pushed on to the defensive, and in spite of stiff last-ditch resistance and some wild fielding in the closing stages nothing could prevent the West Indies from winning. The tourists were cheered enthusiastically by the sporting crowd.

This progress was set back by another frustrating tour to England in 1933. The very hot summer could not be blamed for the disappointment. Irresolute batting was again the chief cause of two further defeats by an innings. Headley himself went from strength to strength. Although their styles were so different, the Jamaican's trouncing of the English bowlers earned him the nickname 'black Bradman' from the public which had marvelled at the Australian's similar performance in 1930. Headley naturally resented being likened to a second anybody else, but it is interesting to speculate that if the tours had been reversed, or if George had come in 1928, Bradman would have been known as the 'white Headley'. Perhaps that sentiment allows too much for racial tolerance and too little for the power of alliteration. Many bowlers would have fancied their chances more against the Australian than against Headley on a pitch which was deteriorating or had been damaged by rain.

Headley scored exactly 50 in his team's disappointing showing at Lord's. He came to the wicket early at Manchester on Roach's dismissal. The other opening batsman, wicket-keeper Ivan Barrow, helped him put on 200 runs for the second wicket. The two Jamaicans dealt firmly with the English attack as 'Nobby' Clark strove hard to take over Larwood's mantle in terms of speed and intimidation. Headley continued to score fluently even after Barrow was out. When the last wicket went down he was 169 not out from the 375 runs total. It was the first century by a West Indian in a Test Match in England.

The selectors underestimated the strength of Caribbean cricket by sending out a second-rate team in 1934/35. They paid for their presumption by losing two matches and the rubber. The difference would have been even greater but for the strange affair at Bridgetown. Only 309 runs were scored in the four innings. Ken Farnes, the one world-class bowler in the side, broke any confidence the West Indians had by dismissing George Carew for 0, Roach in his last Test Match, Charles Jones and Derek Sealy while the side was still settling in. In these atrocious and unpredictable conditions Headley kept his head while all those about him were losing theirs. He made 44 out of the 102 runs scored. This masterpiece of courage and determination was worth more than many double centuries. Even then he denied the bowlers his wicket by being run out. Batting became increasingly bizarre and hazardous as England scrambled home by 4 wickets.

Although he did not reach three figures until the final fixture, Headley made his team's top score in all four Test Matches. He scored 93 at Port of Spain, slightly ahead of Sealy and Constantine, and 53 in the colourless draw at Georgetown. That year runs were unusually scarce by the usual Caribbean standards. In the English team such potentially heavy scorers as Walter Hammond, Patsy Hendren, Maurice Leyland, Bob Wyatt and Leslie Ames could not get going either. The floodgates had to open some time, and this they did with a vengeance at Kingston. The touring bowlers had little time to congratulate themselves on the quick dismissal of opening batsmen Barrow and Cyril Christiani before Headley and Derek Sealy battered them with 202 runs for the third wicket. Spin bowler George Paine stopped the flow for a while, but Rolph Grant helped Headley put on another 147 runs for the seventh wicket. The bowling was savaged in an orgy of run-scoring born out of the pent-up frustration of earlier disappointments. By the time Jackie Grant declared at 535–7 Headley had scored 270 not out in possibly his best attacking innings. His triumph was made the sweeter by being in front of his home crowd. George was only sixty-odd runs away from the world individual Test Match record, and it remained the highest score by a West Indian until Gary Sobers set up the present record against Pakistan on the same ground in 1958. After such a tremendous start the West Indies won easily by an innings and 161 runs.

The revival in batting confidence inspired by Headley's mastery was evident on the 1939 tour to England. As 'King George' tore all bowling apart in his progress through the counties, the younger players were given an example to follow and an opportunity to learn skills which had been denied to their predecessors. If anything the champion was even better than on his previous visit, for by now he had developed a mature confidence and charisma. The thirty-year-old Jamaican had had an amazing run of success, going into the last week of August. In his last eight Test Match innings he had scored one undefeated double century, two single hundreds in the same game, and four half-centuries. There seemed to be no limit to his potential, but his achievements were curtailed by the action of an Austrian former corporal who knew little enough of cricket.

Headley began the rubber with a century in each innings at Lord's. He was only the second batsman of any nationality to record the feat on two separate occasions. Though beaten by 8 wickets in poor light—chiefly through the failure of the bowling—the West Indian batting was better balanced than it had ever been in England before. Headley scored 106 and 107 against the combination of pace from Bowes and Copson and spin from Verity (in his last Test Match before his death in the war) and Wright. He followed this with 51 at Manchester in a game which was contested throughout in that city's traditional rain, which made batting extremely difficult. After Rolph Grant had thrashed a hasty 47, Headley defended successfully, while fast bowler Bill Bowes whipped out the other batsmen.

George Headley

The West Indies lost an early wicket at the Oval, so that George Headley and teenager Jeff Stollmeyer had to restore their team's position as they had done at Lord's. They put on over a hundred runs in an attractive display of strokes which humbled the bowling and prepared the way for some lusty hitting. These two batsmen were out within six runs of each other. Headley was run out for 65 when he seemed set for yet another century. His running had already cost him his wicket several times, but on this occasion at least his partner, Victor Stollmeyer, nervous on his Test Match debut, contributed to the misunderstanding by apparently not seeing the fielder who threw in the ball. It was Headley's last vintage innings. This day's play has sentimental associations for my parents, and so for me. My father's love of cricket was the only stumbling-block to his courtship of my mother, who could not stand the game. Eventually she agreed to go with him to the Oval, where she was so enchanted by Headley's batting that she accepted him.

Perhaps, on reflection, he should have retired then from playing at international level. Yet there seemed no reason to think so when post-war cricket started in 1947/48. He had retained his pre-eminence in inter-territorial matches in the intervening years, and, as he was still under forty, his experience was needed more than ever. All the same, controversy clouded his future. Headley, the outstanding candidate for the captaincy, was passed over for all but the first and fourth games. His colour was a disadvantage in those less liberal times. George did not show any open resentment, but when I discussed the matter twenty-five years later with his son—who was himself considered a possible successor to Gary Sobers—there was a definite impression that West Indian cricket had not played fair by the family. The elder Headley's disappointment was made more acute in the first match at Bridgetown by a strained muscle which caused him to bat last in the second innings. The injury kept him out of the rest of the series.

The following year Headley went to India with John Goddard's party, but returned ill after only one match. That should have been the end, but it wasn't. At forty-four, and without a substantial innings for almost fifteen years, Headley was recalled from England, where he was still playing in the leagues, to face Freddie Trueman and Brian Statham at Kingston in 1953/54. He played the fast bowlers adequately before falling to a controversial delivery from left-arm spinner Tony Lock. So he ended his career in a low key on the same ground on which his two previous Test Match innings had realized 493 runs for once out.

His son, Ron Headley, represented Worcestershire as a left-handed opening batsman from the late 1950s to the early 1970s. He was born two days after his father had completed his second century at Lord's in 1939. Headley was a regular member of the team which won the county championship in 1964 and 1965, and, even if his right shoulder did seem to point too far towards midoff in his stance, he was a close rival to Geoff Boycott and Bob Barber for selection to Mike Smith's touring party to Australia in 1965/66. Several seasons later the Jamaican captained Worcestershire in winning the John Player League limited-over competition. He was possibly past his best when he was chosen to open the innings with Roy Fredericks for Rohan Kanhai's side in 1973. After two moderate games he gave up his place to the more pressing claims of Lawrence Rowe and Gordon Greenidge.

Clifford Roach, the Trinidadian opening batsman, exemplified all the virtues and all the weaknesses of pre-war West Indian batting. For a time he was regarded on a par with Challenor, and although he did not live up to that expectation he gave the public much pleasure. Roach scored his country's first century and first double century, and made several quick-fire fifties. On the other hand, he was run out without scoring on his debut, and twice made a 'pair'. Roach was in such a hurry to score runs and to entertain that he ignored tactical considerations at his peril. He would have suited present-day instant cricket, and would have interested the patrons of the commercial game. In view of his quick running, it is a special tragedy that he has had to spend his later years without the use of his legs.

Challenor and Roach provided a sound start to the second Test at Manchester in 1928. When the former was run out Roach, who showed a more sound defence and greater patience than he did later, and the circumspect Martin took the score to 94-1. Then the Jamaican became the second victim of misjudging the field, and Roach, having reached his 50 quite easily against the fast bowlers, gave spinner 'Tich' Freeman the first of his five wickets. The second-innings dismissal of both openers in murky light before they had scored ended any chance of avoiding defeat. The Oval Test Match went much the same way. Roach made 53 and Challenor confidently played Maurice Tate's accuracy and the thunderbolts of Larwood in putting on 91 at less than a run a minute. It was Challenor's best performance of a season in which he was clearly past his prime. The rest of the batting folded up sharply after that good beginning.

Roach was the stem on to which the selectors grafted the new batting talent in 1929/30. He was a much better player in the Caribbean, and he did not disappoint them. The Trinidadian received the first ball bowled in a Test Match in the West Indies, and went on to score the first century. He made 122 in shepherding his young colleagues through this daunting experience, and hit 77 in the second innings. Fortune's fickleness, or temperamental instability, led to a poor performance in the very next match at Port of Spain, where Bill Voce bowled him twice for a duck. Roach was so upset that he asked to be dropped from the side. The request was refused, and at Georgetown he made the bowlers pay in full for the indignity. He scored 340 runs with Errol Hunte and Headley for the first two wickets. Runs flowed easily when Roach was in such a masterful mood, and when he was finally out for 209 the West Indies were well on the way to their first victory. Alas, his batting did not reach such heights again.

After only one half-century in Australia and another 'pair' at Lord's in 1933 Roach made some amends with a bright second-innings 64 at Manchester, where left-arm spinner James Langridge took 7 wickets. The third Test was lost by poor batting against 'Father' Marriott in his only international game. The Kentish slow bowler cunningly kept the batsmen guessing by not spinning the ball too much. Roach enlivened the final moments by trying to knock the bowlers out of their stride. Facing a deficit of 212 runs, he struck a lightning 56 in just over half an hour. It was magnificent, but it was hardly professional warfare.

Batsmen Joe Small and 'Snuffy' Browne, two of the more successful tourists in 1923, did less well five years later. Browne, the first Guyanese to play regularly in Test Matches, was seemingly superfluous to an attack in which Learie Constantine had improved and to which Herman Griffith had been added, and Small now batted as low as number nine. Their big moment came in the first Test at Lord's. When they followed on 224 runs behind the West Indies lost six more wickets for 55 runs. Small, who failed to score at his first attempt, recalled his earlier ability by making 52. Browne scored 44 in helping him raise the total to a more respectable 166. 'Snuffy' made one of the fastest Test Match half-centuries with 70 not out at Georgetown in 1929/30.

Caribbean Cricketers

Karl Nunes, the first captain, had a lean season. He bore the added responsibilities of leading his side in their first international series and, with George Dewhurst left at home, keeping wicket to the world's fastest bowlers. His best match was at Kingston in 1929/30. Karl seemed more at ease in opening the batting, and with a specialist wicket-keeper, Ivan Barrow, also in the team. The Jamaican captain's 66 against the tide was the top score in the first innings, and by scoring 92 he partnered Headley for much of the second.

Frank Martin, a left-hander, did not get the runs or the credit he deserved. His progress was inexplicably complicated. Martin failed to take advantage of conditions which were in his favour, and in 1933 missed the Tests by treading on a ball and injuring his foot in the game against Middlesex early in the season. He could master some of the most difficult bowling and then get out to a simple long hop. Frank had a tight control which should have made him a very good opening batsman. Indeed, he was the most secure member of the team in 1928 when he reached 40 twice. Just when it seemed that he would not measure up to international requirements he played an innings of rare quality. He could not have picked a better time or place to do it than the fifth Test at Sydney in 1930/31. Martin batted as well as at any time in his enigmatic career. He was still going strong with 123 not out when Jackie Grant declared at 350–6.

Derek Sealy made history by playing at Bridgetown in 1929/30 when he was only 17 years and 122 days old. It is still the youngest age for a West Indian. He showed that his selection was no mere gimmick by scoring 58 at his first attempt. Sealy did even better five years later when he made 92 at Port of Spain and 91 at Kingston. Although he was chosen mainly as a wicket-keeper and batsman, he produced some unusual bowling performances in the early 1940s. Sealy took 8 wickets for 8 when Barbados bowled out Trinidad for only 16 runs, and he played regularly in inter-territorial matches after the war. His greatest influence was in coaching the next generation of Barbadian batsmen.

During the 1930s a succession of wicket-keepers were drafted as opening batsmen. Ivan Barrow came off best in scoring 105 in a double-century stand with Headley at Manchester in 1933. He played above himself then, and did not do so well again. Errol Hunte and Cyril Christiani filled a similar position, and the first three batsmen at Kingston in 1934/35 were specialist wicket-keepers. Hunte went into cricket administration and Christiani died young from malaria. As recently as 1957 Rohan Kanhai's brilliant career was almost stifled at birth when he was expected both to open the batting and to keep wicket on his first tour.

Jackie Grant, a Trinidadian who had gone to Cambridge University, was appointed captain of the touring side to Australia without experience of leadership, and with little prior contact with the players under his direction. The selection worked out well, and he was the first captain to retain his appointment for more than one series. With continuity of leadership the team's approach and confidence improved, so that Grant was able to guide the West Indies to their first victory in a Test Match rubber. When he retired from sport to become a missionary he was succeeded by his younger brother, Rolph.

Jackie won his team's respect by his brilliant close fielding, and with scores of 53 not out and 71 not out in the first Test at Adelaide. His bold declarations at Sydney, where others might have settled for a draw, gave the West Indians a chance to win. In this above all he showed a faith in his bowlers which they did not have in themselves, and which could not be justified by previous events. Grant harnessed that psychological stream whose flow and ebb gave such an exciting variation to West Indian performances until Frank Worrell instilled the team with greater professionalism thirty years later. The knowledge that they could beat Australia, and had done so, did more for morale than any one-sided victory over lesser opposition.

Rolph Grant was a useful all-rounder without being a great cricketer. With his long reach he was an agile short leg and a reasonable off-spinner whose catching and bowling were important in winning at Port of Spain, and he scored 77 at Kingston in that series. Grant did not reach 50 against England in 1939, where he attempted to solve the opening-batsman problem by going in first himself. He hit a whirlwind 47 with three sixes at Manchester in scoring as many runs as possible before the pitch became unplayable.

Frank De Caires, Edward Lawson Bartlett, Lionel Birkett and Kenny Wishart each had one good year without becoming a full-time player. Bartlett started well in Australia, but injured himself fielding in the second Test at Sydney. *Wisden* published his untimely death among the obituaries for 1933. Bartlett had the last laugh, because he lived for another forty years. Even cricket's bible can be wrong sometimes.

The younger batsmen made their presence felt at the Oval in 1939, where the West Indies outplayed their hosts for the first time in England. Only second-innings centuries by Len Hutton and Walter Hammond saved the home side from defeat. Jeff Stollmeyer was the unexpected discovery of the series. He was selected for the tour primarily as an understudy to his brother. On the latter's illness Jeff was taken in first at Lord's. He scored 59 both there and at the Oval, adding over a hundred runs with Headley each time. Victor Stollmeyer was not outshone by his brother. In the third Test he recovered from the unfortunate experience of running out Headley, and was soon in control of the bowling. With his score at 96 Stollmeyer missed a ball from Tom Goddard and was stumped. Maybe he consoled himself with the thought that there would be time enough for a century later on. He did not play again. When the war was over only one Stollmeyer, Jeffrey, came back into the team. Jamaican left-hander Kenny Weekes was in a similar position. Playing in only his second Test, he launched a memorable attack on the bowlers by scoring 137 at a sizzling rate with a series of forcing shots. Weekes's career, like that of many others, was curtailed by the war.

CHAPTER FOUR
Frank Worrell

Frank Worrell was the comprehensive Caribbean cricketer. His batting was beautiful and talented. He bowled accurate left-arm seam, and was nimble in the field. In middle age he became his country's most successful and best-loved captain. As Shakespeare said—some men in their lives play many parts. Worrell was one of the few to do it all at the same time. There was no aspect of the game, except wicket-keeping, to which he did not turn his hand. It is difficult to know quite where West Indian cricket would have been without him between 1947 and 1963. Sir Frank—and no sportsman deserved the honour more than him—is remembered today mainly for the dignity he brought to a game whose very name is a byword for good conduct. His own batting and bowling achievements are often overlooked in the general approval of what he accomplished in his last five years as a cricketer.

Worrell, who was born in Barbados but played most of his first-class cricket for Jamaica, raised Caribbean cricket to a new standard of international respect through his own example on and off the field. After coming into the side for the first post-war rubber against England he was the forefront of the brilliant and successful batting of John Goddard's triumphant team. Later he struggled almost alone against great odds on the disastrous tours of Australia in 1951/52 and England in 1957. Admittedly he had his own lean spell in between, but Worrell could always find that extra touch of genius when it was most wanted. That was only the first chapter of his extraordinary life. The consistent success of the 1960s was built around his experience and expertise.

Caribbean Cricketers

Few batsmen have quite caught the public imagination as much as the alliterative Worrell, Weekes and Walcott immediately after the war. Whereas the other two depended on the power of their strokes, Worrell coaxed his runs from the bowlers with a gentle and more deadly grace. Fielders wondered at his style and applauded it. Spectators were entertained by the freedom of his batting against bowling already softened by opening batsmen Rae and Stollmeyer, and admired his raw courage against pace and bumpers when things were not going so well. The adopted Jamaican was occasionally spectacular rather than consistent. He played better in England and Australia than at home.

Pressed into service as an emergency opening batsman in 1957—a position where he had already failed once before—Worrell carried his bat at Nottingham for 191 not out, one of the great Test Match innings. His seam bowling filled the gap during the speed famine of the early 1950s. Although he was well below genuinely fast, Frank was quite effective at the start of play when there was movement off the pitch. He shattered Australia's batting at Adelaide, and in 1957 was the only one to check the powerful English batting once it had got into its stride. While he did not rank with Gary Sobers or Learie Constantine among the outstanding all-rounders, Worrell represented all the brilliance, scintillation, inconsistency and determination of West Indian teams in the 1940s and 1950s.

Frank Worrell grew up amid the upsurge of young Barbadian batting talent during the war years. He was picked initially as a bowler batting at number eleven. A temporary promotion as nightwatchman changed the whole shape of his career. He did so well that he made the place his own. Shortly after this the nineteen-year-old Worrell and John Goddard put on 502 for the fourth wicket against Trinidad. That record did not last long. Two years later Clyde Walcott and Worrell himself scored 574 runs without being separated for the same wicket and against the same opponents. It was about this time that a schoolmaster called the young cricketer arrogant because he devoted so much time to the sport at which he excelled. Frank moved to Jamaica in shame to get away from the imagined stigma. He was in his new home when England, represented by a mixed bunch of old-timers and novices, toured in 1947/48 and did not win a single game. The West Indies won the third and fourth Tests and drew the other two.

Worrell missed the opening match through illness, and failed by

Frank Worrell

only three runs to make a hundred on his debut at Port of Spain. He played with confidence following the unheralded success of the temporary first-wicket pairing of George Carew and Andy Ganteaume. Wicket-keeper Godfrey Evans caught him off Ken Cranston. Jack Robertson's rearguard century and rain blunted the West Indians' chance of turning this advantage into victory. The next game at Georgetown was entirely different. Poor weather gave the batsmen little opportunity to get going. The West Indies experimented with yet another opening partnership, and lost three quick wickets. Worrell and Robert Christiani improved matters with the best batting of the entire match. They were two of the most entertaining batsmen ever to be at the crease together. The former scored 131 not out in the 297–8 dec total. Nobody else on either side made half that number. England could not cope with spinners Goddard and Ferguson, and were beaten by 7 wickets. Worrell's rapid development made up considerably for Headley's injury and his withdrawal from the series.

Worrell missed the 1948/49 tour to India, where the West Indies confirmed their new ability with a string of high scores. There was some argument over the terms offered to the players, and Worrell went off instead to the Lancashire League club Radcliffe. The move had two important lessons for the future. Although he was gentle and dignified, Worrell would not let anybody push him around, and he recognized even then the value of a professional grounding. He visited India later with the combined Commonwealth teams which played so much good cricket there in the early 1950s. Worrell delighted the spectators with his batting against slow bowlers on generally lifeless pitches which gave him every opportunity to perfect his stroke-play. He rated the 223 not out at Kanpur as the best innings of his entire career.

Most of the Commonwealth tourists were drawn from the leagues in the North of England. Worrell was as popular at Radcliffe as Constantine had been at Nelson, and the flags on the town hall flew at half-mast when he died. The ten years from 1947 to 1957 were the high point of League cricket. The northern towns attracted some of the best players from throughout the world. In just one summer Worrell could play with as many international cricketers and against as many different styles of batting and bowling as he would otherwise face in a lifetime. He took to the Lancashire way of life, settled there and qualified in economics at Manchester University.

Caribbean Cricketers

The 1950 tour was a landmark in cricket history. The West Indies were keen to show that they could win in England, and win well. Their opponents' discourtesy in selecting less than their best side three years earlier had only increased their determination to succeed. The rubber began with a heavy defeat on the spinning track at Manchester. Previous West Indian teams would have lost confidence, and their will to win would have evaporated there and then. This one was different. Led by Worrell, Walcott, Weekes and Rae, the batsmen thrashed the English bowlers as completely as had Bradman's Australians in 1948, and it was their hosts' turn to break. The tourists won the last three matches by increasing margins.

Worrell was overshadowed at Manchester and Lord's without being disgraced. He was saving his energy for the big moment, which came in the third Test at Nottingham. England's batting breakdown in the opening session was unexpected. Operating with Hines Johnson, the tall fast bowler, Worrell sent back Cyril Washbrook and John Dewes. Trundling in, he moved the ball across their bodies. When the tail showed some defiance he bowled top-scorer Derek Shackleton as well. That was nothing to what was to come. Frank demonstrated the innocuous nature of the pitch with a double century of delightful charm. His brilliance eclipsed the normally pugnacious Weekes, with whom he put on 283 runs for the fourth wicket. Sir Pelham Warner—who knew a thing or two about world cricket, and about West Indian cricket in particular—described that partnership as the best batting he had seen in a lifetime of playing and watching. Worrell was eventually caught off Alec Bedser for 261 runs, compiled in ideal conditions with almost every stroke in the book. It remained the highest score by a West Indian in a Test Match in England until Viv Richards beat it in 1976. The remaining wickets fell quickly, but in spite of England's second-innings fightback the West Indies won comfortably by 10 wickets.

Worrell's century at the Oval was in an altogether different mood. The home selectors had picked their best attack of the season. Trevor Bailey and Bedser brought greater pace and penetration to the new-ball bowling and, above all, leg-spinner Douglas Wright gave every batsman trouble in taking 5 wickets for 141. He pinned the batting down, and forced Worrell, among others, to abandon his cavalier approach and to graft for runs. The West Indians, like the Australians before them, were dumbfounded that Wright was not chosen more often. The tourists resisted the temptation for some

Frank Worrell

spectacular hitting and built an unassailable total on a pitch which became progressively worse. Worrell suffered from dizziness, and retired for a time after reaching his hundred. By the time he came out again Gerry Gomez and John Goddard had put the game beyond England's reach. Wright had him lbw for 138. These two consecutive innings, the brilliant and the courageous, showed the two sides of Worrell's personality and his double value to the team.

The 1951/52 tour to Australia was even more disappointing than the previous visit thirty years before. The West Indies were beaten soundly by four games to one. The batting which had looked so good in India and England crumbled against the extreme speed and hostility of fast bowlers Ray Lindwall, Keith Miller and Bill Johnston. The fury of balls zipping into the body from below-standard wickets was something they had not experienced before. With most of the side injured or out of touch, Worrell was required to take over almost everything at once. Although he did not repeat his former high scoring he fared much better than anyone else. The Jamaican all-rounder won the Adelaide Test Match in the opening overs, and prepared a victory at Melbourne which was thrown away by poor fielding and lapses of concentration.

The West Indies went to Adelaide already two games down, but they were given an unexpected break before the game started. Lindsay Hassett, the diminutive but determined Australian captain, was declared unfit to take part. He was replaced by a bowler instead of by Sid Barnes, the tough but controversial opening batsman, who next year showed his pique by withdrawing from the New South Wales team and wearing a butler's coat to bring out the drinks. The Australian batting was unusually thin, with the tail starting at number six. They were rocked by Worrell's early success, and 22 wickets went down for only 207 runs on the first day. Frank said afterwards that the young Australians panicked when they saw moisture on the pitch and contributed to their own downfall. As usual he was over-modest about his own part in the proceedings. Worrell bowled acting captain Arthur Morris, and also had Jimmy Burke and Keith Miller caught in that decisive first session. He finished with 6 wickets for 38. The West Indies survived their own batting shocks to win by 6 wickets.

The tourists' first innings at Melbourne was a personal duel between Worrell and Keith Miller. The Australian all-rounder was then in full cry. He was a flamboyant extrovert who was always in the game, whether batting, bowling or fielding. Miller relished competition with a worthy opponent, and he rejected the idea of setting up records for records' sake. He got himself out for a duck in protest against the Australians piling up over 700 runs in a single day against lowly Essex in 1948. Keith could open the bowling with an off-break or a bumper and was so dangerous because he was unpredictable. Worrell has related how Miller told him in advance when he would release his short-pitched deliveries to bring the crowd to its feet. This time he was in deadly earnest. The Australian scuttled the West Indian batting with a devastating burst of speed. Worrell, who was injured early in the innings, batted one-handed with great courage in scoring 108 out of the 272. Even in these dire straits he did not lose his composure or his grace of movement. Frank tried lifting the bumpers over the heads of the slips. The victory which was apparent for most of the match was frittered away as the last two batsmen, Doug Ring and Bill Johnston, sneaked home by one wicket.

The West Indians needed the short tour of Test Matches in New Zealand to gather their wits and recover their confidence. The bowling was much more gentle than that which they had endured in recent weeks. All the batsmen took the chance to score runs. Worrell made 71 and 62 not out, the top score in each innings, when they won at Christchurch and hit exactly 100 in a stand of 190 with Clyde Walcott in the rain-affected draw at Auckland.

The strain of the responsibility showed in his relapse over the next three home series. Everton Weekes and Clyde Walcott regained their form as soon as they were back in the Caribbean, but Worrell played only one notable innings in each rubber. He failed to take advantage of the high-scoring games against India in 1953. Worrell closed an otherwise disappointing year by scoring 237 in the fifth Test at Kingston in partnerships of 197 with Weekes and 213 with Walcott. It was the first of only two occasions when all three Ws scored hundreds in the same innings. Vinoo Mankad, a slow bowler who relied on flight, and leg-spinner Subhash Gupte took 5 wickets each, but gave away over 400 runs between them. Pankaj Roy and Vijay Manjrekar saved the Indians from defeat, even though they were 264 runs behind on the first innings. The West Indies won the series on the strength of their victory in the second Test at Bridgetown.

Neither the players taking part nor the public enjoyed the 1953/54 rubber with England. The matches themselves and the social atmosphere were affected by bad temper and 'incidents' on the field, by crowd disturbance, and by a breakdown of communication between the teams. To make matters worse the traditional West Indian batting brittleness reasserted itself and prevented the side from winning the rubber after they had gone ahead in the first two matches. Worrell, who was now vice-captain, was affected by the general malaise. He missed the opening game at Kingston, and failed to score in two out of his next three innings. Although his 167 and 56 at Port of Spain looked best on paper, his most valuable batting was really the 76 not out at Bridgetown. His unbroken stand with John Holt made defeat virtually certain for England, who had to bat last. The West Indian run-scoring potential, which seemed so reassuring in three of the matches, collapsed completely at Georgetown and in the fifth Test at Kingston. Worrell's failure was due partially to the attempt to make him an opener. His natural desire to score freely was ill suited to the requirements of the position.

The West Indies suffered an even greater humiliation against Australia in 1955. The bowling was impotent to stop the avalanche of runs. Apart from Clyde Walcott, Everton Weekes and one innings by Denis Atkinson the batting had no answer to the varied bowling talents of Ray Lindwall, Keith Miller, Ron Archer, Bill Johnston, Ian Johnson and Richie Benaud. Worrell passed 50 only at Georgetown —though that was commendable in the only low-scoring game of the season—and at Kingston. His career was in decline. He was dropped from the vice-captaincy, and was omitted from the predominantly youthful party which toured New Zealand in 1956.

The visit to England the following year is still a mystery. A West Indian team containing some of the greatest names in its history was outplayed in all five Test Matches. While few players returned with their reputations intact, Frank Worrell and Collie Smith—perhaps alone—added to theirs. Throughout much of that summer Worrell was plagued by injury and preoccupied with his university studies. The series began embarrassingly well at Birmingham. After Sonny Ramadhin bowled out England on a good batting wicket the West Indies took a first-innings lead of 288 runs. They owed their position to a sixth-wicket partnership of 190 runs between Worrell—who had to use a runner because of his damaged thigh—and Smith. In the event Peter May and Colin Cowdrey replied with 411 runs for the fourth wicket in England's second innings. The tired West Indians, losing wickets steadily in the final two hours, had to hang on for a draw at 72-7. They were not in the fight again after that.

The team spirit had disintegrated so much by the third Test at

Nottingham that Worrell was required to open both the bowling and the batting. He began the game by moving a ball sharply through the air to have England's new first-wicket batsman, Don Smith, caught at the wicket for a single. Then he watched Tom Graveney, Peter Richardson and Peter May take the eventual total to 619–6 dec. Frank Worrell and Gary Sobers went in first against Freddie Trueman, Trevor Bailey and Brian Statham, possibly the best English pace attack in the post-war period. The seam bowlers were supported by off-spinner Jim Laker just one year after he had taken 19 wickets in one Test against Australia. At first, helped by an even-paced pitch, the batsmen succeeded beyond their highest hopes. In defying some excellent bowling and fielding Worrell played his best innings since the tour to Australasia. The score reached 295–3 by the evening of the third day. Immediately on the next morning Trueman produced one of those whirlwind spells for which he was famous. He broke through the batting so completely that the tourists were all out for 372. At one stage 6 wickets went down for 22 runs. Worrell, who watched the débâcle from the other end, added 55 match-saving runs with Ramadhin for the last wicket. He was 191 not out when the innings ended. In technical merit and value to his side this performance equalled and probably excelled his own double century on the same ground in 1950. The batsman himself was less enthusiastic. He considered that the pitch was so docile any good player should have got runs. Maybe his self-deprecation was a good-natured criticism of his less successful colleagues. Worrell had been on the field for over twenty hours. He went in first when the West Indies followed on 247 runs behind. Understandably tired, he was bowled by Statham for only 16. Collie Smith's heroic second-innings century achieved the draw.

Worrell's bowling was called on in the next match at Leeds. Replacement fast bowler Peter Loader routed the tourists for 142. His 6 wickets for 36 included a hat-trick. In fact, the last four wickets fell to successive deliveries. The West Indians seemed to be mesmerized by the quick bowling and sharp catching. However, England were made to fight harder for victory than seemed possible at the time. Worrell bowled Don Smith for 0 and had Peter Richardson caught at the wicket as the score wobbled at 42–3. David Sheppard (who is now an Anglican bishop), Peter May and Colin Cowdrey stopped the collapse by scoring over 60 runs each. Because of the Jamaican's persistent accuracy the batsmen could not reach a total anything like the high aggregates of their last three innings. Worrell dismissed Cowdrey and Sheppard in his 7 for 70. The final wicket went down too late for the West Indies to begin their second innings that night. The following morning the over-used Worrell received the first ball from Trueman, and shortly afterwards was brilliantly caught by Cowdrey for 9. The batting was even more feeble than before. In spite of Worrell's bowling marathon the game was lost by an innings, and was followed by an even heavier defeat at the Oval.

The disasters of 1957 brought about the end of several hitherto traditional and impractical attitudes. The West Indies could no longer rely solely on sheer talent and individual initiative in an increasingly competitive and professional world. The methods of appointing captains and selecting teams had to be overhauled. The older generation would retire soon, and the younger players had not yet matured. Frank Worrell—who must have seriously considered whether to retire from cricket in favour of a career in politics or economics—was the bridge between these two distinct eras. After a short interval he led the West Indies out of the twilight of their first golden age into the bright new dawn of the 1960s.

That is another story.

CHAPTER FIVE
Weekes and Walcott

A great explosion of batting energy and enthusiasm in the small island of Barbados propelled the West Indies to the forefront of world cricket as soon as the war was over. A new generation of gifted schoolboy batsmen matured rapidly during the early 1940s to challenge Trinidad's traditional leadership. For the first time the West Indies could call on three or more middle-order batsmen who could score centuries consistently. Frank Worrell moved to Jamaica before Test Matches were resumed, but Clyde Walcott and Everton Weekes were still going strong in their homeland. Hitting the ball hard and often, they were the foundation on which the opening partnership of Rae and Stollmeyer and the bowling of Ramadhin and Valentine were established. The prospect of one W following another to the wicket was daunting enough for any bowler.

Weekes was comparatively short in stature, with great power in his arms. He murdered any bowling but the very best, and often that as well. Weekes was particularly severe in front of the wicket and on the offside. Perhaps more than any other he had the finishing quality which is called the 'killer instinct' in boxing parlance. Once Everton decided to knock any bowler out of the attack his victim rarely survived the ordeal. Weekes moved down the pitch to spinners and medium-pacers with terrifying effect. He had no basic coaching until after he had established his place in the game, and, more so even than Headley, was the Caribbean's answer to Bradman in his attitude to run-acquisition.

Walcott, tall and powerful, also struck the ball with tremendous strength. He drove like dynamite, and could hook off the front foot.

His ability to meet bumpers at the point where they pitched helped him deal more efficiently than many of his colleagues with intimidatory leg-stump bowling. Towards the end of his career Walcott played against Kent at Canterbury, a match which I was privileged to see. At one point in the afternoon he stepped back towards his stumps in an apparently defensive position, and yet he still punched the ball effortlessly for six over square-leg. It was well nigh impossible to bowl to a man like that. Walcott, who was guided by Derek Sealy in his formative years, was an all-round athlete in his youth who could have succeeded as a runner or footballer. For several years he was the regular Test Match wicket-keeper. Sometimes he took off the gloves and went into the field. In the second innings at Manchester in 1950 he even opened the bowling.

The English touring team to the Caribbean in 1947/48 was exceptionally prone to injury. The jinx first hit the captain, veteran fast bowler 'Gubby' Allen, on the boat going out, and it did not let up. Although the team was strengthened later by Len Hutton's arrival, it could not contain the enthusiastic young West Indians. In the first three games, in which his top score was 36, Weekes gave no indication of the deluge of runs which would soon flow from his bat. He was dropped from the original team for the fourth Test at Kingston. When Headley had to withdraw Everton was summoned belatedly to the ground. It was appropriate that he should take over from the master so directly. Weekes hammered the under-strength English bowling for 141, the highest individual innings of the rubber, which started his record-breaking sequence of centuries.

Walcott had attracted a good deal of attention while he was still a schoolboy. His batting feats included that record 574 runs stand with Worrell. Yet he had to open the innings on his Test Match debut, the ritualistic initiation for an aspiring wicket-keeper, and had a very poor season. With so many other world-class batsmen pressing their claims, Walcott was kept in the team for the Indian tour in 1948/49 only because he was competent behind the stumps. Once there he made sure that he was not forgotten.

The West Indians were the first side apart from England to attempt a full itinerary of the Indian sub-continent. The long journeys by train from one province to another, the variable climate and the problems of diet could have upset their rhythm and performance. Instead the batsmen played well above themselves, and the team's resolve was moulded by the common effort to win. The captain took some time to settle the batting order. In spite of Frank Worrell missing the tour, Weekes batted only seventh in the first Test Match at New Delhi. He came in after the substantial partnership between Walcott and Gomez hastened his promotion to his regular position at second wicket down by scoring 128, and was on his way.

At Bombay he savaged the bowling in the style which quickly became his trademark. Defeat was already out of the question when he was caught at the wicket for 194. The Indian bowlers did not know where to pitch the ball or how to set their field. Then Weekes upstaged even himself at Calcutta. While seamer Sunil Banerjee and Ghulam Ahmed's well-controlled off-spin troubled the other batsmen Everton stood out in making 162 out of the 366 runs. His 101 in the second innings set up a new world record of hundreds in five consecutive Test Match innings. He almost got another at Madras. Dattu Phadkar made the ball fly nastily after the West Indian first-wicket partnership of over 200, but Weekes weathered the storm in scoring 90 before he was run out. Not everybody agreed with the umpire's decision. The Barbadian completed a very good tour for him with 56 and 48 in the fifth Test at Bombay.

Walcott was only just behind his compatriot in the chase for runs. He was ushered quickly to the wicket at New Delhi, where the tourists lost their first three batsmen cheaply. It was the type of challenge he relished. Clyde flayed the attack with 152 in a 267 runs stand with Gerry Gomez. Poor Rangachari, the medium-pacer who had caused the minor collapse, was hit for over a hundred runs. The bowlers' torment ended only when Walcott was run out. Encouraged by his example, three other players made hundreds in the innings. Walcott scored 54 and 108 as second fiddle to Weekes at Calcutta. He showed characteristic fighting spirit in the final fixture where India came very close to winning and drawing level in the series. Phadkar was going well, but, as Pat Sen was injured, his partner, Ghulam Ahmed, was the last real batsman. In the closing overs Walcott cut down the possibility of extra runs by throwing off his glove and chasing the ball towards the boundary. Every run saved was vital. His effort was well worth while because India failed to win, by only 6 runs.

The West Indians overcame similar problems of weather, food and a strange social environment to beat England in 1950. The summer was often cold and wet. It is strange to recall now that the West Indian community in Britain was then very small, and had almost no influence on the national way of life. Walcott has explained the

Weekes and Walcott

difficulties of obtaining even such a basic ingredient as rice. (Rice pudding, however, probably did more to upset them than all the English bowlers!) All the same, the situation was not so bad as some of the early stories make out. While passers-by might well have touched the dark-skinned tourists to see if the colour rubbed off, the West Indians themselves were better acquainted with white society. Learie Constantine had his tongue in his cheek when he said that all white men looked alike to him on his first tour in 1923. He was supposedly confused into thinking that an incoming batsman was the same one who had just been dismissed. Many of the early tourists were themselves white, several of whom had spent quite a bit of time in this country.

In their first post-war tour the West Indies won their first Test Match in England and went on to take the rubber. Until then the merest hint of a setback had sapped their confidence. Perhaps the almost complete break in team continuity from 1939 to 1947 had rescued the newcomers from the pessimism of their predecessors. After losing at Manchester on a pitch which broke up too easily the tourists won the other three games with assured superiority. Walcott was magnificent in the famous 'calypso' Test Match at Lord's. The wicket-keeper, extremely agile in spite of his size, contributed much to the breakthrough of the young spinners Ramadhin and Valentine. He stumped both of the English opening batsmen, Len Hutton and Cyril Washbrook, who had started so well, and then quickly caught Bill Edrich to expose the inexperienced middle-batting. Because the West Indians had thrown away such advantages before, the result was still in balance when they batted a second time. Walcott made sure that there was no let-up now. He hit a really powerful 168 not out against the same spin bowlers who had worried them in the previous game. In that one innings he exorcised English slow bowling of the kind which had haunted the pre-war batsmen. Clyde attacked while Gomez defended in a match-winning stand of 211 runs. He had little batting success in the rest of the series, but he was not really needed again.

Everton Weekes rolled over the English county bowling without quite hitting the heights in the Test Matches. Frank Worrell's brilliance and Allan Rae's dependability were more important in winning the rubber. Weekes's part should not be forgotten, however. His performance would have been outstanding in a less gifted age. His reputation of murderous determination might well have deterred most bowlers. Everton sacrificed his own well-being for the team's benefit, and was at his best when the chips were down. He began the season with a top score of 52 against spinners Bob Berry and Eric Hollies in almost unplayable conditions at Manchester. In the second of his two knocks of 63 at Lord's he was out when going quickly for the runs. Everton's best achievement was 129 in a stand of 283 with Worrell at Nottingham. His fielding was a constant threat to opposing batsmen as he poached catches put up off Ramadhin and Valentine—never more so than when he held five in England's collapse at the Oval.

The side which went to Australia in 1951/52 bristled with potential runs. Its reliance on spin bowling as well may have led to its undoing. Since Martindale and Constantine had retired the West Indians had had no experience of playing their own fast bowling, and they had encountered nothing worth talking about in India and England. When they came up against the Australians they did not know what hit them. The tourists managed only two centuries in the whole series, though, to be fair, the other team did not do much better. Some of the pitches left a lot to be desired as far as batting was concerned. The players were also critical of the administrators for arranging a schedule which pitched them straight into the Test Matches after only one other first-class game.

Weekes suffered more than most because so much more had been expected of him. When the West Indians ran into bumpers for the first time at Brisbane his second innings 70 was a minor masterpiece of positive batting. If he had been able to continue in that vein the ultimate overall performance would have been much better, but his scope for playing strokes was cut down by injury and by tight fast bowling. For his part, Walcott's career was changed drastically by the events of the tour. He suffered a broken nose and also a strained back which forced him to give up wicket-keeping. From then on he played as a batsman and an excellent slip fielder. Walcott showed his aptitude for the new role by scoring 115 at Auckland and 65 at Christchurch on the short visit to New Zealand.

The West Indian batsmen had a point to prove, and they made the Indians suffer for it. Weekes went out for runs right from the start of the first Test at Port of Spain. He scored 207, and shared a double-century partnership for the fifth wicket with young Bruce Pairaudeau. At this stage in his career the Barbadian was a better player against slow bowling—where he would move down the wicket—than against pace on a bad pitch. He developed a seemingly insatiable appetite for Indian bowling, and did not care whether it turned or was flighted. Weekes followed this grand opening to the season with 161 and 55 not out in the third Test, also played in Trinidad, and 109 at Kingston. His innings of 86 in the rain-spoiled play at Georgetown was quite modest in comparison.

Walcott showed his value in a crisis this year. The West Indian crowds were watching their first home series for just under six years, and he gave them something to remember. There was little between the two teams in the hard-fought second Test at Bridgetown until the visitors' batting collapsed on the last morning. Up to then it had been touch and go. Walcott was lbw to Phadkar for 98, given out by his uncle, the umpire. He stood between an early defeat and giving his own spinners the fighting chance which they took. Then Clyde closed the season majestically with 125 at Georgetown and 118 at Kingston.

The West Indian batting against England in 1953/54 was disappointing. It had the measure of the opposing bowling often enough, but two inexplicable breakdowns wiped out the early lead. This sort of thing had happened overseas in the 1930s. Weekes stood firm throughout the season. He scored 55 and 90 not out in the first Test Match at Kingston against the very good English attack of Trueman, Statham, Laker and Lock which had just won back the Ashes from Australia. After missing the next game Weekes scored 94 at Georgetown, a superb innings in a weak team batting performance. Then he led the way with 206 among the five centuries at Port of Spain. Weekes's tough tussles with Brian Statham—perhaps the most accurate of all fast bowlers—belied those who said he could not play genuine pace.

In these next two years Clyde Walcott could justifiably claim to be the best attacking batsman in the world. He began the 1953/54 series with a quiet 65 at Kingston. In the following match at Bridgetown he came in with the innings in tatters through the dismissal of the first two men without scoring and with Weekes out of the side through injury. Walcott imposed his will on the bowlers and changed the whole course of the game by hitting 220 out of the 383 runs total. Few batsmen have monopolized their side's scoring so completely. In view of the critical situation and the quality of the bowling this was probably his greatest innings in international cricket. This assessment does not exclude Lord's in 1950 or any of his subsequent feats against Australia. Clyde made 124 at Port of Spain, the second time all three

Ws made hundreds together, and he was the only West Indian batsman to cope in the disastrous fifth Test Match at Kingston. The West Indies needed only a draw to win the rubber. They were encouraged by having first use of a good pitch, albeit with a little early-morning life. Their illusions were soon shattered. Trevor Bailey took 7 wickets for 34 in bowling them out for 139. The English all-rounder's bowling is not always given the credit it deserves. He was selected as a bowler before he became famous for his stone-wall batting. I have watched him enough times in county matches to realize that he swung the ball as much as anyone. Maybe he found a touch of Clacton or Leyton in Sabina Park. Walcott made 50 after the first four wickets had tumbled, and hit 116 in the second innings when the issue was already decided. It was a foretaste of things to come.

The Australians swept through the Caribbean in 1955, dominating each of the five Test Matches. The batsmen should not be blamed too much. Indeed, Clyde Walcott was the outstanding personality of the season. He compiled five centuries in his 827 runs aggregate, while his compatriots stumbled and fell to the combined speed and spin. Walcott prospered because he did not go on to the back foot to hit the short-pitched bowling—which would have exposed him to the ball that kept low—but met the fast bowlers coming forward. In outscoring the run-hungry Australians he became the first—and to date the only—batsman to score a century in each innings of a Test Match twice in the same series.

Walcott started with 108 at Kingston, where the tourists early stamped their authority on the proceedings. He and Weekes achieved an honourable draw at Port of Spain. In spite of the trouble which Ray Lindwall gave most of the other batsmen, Clyde seized the initiative with 126 and 110. Lindwall's smooth bowling action was almost poetic, and he could make the ball rise head-high from a near-perfect length. Walcott made 73 at Georgetown and 83 at Bridgetown in building up to the climax in the fifth Test Match at Kingston, where batting records abounded and Australia won by an innings and 82 runs. Double-centurion Neil Harvey, Ron Archer, Colin McDonald, Richie Benaud and Keith Miller scored hundreds in their massive 758–8 dec, but even they yielded pride of place to the big Barbadian. He hammered a regal 155 in the first innings, when the next highest score was only 61, and made another 110 in the second. Gary Sobers helped him put on 179 runs for the fourth wicket. There was very little resistance once they were out. Clyde Walcott batted throughout the

Weekes and Walcott

series with complete assurance in what was probably the best performance by a batsman on the losing side.

Weekes kept pace with his partner in the early matches. He was most effective in the second Test Match at Port of Spain, where he scored 139 and 87 not out in their third-wicket stands of 242 and 127. Nobody bettered his 81 at Georgetown on the only pitch which favoured the bowlers all summer. His admirers waited expectantly to see how he would react to Walcott's challenge as the side's leading run-scorer. They soon found out.

Most of the established players were left out of the touring team to New Zealand in 1956. The younger men were given every chance to prove themselves. Weekes was included for the benefit of his experience and his example. What an example it was! He celebrated with centuries in his first five first-class innings, including two in the Test Matches. The mild, medium-paced New Zealand bowling was all grist to his mill. Weekes scored 123 in a stand of 162 with Collie Smith for the fourth wicket at Dunedin, a dynamic 103 at Christchurch and another 156 at Wellington. The other batsmen became little more than spectators. Although the opposing bowling was not particularly strong, nobody else reached a hundred in any of the four matches. Every time Weekes scored a century the West Indies won by an innings. When he failed at Auckland, though hitting the top score of 31 in the second innings, the tourists were beaten. Here New Zealand won their first Test Match victory after trying for 25 years.

Clyde Walcott and Everton Weekes were all too obviously in peak form. Not surprisingly, England regarded the West Indian visit in 1957 with some trepidation. The batsmen, especially Walcott, moved through the early county games, putting the bowling to the severest edge of their bats like the Norsemen of old. It was 1950 all over again. Then the bubble burst suddenly and beyond recall. Injury and lost form came together, just in time for the opening of that ill-fated Test Match series.

Walcott was restricted by a damaged thigh, but made 90 in the first game at Birmingham. He did not reach fifty in any of the remaining matches. The powerful Barbadian, toying with the little bat in his hands, looked as imposing as ever. Surely it was only a matter of time before he avenged the indignities he had to suffer? But he could not get going again.

Weekes's own run of success came to an end at the same time. Troubled by ill-health, he failed totally, apart from a gallant fighting innings at Lord's. Defeat was inevitable from the moment Trevor Bailey, taking 7 wickets for 44, bowled the West Indies to a first-innings deficit of 297. On the last day Weekes stood up to the formidable battery of Trueman, Statham and Bailey on a spiteful pitch from which the ball jumped sharply and damaged his finger early on. He attacked the bowling with an impressive array of strokes until he was caught at the wicket for 90. It was as good an innings as he ever played, and deserved a hundred. He lost his way after that, suffering from double-vision towards the end of the tour. Everton's difficulty in timing his shots distressed those of us who remembered his spectacular hitting of recent years.

There was a happy ending to both stories. Everton Weekes ended his Test Match career in the way he would have wanted it. The clean Caribbean air was more agreeable to his impaired vision, and he scored 197 against Pakistan at Bridgetown in 1957/58. He put the West Indies so far ahead that little Hanif Mohammad had to stay at the crease for a record 16 hours and 13 minutes to keep his team in the game. He softened the bowlers' resolve in preparation for Gary Sobers's record-breaking spree. Weekes scored half-centuries in the two matches played at Port of Spain. Like Rocky Marciano—to whom his professional approach has been compared—Everton is quiet and good-natured to everybody but his professional opponents on the field. I suspect that most West Indian fans have greater affection for him than for any other batsman of his age, and that, in spite of his sequence of centuries in India and New Zealand, he was happiest playing at home.

Clyde Walcott's bold batting was also suited better to the Caribbean, and he had one more successful season before he retired. Everything that had gone wrong in England came together well against the Pakistanis. Walcott, who scored 88 not out, was at the wicket when Gary Sobers surpassed Len Hutton's highest individual score in a Test Match by making 365 not out at Kingston. They were at the crease again in adding 269 for the second wicket at Georgetown. Walcott was back to his masterful best as he attacked the wily and patient sixteen-year-old left-armer Nasimul Ghani. The young Pakistani had his revenge in taking 6 wickets at Port of Spain, where the West Indies suffered their only defeat. Even there Walcott did not falter, with 62 out of 227.

Everton Weekes and Clyde Walcott retired together at the end of that series. The latter was persuaded to come back for a final appearance in the hotch-potch rubber with England in 1959/60. His 53 in the fifth Test Match at Port of Spain was a refreshing contrast to much of the dull batting which had gone before. Walcott was never dull, always exciting. His contribution to West Indian cricket did not end with his retirement from the field of play. He has had a very successful second career in management and administration. When John Goddard was indisposed it fell to Clyde to broadcast the concession of victory to England at the Oval in 1957. Few who heard him speak could not have been touched by his dignity in defeat and his conviction that the West Indies would rise again from that humiliation. It was only fitting, therefore, that Walcott managed and directed the invincible team which humbled England in 1976.

Clyde Walcott changed the balance of cricket in the Caribbean in another more fundamental way. For many years Guyana had been a comparative backwater of international sport, until he moved there from his island home on a coaching assignment in the mid-1950s. The local talent developed rapidly under his appreciative eye. Walcott, who was then vice-captain, took Rohan Kanhai with him to England in 1957. Basil Butcher, who had come very close to selection for that team, and Joe Solomon were ready for the next tour to India and Pakistan just over a year later. They started a line of strong Guyanese batting which through Clive Lloyd, Roy Fredericks and Alvin Kallicharran has replaced the previous Barbadian near-monopoly.

CHAPTER SIX
Rae and Stollmeyer

Each country has at least one opening partnership with which it is always associated. Allan Rae and Jeff Stollmeyer are as much part of the West Indian folk-tradition as are Jack Hobbs and Herbert Sutcliffe in England, Billy Woodfull and Bill Ponsford in Australia, and Vijay Merchant and Mustaq Ali in India. There is one important difference, nevertheless. They were their country's only stable first-wicket pairing until Gordon Greenidge linked with Roy Fredericks in the mid-1970s. The value of a sound start to the innings is worth far more than the runs on the board or the duration of the batsmen at the wicket. They have to break down the morale of the opposing bowlers so that the later batsmen can go for their shots. If they fail every wicket lost boosts the fielding side's confidence and adds to the burden of responsibility on those that follow.

The West Indies have nearly always had one reliable opening batsman. The cupboard has rarely been entirely bare. Over the past eighty years Charles Ollivierre, George Challenor, Clifford Roach and Conrad Hunte have spearheaded their team's batting challenge. Even with all their considerable individual talent these players could not bat at both ends at the same time and prevent the steady fall of wickets. The absence of a second regular opener was the one weak spot in several otherwise balanced and successful West Indian sides, including Frank Worrell's triumphant team of the early 1960s.

There was no recognized partnership until twenty years after the first Test Match. Challenor's power declined after he passed forty. Roach was inconsistent. The failed experiment of deputizing non-specialist batsmen made for greater uncertainty in the one position where stability was required most. For a time wicket-keeper Ivan Barrow went in first, particularly overseas. There was even less continuity at home. Roach had four different partners in 1929/30. Each game five years later had a different pairing. As the era closed young Jeff Stollmeyer was the only experienced opening batsman with any promise for the future.

The problem was not resolved at once in 1947/48. Veteran George Carew came into the side when Stollmeyer was injured before the second Test Match at Port of Spain. In his only previous innings he had failed to score on the Bridgetown quagmire thirteen years beforehand. His partner, Andy Ganteaume, a sound but hardly entertaining batsman, was new to Test Match cricket. Both scored centuries in the then record West Indian first-wicket stand of 173 runs. The whole match was marked by unexpected feats from unusual opening batsmen. Billy Griffith, the English deputy wicket-keeper, was drafted to go in first, and made his maiden first-class hundred on his international debut. It was that sort of game. Ganteaume did not bat in the second innings, and although he had played very well, he was dropped from the side. He was replaced in the opening position by John Goddard, a left-arm spinner who had achieved some batting success in inter-territorial competition. Consequently Ganteaume is the only player of any nationality to score a century in his one Test Match innings. (New Zealand's Redmond made 107 against Pakistan at Auckland in 1972/73, but although he did not play again, he did bat in the second innings.) Carew went to India as Stollmeyer's prospective partner. He yielded his place to newcomer Allan Rae in the Test Matches.

Jeff Stollmeyer's career straddled the periods of pre-war amateurism and post-war professionalism. He was a cultured batsman, remembered best for his elegance and style. Accidents at awkward times kept him out of the captaincy in the 1940s, and curtailed his leadership in the early 1950s. While still in his teens, the younger of the two Stollmeyer brothers from Trinidad scored 59 at both Lord's and the Oval in 1939. Then he was just one of several young batsmen who showed promise for the future. Whereas others fell by the wayside during the war years, Stollmeyer consolidated his position with some fine innings in domestic cricket. He was an automatic choice to play against England in 1947/48, and he made 78 in the first Test Match at Bridgetown. He missed the next two games through injury. One of these was the fixture at his native Port of Spain where he had been nominated captain. Jeff came back only for the match at Kingston. He was vice-captain to Goddard on the tour to India.

Run-scoring was embarrassingly easy on the tropical pitches. Apart from occasional flurries by all-rounder Dattu Phadkar, the bowling was gentle-paced and the West Indian batsmen were not afraid to use their footwork in getting after the spinners. The great Indian fast bowlers of the past decade, Amar Singh, Mohammad Nissar, Jahangir Khan (the father of Majid Jahangir Khan), were either retired or dead. Their breeding-ground in the north-western provinces had passed to Pakistan in the political partition of 1947.

Allan Rae, a Jamaican left-hander whose father had toured England with Karl Nunes's team in 1928, seemed fortunate to be preferred to Carew. In spite of a hesitant start, he developed quickly into an excellent batsman with an ideal temperament whose sound defence complemented Stollmeyer's artistry. Bowlers and critics testify to Rae's great patience. That goes without saying, but I can remember his exhilarating exhibition of hitting in a charity match at Gravesend in 1950. He lifted the ball repeatedly into near-by Trafalgar Road. It was the first time I had seen a real Test Match player in action. Irrespective of his general reputation, that memory is not forgotten easily.

The partnership made its first important impact in the second Test at Bombay. In an innings marked by strong driving, Rae scored 104 before hitting a return catch to Phadkar. The stand realized 134 runs. The same batsmen had a decisive influence on the game at Madras, where an innings victory broke the sequence of drawn matches. Stollmeyer, who made an undefeated double century in the preceding engagement against South Zone, again scored confidently. As the batsmen's supremacy became obvious the Indian bowlers made the mistake of attempting a modified leg-theory. Their great stroke-player Rusi Modi, who was fielding at the time, remarked on the futility of bowling bumpers against players who were already well set. Stollmeyer and Rae thrived on this short-pitched attack in putting on 239 runs for the first wicket. They scored 160 and 109 respectively. The left-hander's defensive talent also served his side well in the fifth Test at Bombay. The tourists were 93 ahead at the halfway stage, but ran into trouble in their second innings against a steady rather than penetrative attack. Rae fought stubbornly until he was caught by Mankad off Phadkar for 97. His effort held up India long enough to prevent them squaring the rubber.

The reliability of the opening partnership went a long way towards beating England in 1950. For the first time since Ollivierre was paired briefly with Pelham Warner the West Indians could take the edge off the bowling. The powerful middle-order batting revelled in the luxury to record some very high scoring. The achievements of the openers that summer were more important than mere statistics, though these too were impressive enough. The first Test at Manchester was little more than a contest between the skills of the respective slow bowlers. With the game already lost, Stollmeyer hit 78 in a display of attractive strokes. He moved his feet well to get to the pitch of the bowling of Jim Laker, Bob Berry and Eric Hollies. It was the classic case of the vice-captain being the last man to go down with his ship. The Trinidadian was usually at his best when the other batsmen failed. He was remarkably consistent throughout the series, in which he was not dismissed once for under twenty.

Rae was the lynch-pin on which the triumph at Lord's was founded. His 106 on the first day went a long way towards winning the match. He kept out the best deliveries and hit the bad balls hard. The Jamaican saw off the innocuous attack of Alec Bedser and Bill Edrich and shattered the bowling in substantial partnerships with Frank Worrell and Everton Weekes. The West Indies had a comfortable lead of 175 runs, and did not look back. Rae was just as secure on the feather-bed pitch at Nottingham where the feeble English batting did little justice to the conditions. He made 68 before he was stumped, and Stollmeyer was out four runs short of his half-century. They pointed the way to a large total with a stand of 77. In the second innings they knocked off the 102 runs needed to win without loss.

Rae's tight, unspectacular batting made sure that the Oval Test would not be lost from as early as the first day. His soundness blunted potentially the best English bowling of the summer. After the usual competent start of 72 Rae exasperated the bowlers with another patient century. He and Worrell scored 172 runs for the second wicket. After that their own spinners got the upper hand, and the West Indies won by an innings and 56 runs.

The batting shattered on its first impact with Australian fast bowlers Ray Lindwall and Keith Miller in 1951/52. Rae took the first strike at Brisbane. He failed to come down quickly enough on Lindwall's rapid full toss and was bowled for a duck in the very first over of the series. The tourists did not recover from such an ill-

Caribbean Cricketers

omened start. Some joker in the team suspended a razor-blade in their changing-room so that they could complete their suicide. The bowlers hustled them out with a stream of bumpers which cramped Stollmeyer's stylish strokes and cancelled out Rae's effectiveness. Various ill-judged changes to the batting order, including the use of wicket-keeper Simpson Guillen as temporary opener, did not give the side a chance to settle down. A third opening batsman, Roy Marshall, was brought in to bolster the flagging middle-order batting which had been weakened by injury. Later in the decade Marshall charmed spectators in England with his bright batting for Hampshire in the county championship. His unorthodox methods of scoring led to the downfall of several would-be imitators. The morning after the daily newspapers gave extensive coverage to his cutting a six over point I saw an Essex opening batsman get himself caught trying to repeat the same stroke at Leyton.

Stollmeyer's best innings was again played in forlorn circumstances in the fifth Test Match at Sydney. Replying to Australia's shock dismissal by Gerry Gomez for only 116, Keith Miller hit back with speed and fury which wrecked the West Indies in turn for 78. Stollmeyer had taken over the captaincy when Goddard withdrew on the eve of the game, and he batted wonderfully in furtherance of his lost cause. His 104 was by far the highest individual score of the match. Even though he was in poor health, Rae made 25, the next best in the innings, and the tourists reached 137–2. Now it was Lindwall's turn to move in attack. Under his bumper barrage 7 wickets went down for 24 runs. That was that.

The batsmen found their feet again in New Zealand. Stollmeyer batted beautifully for his 152 at Auckland. He was appointed captain on Goddard's retirement when the team returned home. The task ahead of him was difficult. Under the influence of defeat and dissension team loyalty seemed to be fragmented on territorial lines. Stollmeyer led them to victory over India, and shared the honours with England. Further injury limited his appearances against Ian Johnson's Australian side and precipitated his premature retirement in 1956. Stollmeyer had hoped to lead the West Indies in England. His departure left them without a unanimous choice as either captain or opening batsman.

Batting in his first home series, Allan Rae scored 63 not out against India at Port of Spain in 1953. He had an unbroken stand of 142 with Stollmeyer in the second innings. It seemed that the 'old firm' was back in business. Yet, surprisingly, this was the last time that they went in first together. The partnership was dismantled to give an opportunity to young Bruce Pairaudeau, who scored 115 in the first innings of the same match. Rae was unlucky to be dropped because his batting had improved from its lowpoint in Australia. Meanwhile Stollmeyer himself had a successful series in scoring 76 not out, 54 and 104 not out in the first three games. It was the first time he had played right through a rubber in the Caribbean, fourteen years since his Test Match debut.

With John Holt, another Jamaican, as his regular partner Stollmeyer should have done well against England in 1953/54. In fact he was frustrated both as captain and as batsman. Jeff made 60 at Kingston where, following his controversial decision not to enforce the follow-on, the West Indies won by 140 runs. He was run out without scoring at Bridgetown, made 40 in each of the next two games, and hit 64 in the fifth Test. That was little consolation, as England won by 9 wickets. They had pulled up from a 2-0 deficit to level the rubber. Stollmeyer played twice against Australia the next year, but did not reach 50. Further aggravation to his injury caused him to retire in the domestic season leading up to the 1957 tour to England. His specialist experience might have made all the difference in that disappointing year.

Allan Rae and Jeff Stollmeyer still team up to withstand an attack on West Indian cricket: as leading administrators, they had to bear the brunt of Kerry Packer's intervention in the Caribbean. Stollmeyer's quiet dignity, which made him slightly aloof as a player, has been an asset in these very difficult negotiations. He has admitted his regret at the seeming inability to prevent the conflicting demands of conventional and commercial cricket from breaking up the West Indian team. The fact that the rupture has not become permanent is a tribute to his diplomacy. He was always at his best in a crisis.

Bruce Pairaudeau's subsequent career suffered greatly from the immediate favourable impression of scoring 115 at Port of Spain and 58 at Kingston in his first series. He was moved up to open the innings but did not come off as expected. Pairaudeau scored those early runs against a primarily spin attack. His later failures against fast bowling have been attributed to his wearing spectacles and his better suitability to the middle order. England's Mike Smith, who also wore glasses, moved down the order with considerable success. Pairaudeau regained his place in the side with 68 against New Zealand at

Caribbean Cricketers

Wellington in 1956. He failed along with the other opening batsmen in England the next year. Freddie Trueman bowled him quickly for a single in the first Test Match at Birmingham, but Pairaudeau spent nearly the entire first innings at the crease as runner for Clyde Walcott and Frank Worrell. He was there while 387 runs were put on. Bruce went to live in New Zealand for the rest of his cricketing life.

Hammond Furlonge, a member of the large Trinidadian family, was an unlucky omission from the England tour. The previous year he had scored 64 at Auckland when all the other batsmen disappointed. That innings showed his ability to keep going when things were far from well, and he must have been very close to selection. The selectors banked on maturity instead. Young Furlonge did not play in another Test Match.

John Holt, whose father had toured England with Harold Austin's second team thirty years earlier, took over from fellow-Jamaican Allan Rae against England in 1953/54. He had been knocking on the door for some time. Holt was very successful at first. Later he was omitted from the tours to New Zealand and England after a spate of dropped catches and a lean time against the Australian fast bowlers. His international career began dramatically. When Michael Frederick, the preferred opening batsman, did not score, Holt and Stollmeyer added 135 runs for the second wicket at Kingston. Statham had him lbw only 6 runs short of what would have been a famous century. The dismissal decision produced a riot among his partisan home crowd.

The Jamaican had an even better match at Bridgetown where he went in first. He helped Frank Worrell score over 200 runs for the second wicket before he was caught and bowled by Statham for 166. Holt's batting enthralled all who saw it, a far cry from his castigation for slow scoring in later years. England could not match such tall scoring, and were beaten by 181 runs. The West Indian batting crumpled twice in the next game at Georgetown, where the tourists turned the tables in winning by 9 wickets. With Holt batting at number nine because of injury, Worrell, the replacement opener, was out for a duck and wickets fell regularly. McWatt and Holt slightly retrieved the position with 99 runs for the eighth wicket. The wicket-keeper's run-out for 54 sparked off perhaps the worst crowd disturbance of that troubled season. Holt, who made 48 not out, resumed his place with Stollmeyer for the second innings, and hit the top score with 64.

Rae and Stollmeyer

Few selections have given rise to as much controversy as the composition of the 1957 team to tour England. With Stollmeyer ruled out already the three other leading candidates were also overlooked. They were Holt (Jamaica), Furlonge (Trinidad) and Hunte (Barbados). Their places were taken by Bruce Pairaudeau, Andy Ganteaume and Nyron Asgarali. This trio failed so often that Frank Worrell, Gary Sobers and Rohan Kanhai were pressed into service. Ganteaume, who had been passed over when he was at his best, had left it too late to come back to big-time cricket.

Holt was brought back to partner Hunte for the double-tour of India and Pakistan in 1958/59. He had played there before with one of the Commonwealth sides. The openers were so much at sea against India's moderate pace bowling in the first three games that their places were in jeopardy. Holt had his best match for five years at Madras. He scored 63 and 81 not out, and was better still in the fifth Test at New Delhi. Hunte and Holt scored 159 before the first wicket fell. John's rather dour 123 was the springboard for the more spectacular hitting by Collie Smith and Joe Solomon. When they did badly in the first two matches against Pakistan, Holt and Hunte were replaced by young Robin Bynoe and wicket-keeper Gerry Alexander without any better result. Unlike his partner, who went on to greater fame, John Holt was not recalled. He was the last in the line of direct descendants to Rae and Stollmeyer.

CHAPTER SEVEN
Ramadhin and Valentine

Sonny Ramadhin and Alfred Valentine ('those little pals of mine') are linked indelibly in calypso and in cricket history. Few other careers have been as remarkable in their unexpected initial success. One day they were unknown, the next their names were household words. They were the first two West Indian world-class spin bowlers to work together, and to date the only ones. Apart from the occasional spells of Tommy Scott and Ellis Achong, pre-war slow bowling was the part-time occupation of batsmen. It was not taken as seriously as pace. The decline in the standard of fast bowling, plus the ageing of the established bowlers themselves, coincided with the preparation of pitches more suited to spin. The West Indies needed a change by the time the English team arrived in 1947/48.

Off-spinner Jim Laker took 7 wickets in the very first innings at Bridgetown. The other bowlers would have to rethink their approach along these lines. The West Indian slow bowlers won the moral victory at Port of Spain, and actually carried it off at Georgetown. The young batsmen in the experimental touring side had been deprived of first-class cricket for five years. They had next to no experience against any type of good bowling. Their own attack lacked 'bite', depending as it did on the seam bowling of 'Gubby' Allen, then well in his forties, and Ken Cranston.

Wilfred Ferguson made his first mark with 56 not out at Bridgetown. He was an even better bowler, and took 11 wickets at Port of Spain, almost enough to win the game. When Jack Robertson was run out early on the Trinidadian bowled Jack Ikin, caught and bowled Cranston, and dismissed three lower-order batsmen. In the second innings he gave the West Indies a great chance by catching Billy Griffith off Gomez and having Ikin lbw. He took another 2 wickets while the issue was still open, but Smithson stayed with Robertson long enough to deprive the West Indians of sufficient time to win. Ferguson still had the last word by dismissing both batsmen and bowling last man Harold Butler for 0. It was the most comprehensive bowling performance to date by a West Indian spinner. The home side, who had outplayed their opponents at every turn, finished only 68 runs behind with 7 wickets in hand.

England had the worst of the wicket at Georgetown where the rain poured down after the West Indians scored 297–8 dec. The deadly left-arm spin of John Goddard, the new captain, swept away the main body of the batting by having Hutton, Robertson, Place, Ikin and Howorth all caught at a personal cost of only 31 runs. Goddard seemed so innocuous holding the ball in front of his body with both hands as he approached the stumps. Ferguson held three of the catches and also took another 3 wickets of his own. When they followed on 186 runs behind England were soon in further trouble. Almost immediately Ferguson had Robertson lbw and bowled Hutton and Place. Joe Hardstaff got enough support from the tail to make the West Indies bat again. Just when it seemed that they would wriggle off the hook once more Ferguson dismissed Howorth and finished the innings by having opposing captain Allen lbw. The batsmen easily scored the runs required to win by 7 wickets. The blueprint for future victories was already there.

Fast bowler Hines Johnson clinched the rubber at Kingston. Fast-medium Prior Jones and John Trim found enough life in the pitch at Madras to decide the one game that mattered in India. Spin bowling was pushed into the background again. Ferguson, who was by now regarded as the best spin bowler in the world, was the chief casualty of that tour. He did little after taking 4 expensive wickets in the first innings of the second Test Match at Bombay. The Indian batsmen had been reared on a diet of their own spinners Wilfred did not puzzle them on those soulless pitches. All the same, it was still a major surprise when he was left out of the team to tour England in 1950. Neither of his successors, teenagers Ramadhin and Valentine, had any worth-while first-class experience. The way in which they succeeded shut the door on any chance of Ferguson coming back.

These slightly built youngsters were unknown even in their own islands at the start of the year. Their appearance contrasted starkly with the mature tradition of Manny Martindale, George Francis and Herman Griffith. They bewildered even their most skilful opponents at the first meeting, and destroyed them in the second. Their styles of delivery were unconventional. Ramadhin bowled with his sleeves buttoned down and still wearing his cap. Everything about him was a mystery. His initials were given variously as 'S' or 'K.T.' without any apparent comment from the player himself. Sonny is described as being so inexperienced that he did not even recognize Len Hutton when he dismissed him early on the tour. Some of his team-mates have testified to this incident. The record-books show that he did not dismiss Hutton at any time that season. Such stories are the lifeblood of legend. Ramadhin perplexed the batsmen with his flight, and by spinning the ball either way without any obvious change of action. He got less turn from the pitch than his partner, and deceived his opponents through the air as much as off the wicket. Jack Hobbs scotched the South African googly menace in 1907 by playing forward and killing the spin where it pitched. His successors who attempted similar tactics against Ramadhin were often confused, and were usually bowled or stumped.

Valentine, gauche, gangling and wearing glasses, struck a length and spun the ball appreciably. His whole approach and delivery seemed at odds with the text-book. Although he did not bother to mark out his run, there was little mystery about the Jamaican. The only doubt was by how much he would beat the bat. Alfred could be lethal whenever the wicket was responsive, especially with the delivery which dipped in to the batsman. He mastered the intricacies of flight and changes of pace to bowl persistently when conditions were against him. Valentine was the perfect foil to Ramadhin. His attitude to the game seemed so casual that he did not know he needed spectacles until he found his vision blurred in trying to read the scoreboard.

Valentine was somewhat lucky to be chosen for the first Test Match at Manchester. He had not bowled too well on tour and his captain, Goddard, was expected to be the main left-arm spinner. His good performance in a county match against Lancashire on the same ground may have swung the verdict in his favour. This type of bowler had caused havoc with West Indians in the past. Now the boot was on the other foot. By lunchtime on the opening day England were 88 with five men out, and Valentine's name was broadcast round the world. Valentine seized his chance when opening batsman Hutton retired through injury. He struck with deadly accuracy, and was supported by some fine close fielding. Gomez caught Bill Edrich, Tom Dollery and Norman Yardley, and Reg Simpson and Hubert Doggart followed them out in the pre-lunch session. The Jamaican had taken all the wickets. When he was rested Trevor Bailey, a stubborn all-rounder nicknamed 'barnacle' for his habit of clinging to the crease, and Godfrey Evans, the pugnacious wicket-keeper, saved England in what turned out to be a match-winning stand of 161. Valentine was not finished yet. He caught and bowled Evans, bowled Hutton on his return to batting, and also accounted for Laker. By dismissing the last two batsmen Ramadhin prevented his partner from becoming the first bowler to take all ten wickets in a Test Match innings. Jim Laker, one of his victims then, performed that feat against Australia on the same ground six years later. Valentine bowled superbly in taking 8 wickets for 104. The West Indies lost because they batted last on a wicked pitch and England had greater depth in batting.

From that point on spin was the trump card of the rubber. England picked four slow bowlers for the second Test at Lord's. Although the tourists batted well, Roly Jenkins, a nagging left-armer who took 5 wickets, denied them the large total which seemed possible when Rae was going so steadily. The outlook seemed even more ominous when Leonard Hutton and Cyril Washbrook saw off the fast bowlers without loss and without difficulty. The arrival of the spinners changed all that. Both opening batsmen were stumped as they misread the flight and turn. Neither Hubert Doggart nor Gilbert Parkhouse scored as Ramadhin and Valentine bit deep into the batting. Even Johnny Wardle's forceful late hitting could not turn the tide. In the second innings Washbrook resisted doggedly with a fine 114, but once he was out the steel bands which were a new feature to the game's headquarters could strike up their victory march. His last effective support ended when Valentine had Parkhouse caught for 48. Ramadhin bamboozled the other batsmen in taking 6 wickets for 86. The West Indies won by 326 runs, and broke the significant psychological barrier of winning in England. The young spinners' part in that triumph has been well recorded.

The third Test Match at Nottingham was the only one that summer which was not decided solely by spin. England came back well after batting badly on the first day. In the second innings Cyril Washbrook made another century, and put on 212 for the first wicket with Reg

Caribbean Cricketers

Simpson, an attractive stroke-player. The latter, who was playing on his home ground, was run out for 94. John Dewes and Parkhouse took up the struggle, and seemed to be batting safely for a draw. Then Ramadhin ran through the middle-order and tail. He bowled Yardley and outfoxed Doug Insole before he had scored. Several of the young English batsmen had made their reputation on the near-perfect batting surface at Cambridge University. They were out of their depth when the bowling was less straightforward. The Trinidadian ended another courageous knock from Evans and finished with 5 wickets for 135. There was still time for the West Indies to win.

They scored over 500 at the Oval. As the wicket deteriorated the touring bowlers had the batsmen at their mercy. Left-arm spinners Goddard and Valentine made the ball turn to a frightening extent just outside the off-stump. Hutton kept them out by carrying his bat for 202. It was a superb demonstration of technique. Meanwhile the bowlers whittled away at his changing partners. Denis Compton, who was returning after a damaged knee had kept him out of the side for most of the season, was run out for 44. The other batsmen surrendered in desperation. England, who failed to save the follow-on by only 10 runs, suffered greatly in their second innings. Valentine hustled out the front-line batsmen and completed another famous victory by dismissing Bedser and Malcolm Hilton without a run between them. His figures were 6 wickets for 39. The West Indies had humbled England three times in a row. Even allowing for injuries and frequent team changes, the home side had been thrashed decisively on pitches for which they were supposedly better equipped.

The unexpectedly low scoring in 1951/52 was ample evidence of the bowlers' ability. Nobody performed better than Valentine. He kept scoring so tight that the batsmen had a free rein only in the second Test at Sydney. The Jamaican pitched the ball up quicker in attacking the right-hander on middle and off. The Australians temporarily upset Ramadhin by striking him off the front foot, unlike the Englishmen who played him from the crease. Keith Miller, physically powerful, and the elf-like Lindsay Hassett were chiefly responsible for his decline.

The West Indian bowlers came very close to winning the opening game at Brisbane. Valentine suffered severely from dropped catches, but still took 5 wickets for 99 in the first innings. After Gomez bowled Ken Archer for four in the second, the two spinners sent down almost 81 overs. All the other bowlers managed only five overs between

Nursery of Talent Young cricketers develop their skills in rural Barbados. The seashore, country glade and urban street are the natural nursery of West Indian talent *Patrick Eagar*

Woods *and* **Cumberbatch** – the fast-bowling terrors from Trinidad who wrecked the opposing batting in the 1890s *W. H. Whiteman*

Learie Constantine, all-rounder, the first West Indian international cricket celebrity, hits out on his way to a century against Essex in 1928 *Central Press*

The 1928 Team The first Test Match team was selected from the touring party to England in 1928. *Back row* W. H. St. Hill, E. A. Rae, E. L. G. Hoad, J. A. Small, F. R. Martin, L. N. Constantine, G. N. Francis, O. C. Scott; *Front row* J. Schultz (manager), E. L. Bartlett, M. P. Fernandes, C. V. Wright, R. K. Nunes (captain), G. Challenor, C. R. Browne. H. C. Griffith, J. M. Neblett and C. A. Roach missed this photo session *Central Press*

George Headley was the best bad-wicket batsman, and demonstrated a masterful technique in all conditions. He lashes another boundary in his sparkling 65 at the Oval in 1939. Arthur Wood is the wicket-keeper, and Walter Hammond is the fielder *Central Press*

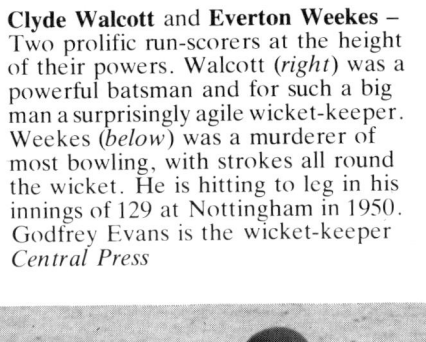

Clyde Walcott and **Everton Weekes** – Two prolific run-scorers at the height of their powers. Walcott (*right*) was a powerful batsman and for such a big man a surprisingly agile wicket-keeper. Weekes (*below*) was a murderer of most bowling, with strokes all round the wicket. He is hitting to leg in his innings of 129 at Nottingham in 1950. Godfrey Evans is the wicket-keeper
Central Press

Frank Worrell, the complete cricketer, was always graceful in the execution of his strokes, and in the delivery of his medium-fast seam bowling *Central Press*

Sonny Ramadhin *(top)* and **Alfred Valentine** *(bottom)*, the 'calypso twins', mesmerized batsmen by mystery and their control of flight and spin *Central Press*

Gary Sobers was the greatest all-rounder of international cricket, whether he was batting, bowling or fielding *Patrick Eagar; Central Press*

Ramadhin and Valentine

them. Ramadhin seemed to have the match won when he dismissed Morris, Hassett, Harvey, Lindwall and Ian Johnson. The Australians were just as vulnerable as the English. Goddard persevered with his exhausted spinners in spite of their earlier exertions. He rubbed the new ball in the dust to help them. Hindered in the field and unaided, they saw Australia creep ahead by 3 wickets.

Valentine took another 6 wickets in the win at Adelaide. He had a more frustrating time on the last morning at Melbourne. The tourists changed their batting order with disastrous results, and Ramadhin and John Trim were needlessly run out. So Australia were given an outside chance of winning a match they seemed to have lost. The final stages became a direct confrontation between Hassett (who played as well as he had ever done) and Valentine. The balance swung backwards and forwards. The bowler took 4 wickets, and then trapped the Australian lbw for 102. He was ninth man out, and there were still another 38 runs needed to win. Doug Ring, who took some risks with his batting, and Bill Johnston were helped by lax fielding and poor field-placing. Too many of the West Indians told each other what to do. The team broke up into its territorial components. Ring could have been caught if the field had been set intelligently. Johnston's batting ability was negligible, so much so that he was a victim of one of Hassett's best practical jokes. The Australian captain wanted to show that statistics by themselves were meaningless. He arranged for Johnston to be out only once on the 1953 tour to England. Although he scored only 102 runs for the whole season, the number eleven had a better average than Bradman! At Melbourne he and Ring squeezed out a tense one-wicket victory.

Ramadhin enjoyed the milder pitches in New Zealand. He took 9 wickets in the win at Christchurch. The home country made the tactical error of playing Bert Sutcliffe and Vernon Scott, their best ever opening partnership, in the middle order. After being away from home for six years the West Indies now had three series straight off in the Caribbean.

Ramadhin and Valentine bowled in front of their own crowds for the first time against India in 1953. The public had heard on the radio about their triumphs, and flocked to the grounds in record numbers. The Test Matches provided a fascinating duel between the West Indian spin bowlers and their Indian counterparts, Subhash Gupte and Vinoo Mankad. There was only a one-wicket difference in the total aggregates of the respective pairs. All four also took some stick from the batsmen. Whereas Valentine was consistent throughout the rubber, Ramadhin was at his best in the first two games. The second Test Match at Bridgetown was the only one to reach a definite conclusion. India seemed to be in command at 204-3 in their first innings. The lower batting fell to Valentine, and the tourists trailed by 43 runs. Going into the last day, India had to score 272 to win. With some moisture in the wicket Ramadhin was at his best since the England tour. The Indians, who were not usually ruffled by slow bowling, could not cover his movement off the pitch. He ended all real resistance by dismissing leading batsmen Vijay Hazare and Polly Umrigar. The West Indies won by 142 runs. In doing so they made sure of winning their third consecutive home series.

With so much rain the game at Georgetown had no more than academic interest. The Indians slipped quickly to 64-5, including Ramchand and Vijay Manjrekar run out without scoring. Vinoo Mankad struggled to put the innings back on an even keel. Although Ramadhin bowled well without success, Valentine was more dangerous in taking 5 wickets. India began their second innings over 100 runs behind, and lost three batsmen to Valentine before rain washed out the last day's play. After that the tourists had to win the fifth Test Match at Kingston to share the rubber. They started with 230-3 with a strong stand between opener Pankaj Roy and all-rounder Umrigar. The other batsmen added only 82 more runs as Valentine took another 5 wickets. He dismissed Umrigar, Manjrekar and Mankad in that critical period. There were still too many runs in the wicket for the Indians to restrict their hosts to a modest total. Valentine sent back four batsmen in the second innings when Roy and Manjrekar played out the draw with a double-century partnership.

The following series with England underlined the decline in West Indian bowling. Alfred Valentine, who had carried so much of the responsibility since he was first chosen, did not bowl as well as usual. He was replaced by another left-arm spinner, Gary Sobers, in the fifth Test Match. Ramadhin played as well as ever, but he was not supported. He had matured over the past two years, and bowled more to a plan. His fortitude in a difficult year laid the earlier suspicion that he could not take punishment. That rumour came about because he left the field in Australia just as his team was about to lose. Sonny took 4 wickets in the first innings of each of the first two Test Matches. England scored 170 and 181, and were well on the way to losing even that early. His best performance was at Georgetown, where he came on as first change to Worrell and Gomez. Len Hutton set out to break the bowlers' morale with a painstaking 169, but Ramadhin stuck to his task and took 6 wickets in the innings.

The Australians destroyed the West Indian bowling in 1955 with totals of 758-8 dec, 668, 600-9 dec and 515-9 dec. Because the opening attack failed to make any impact the batsmen were always well set before the slow bowlers were called upon. Ramadhin and Valentine took only 10 wickets between them in the entire season. Neither of them played in the fifth Test at Kingston, where the tourists hit five centuries in one innings. The least said about this year the better.

One year later the West Indian spinners took a welcome respite from the recent battering. They were included in the low-key and pleasant tour of New Zealand, and were soon back to their old ways. Supported by young all-rounder Collie Smith, they won the first three Test Matches. The New Zealanders themselves relied on medium-paced seam bowling. They had no genuine pacemen, and no world-class batsman, since Sutcliffe's injury in South Africa. It should have been little more than a work-out, a perfect setting for new and rusty talent. The first morning at Dunedin set the pattern for the series. Ramadhin took 6 wickets for 23 in bowling out New Zealand for a paltry 74 runs. He regained all his old magic by hitting the stumps three times and dismissing four batsmen for ducks. It was a much-needed tonic for the team's flagging fortunes. The Kiwis batted with greater resolution in the second innings, but still lost by an innings and 71 runs. Ramadhin spun out the early batting again in another innings victory at Christchurch. This time Valentine and Smith applied the *coup de grâce*, as no home batsmen reached 50 in either innings.

The 1957 side seemed stronger in bowling than their predecessors. Ramadhin and Valentine were bowling as well as ever, and this time they were backed up by Smith and Sobers. In the event the bowling failed completely. Valentine lost confidence, and took a long time to find his length and direction. He was injured on the eve of the crucial fifth Test Match at the Oval, where Tony Lock, a bowler in similar style, was England's match-winner. He had an unhappy match at Lord's and missed an important catch when the sun reflected from his steel-rimmed glasses. When things do go wrong they go wrong. Sobers, and even more so Smith, were needed to prop up the fading batting. Ramadhin spun his way through the early county games with his former flair, and achieved his best ever performance in the first Test Match at Birmingham.

Sonny won the first round convincingly. He shot out England for a lowly 186 on a good batting wicket. With little in either the pitch or the weather to help his spin, he took 7 wickets for 49. The Englishmen repeated all their previous mistakes, and seemed even more mesmerized than before. They just could not tell which way the ball was going, and panicked in the process. Insole (who had played him so badly in 1950), May and Cowdrey were out to catches before Ramadhin knocked over the lower batting. England needed to score 288 at their second attempt to avoid an innings defeat. That target seemed far away when Ramadhin again dismissed Richardson and bowled Insole for 0. It was indeed the beginning of the end, but not quite how the West Indians imagined it. Peter May and Colin Cowdrey, struggling at first, put on a record 411 runs for the fourth wicket. Their main objective was to expose Ramadhin. They smothered his spin and killed off his mystery by pushing forward with bat and pad together in spite of the risk of being lbw. Because so many other bowlers were unfit, the Trinidadian sent down 98 overs almost without respite. He did not complain, but just trudged back a few paces, came in again and turned his arm over again. The West Indies lost more than the advantage in this one game. Ramadhin's hold was broken for ever. He was shut out of the rest of the series, though he did take 4 wickets at the Oval when everything had been decided.

The rebirth of fast bowling spearheaded by Roy Gilchrist and Wesley Hall ended the heyday of West Indian spin in 1958/59. Ramadhin had little to do on the tour to India and Pakistan. He took 4 wickets at Lahore, and again against England at Port of Spain, then retired the following year. In Australia he lost his place to Lance Gibbs, a more orthodox off-spinner. Valentine, who had seemingly retired already, was the surprise selection for the same party. Perhaps the selectors hoped that he would regain the form of his earlier visit to that country. And they were right, because the slow bowlers almost won the series.

Valentine combined well with Gibbs when the West Indies won by 222 runs at Sydney. He took 4 wickets in each innings, including Colin McDonald, the dour opening batsman, and all-rounders Richie Benaud and Alan Davidson twice each. Alfred was also at the centre of the dramatic and controversial defeat in the fifth Test Match at

Melbourne. In the closing stages he bowled burly Peter Burge and captain Benaud in the Australians' surge towards victory. Then he seemed to dislodge Wally Grout's bail. The umpire was unsighted, and ruled the batsman 'not out'. The ensuing runs were allowed to stand. When Grout surrendered his wicket immediately afterwards only 2 runs now separated the teams. Next Valentine beat the prodding bat of gum-chewing stonewaller Ken Mackay. The ball passed so close to the stumps that wicket-keeper Alexander threw up his hands in appeal. Australia won by 2 wickets on the scampered extras.

That was really the end of Valentine's career. Ramadhin and Valentine gave way respectively to Gibbs—who exceeded their achievements in statistical terms—and Gary Sobers, who among his other talents was still a more than competent left-arm spinner. Sonny and Alfred went their different ways after that. The former settled in England, where he played in League, county and minor county cricket. The latter stayed on the other side of the Atlantic.

CHAPTER EIGHT
The Fifties

The first great West Indian side was not fashioned overnight. Frank Worrell, Clyde Walcott and Everton Weekes came together in 1947/48. The partnership between Allan Rae and Jeff Stollmeyer was welded the following year, and the talents of Sonny Ramadhin and Alfred Valentine evolved in 1950. The difference between the early success and later failure was due in some considerable part to a change in the quality of the second-line players in the other positions. There was an abundance of secondary batsmen and bowlers in the years of plenty at the end of the 1940s, but few reliable substitutes were available when the leading members were injured or played below their best. The most serious defects were unstable leadership, the premature break-up of the first-wicket partnership, an almost total dearth of new bowling, and, with the exception of Collie Smith's brief and mercurial life, nobody who could be sure of scoring runs at numbers six, seven and eight. The new generation at the end of these ten years, chiefly Gary Sobers and Rohan Kanhai, played too much in the shadow of their better-known colleagues to make an impact in their own right.

John Goddard won the captaincy from three other contenders in 1947/48. He led the West Indies in winning at Georgetown, where his own bowling was decisive, and at Kingston. As a young man he had once put on over 500 runs with Worrell, but he did not make the grade as a Test Match batsman. Goddard's concentration on leading the side was detrimental to his individual performance. He was replaced by Valentine as the specialist left-arm spinner in England, where his only successful game was at the Oval. He scored 58 not out and took 4

The Fifties

first-innings wickets. Goddard made the top score of 45 on the tourists' first meeting with Lindwall and Miller at Brisbane, and 57 not out in the following fixture at Sydney. He moved himself up the order to bear the brunt of the attack. The ploy did not come off, and he retired from Test Match cricket at the end of that tour. His captaincy was faulted for relying too much on the spin bowlers in the first game, and for not enforcing discipline with a stronger hand at Melbourne.

Goddard continued to represent Barbados, and was player-manager to the team of colts which went to New Zealand. While there he scored a sound 83 not out in the second Test Match at Christchurch. On that evidence he was unwisely recalled for the 1957 tour to England. He did little apart from his defensive 61 in saving the Nottingham Test Match with Collie Smith, and seemed reluctant to bowl himself. Goddard was a little too easy-going for modern international cricket, or keeping his more temperamental players in check under the pressures of competition.

Gerry Gomez had made two appearances before the war. With Headley and Jeff Stollmeyer, he was the only experienced player in the first Test Match at Bridgetown in 1947/48. He was a specialist batsman at that time. The bowling for which he is better remembered now came later. Gomez made the top score of 86 in that first post-war game, but was stumped without scoring in the second innings. He captained the West Indies at Port of Spain when Stollmeyer was out of action. He scored 62, dismissed century-maker Billy Griffith and would have won the match if it hadn't rained. Gomez did not come as close to the captaincy again.

Gerry opened the bowling with Prior Jones in India in preference to John Trim, who was faster. He used the seam well in moving the ball early on. Gomez came in for the first innings at New Delhi with 3 wickets down for 27. He scored 101 in putting on 267 runs with Clyde Walcott before he was stumped off Lala Amarnath. As a bowler he had the Indians in trouble at Calcutta and shared in the triumph at Madras. Gomez bowled stylist Rusi Modi—who usually made a half-century every time he went in—and wound up the victory by dismissing Ghulam Ahmed and Chowdhury, the last two batsmen.

The Trinidadian shared the new ball again with Worrell in 1950. He also held three catches in Valentine's breakthrough at Manchester. He did well with the bat in the two Test Matches held in London. Gomez defended capably for 70 while Walcott hammered

Caribbean Cricketers

the bowling at Lord's, and put on over 100 runs with Goddard at the Oval. He did better than most of the others in Australia. Gerry made 50 in each of the first two games when the main batsmen failed, and bowled superbly on the opening day of the fifth Test Match at Sydney. He drew first blood by bowling George Thoms, and finished with 7 wickets for 55 as Australia made 116. Gerry's calypso refrain about his own ability ('Who is the best player in the West Ind-ez, Gerry Gomez') was never more justified. Unfortunately, the Australian fast bowlers were spurred on to see what they could do. Altogether 19 wickets went down for 180 runs in one day. That was the highpoint of Gomez's career, and he faded after taking 4 wickets for 72 against India at Kingston. Denis Atkinson took his place in the team.

Robert Christiani came within one run of a century in his first match at Bridgetown in 1947/48. Ken Cranston had him lbw for 99 as the batsmen hit out to get ahead of the clock. Christiani was the first regular West Indian batsman from Guyana, and a useful member of the side in more ways than one. He made his runs speedily and attractively, with good footwork and wristy strokes. Christiani did well when the others were in trouble. He shared an entertaining and valuable stand with Worrell at Georgetown in which he made 51. Like brother Cyril, Robert was a good wicket-keeper who stood in when Walcott was injured or wanted some time in the field.

Christiani got his Test Match century at last when he hit 107 at New Delhi. In that same match he showed a new skill by taking 3 wickets as India battled to a draw.

Throughout the series he attacked the slow bowlers by moving out to them, and placed his shots neatly through the field. Although he also made 74 at Bombay the West Indian batting had such depth that Christiani could not bat in the top half of the order. During Walcott's temporary illness at Calcutta he caught Lala Amarnath and stumped both Sunil Banerjee and Ghulam Ahmed off Ferguson to end the innings.

Robert had a disappointing tour in 1950, but he was retained in preference to either Roy Marshall or Kenny Trestrail. He justified the selectors' faith in Australia, where the middle batting to some extent overcame the failure of the first three or four batsmen. Christiani scored 76 in the second Test Match at Sydney, his side's best in the only game in which the bowling was really collared, and he hit the winning run at Adelaide.

Medium-paced bowler E. A. V. Williams enlivened the closing moments of the second innings at Bridgetown in 1947/48 with some spectacular hitting. He reached his fifty in exactly half an hour, and was caught at the wicket for 72. Wilfred Ferguson followed his undefeated half-century in that match with 75 at Kingston, where Jamaica's Ken Rickards, batting higher than Walcott, scored 67 on his home ground. Rickards was one of several enterprising batsmen omitted from the team in the overall boom in talent. It was all a question of whom to leave out.

Hines Johnson, a very tall fast bowler from Jamaica, played first at Kingston in that same series. England openers Len Hutton and Jack Robertson began with a partnership of 129 runs. By this time Johnson had found his direction, and once he had got his first break he carried all before him. The 36-year-old paceman was faster than anybody the batsmen had faced on the tour so far. He dismissed both openers, forced two others to snick catches to the wicket-keeper, and bowled Maurice Tremlett in taking 5 wickets for 41. He started the second innings well by bowling Robertson. Then Winston Place, who made 107, held up his attack with the help of Hutton and Joe Hardstaff. Johnson returned for a further spell in which he bowled Hardstaff and scattered the tail in another 5 wickets. The English batsmen did not doubt that here was a worthy successor to Martindale and Constantine. Hines missed the Indian tour through business commitments and, aside from dismissing Simpson and Parkhouse in the opening overs at Nottingham, he failed in England. Opportunity had come to him too late.

Prior Jones started the 1947/48 season impressively with 4 wickets at Bridgetown, including that of Denis Brookes, a very good county batsman who deserved more representative honours. He did not play again that year, but in Johnson's absence opened the bowling in all five games against India. Jones gave the tourists a flying start at New Delhi by having Vinoo Mankad lbw, but the slower pitches did not suit his medium-fast style. The fourth Test at Madras was the turning-point of the rubber. Dattu Phadkar's use of leg-theory showed the West Indian bowlers how the batting could be unsettled. As a result Jones and Trim brought about the only real batting collapse of the entire season. He bowled with accuracy and inspiration in the second innings, and took the same determination into the final game at Bombay. India had to score 361 in 395 minutes to win. He set the tourists on the right path by dismissing the brilliant though erratic Mustaq Ali, slowed the Indians' advance by bowling Vijay Hazare for 122, and almost snatched a dramatic win by dismissing Vinoo Mankad and S. N. Banerjee in the action-packed climax. If only the other bowlers had done half as well ... Rather surprisingly, Jones did not come off in England, and he played only once on the Australian tour.

John Trim, who came on as first change, had immediate success at Madras. He dismissed Mustaq Ali, whose century had saved India in the previous game, forced the competent Amarnath to hit his own wicket, and finished with 4 wickets for 48. Trim took 3 more wickets in the second innings, but did nothing much after that until his sensational spell at Melbourne in 1951/52. The Guyanese fast bowler dismissed left-hander Arthur Morris quite early, and was rested as Australia moved to 175–3. When he came back to the attack Trim bowled Miller and rounded off the innings with 5 wickets for 34. An injury kept him out of that game's tense finale.

Frank King's success against India at Port of Spain seemed to herald the long-expected revival of fast bowling. He took 5 wickets—all of leading batsmen—and Maka, the wicket-keeper, was forced to miss the rest of the tour with injury. King's physique did not measure up to the demands he put on it by trying to match hostility, speed and bumpers with Freddie Trueman in 1953/54. His stamina broke down several times in the next few seasons. The Australians put him to a particularly severe test. In the fifth Test Match at Kingston he had the satisfaction of dismissing Les Favell before a run was scored, but the batsmen had the last word in totalling 758–8 dec. King's international career ended when his fitness let him down again in New Zealand.

Jamaican fast bowler Esmond Kentish was already in his mid-thirties when he had his one triumph against England at Kingston. He had not played for the West Indies since he partnered the other veteran, Hines Johnson, on the same ground in the first post-war series. Kentish did not take a wicket in the first innings, and laboured in the second as Willie Watson, Len Hutton and Peter May took England towards safety. Then he had May and Graveney both caught. Flushed with confidence, he bowled Evans, Lock and Trueman as 7 English wickets went down for a hardly credible 6 runs. Kentish returned 5 wickets for 49 and the West Indies won by 140 runs. He played no more Test Match cricket, but represented Oxford University against Cambridge at Lord's in 1956 when he was thirty-seven.

Clifford McWatt, who kept wicket in all five games in 1953/54, was also a useful batsman. He made 54 at Kingston, and repeated that score with serious consequences at Georgetown. McWatt and Holt put on 99 runs after 7 wickets had gone cheaply. The former was run out in the excitement of trying to complete the century partnership. The incident evoked an angry reaction from his home crowd. Although he did not fail in any way, the Guyanese wicket-keeper was replaced by Alfie Binns and Clairmont Depeiza for the next series.

Collie Smith was the most exciting discovery of the exceptional rubber against Australia in 1955. He was raised in Kingston's most deprived area, and brought a welcome spirit of adventure to his play which was more in keeping with the era of Learie Constantine than the embattled environment of the 1950s. Smith's smile and joy in playing were infectious. He cared little about the reputations of his opponents. In one crisis he hit a straight six off Brian Statham, a regularly accurate fast bowler. Although this apparent devil-may-care attitude gave rise to some inconsistencies in his early career, Smith showed twice in 1957 and again just before his premature death two years later that he could assume responsibility. When he died he was mourned for the pleasure he had given in bringing a club-cricket attitude to the Test Match arena, and he was missed for the extra entertainment he could have provided in the years to come. Schoolchildren and many adults who did not normally support cricket joined the crowds who paid homage as his body lay in state.

O'Neil Gordon Smith (to give him his full name) showed his uniquely personal qualities as early as his debut at Kingston. He put on over a hundred runs with Clyde Walcott against Lindwall, Miller and Ron Archer at full pace. The young Jamaican went in on the fall of the first wicket in the second innings and scored 104 before he was caught by Harvey, a brilliant fielder anywhere. Four leading players fell short of double figures, and only Holt reached 50. The newcomer had obvious talent and the character for a crisis. He soon learned the variability of fortune and of the selectors.

Collie batted after a substantial stand between Weekes and Walcott in each innings of the next match at Port of Spain. He tried to keep the score moving, and was out for a duck both times. Smith was dropped from the team immediately. The young man was made to realize that not everybody considered Test Match cricket was fun or entertainment.

He was one of the bright young men taken to New Zealand. Smith struck a lively 64 in his 162 runs fourth-wicket stand with Everton Weekes at Dunedin. The two batsmen delighted the spectators with some hard and sparkling strokes. Collie was an extremely agile runner between the wickets. Several times I have seen him lap his partners in the desire to get on with the scoring. Smith teamed with Ramadhin to bowl out the New Zealanders, and his off-spin was even more decisive at Christchurch. When the home country needed 228 runs to avoid an innings defeat he had Bert Sutcliffe and John Guy stumped, bowled John Reid, the batsman most likely to succeed, and caught and bowled Sammy Guillen.

Smith played two innings of exceptional quality in 1957. His class showed up the other batsmen, who floundered against some very good English bowling. Fast bowlers Freddie Trueman, Brian Statham, Trevor Bailey and Peter Loader provided life, penetration and variety, and Jim Laker and Tony Lock were the world's leading finger-spinners.

Collie's century in the first Test Match at Birmingham had two distinct parts. At first he grafted for his runs in the knowledge that Walcott and Worrell were injured. Once the West Indies were in front he hit out in a 190 runs sixth-wicket stand with Worrell. When Laker had him lbw for 161 the game was weighted very much in the tourists' favour. In their fight-back May and Cowdrey nullified Smith's soft spin with excessive pad-play. Even then he consoled himself by breaking their record partnership.

The Jamaican's hundred in the second innings at Nottingham was completely different in character. He showed once and for all that the erstwhile novice who took pride in his lack of any inhibition was now a mature, discerning batsman. The West Indies were 247 runs behind at the halfway point. They lost another five batsmen for 89, including Worrell, who had carried his bat through the first innings. Between them Trueman and Statham revived memories of the tourists' alleged vulnerability to outright speed. Few people would have laid any odds on quick-hitting Smith's survival. He put his head down and batted with surprising though necessary caution, while still keeping the bowlers guessing by the occasional flash of aggression. Collie added over a hundred runs with Denis Atkinson, but the match entered a more critical phase when Statham had the Barbadian caught at the wicket with the new ball. Smith and Goddard survived a torrid session before they saved the match, with 154 runs for the seventh wicket. When Trueman bowled the former for 168 England had no time to finish the match.

Collie Smith's personality was the one bright spot in a dismal summer. His face and hands reflected alternating joy and despondency at each stage of the game. His participation off the field was equally as whole-hearted. He was one of the few members of either team to attend church on the Sunday of a Test Match, and he signed autographs for delighted schoolboys from the back window of the pavilion when the authorities had forbidden it on the playing area. In spirit he was still one of them. His commitment to cricket and to life was total.

Smith batted and bowled consistently against Pakistan in 1957/58. Gary Sobers overshadowed him with the bat, and he was pushed aside by the new breed of fast bowlers. The best of his three half-centuries was the 86 in the fifth Test Match at Port of Spain, where the West Indies were beaten. Smith showed his determination in almost lone resistance to Fazal Mahmood, the great medium-paced bowler and off-cutter. Collie's spin bowling went a long way to winning the second Test, also at Port of Spain. He dismissed Hanif Mohammad, one innings after his monumental triple century, Imtiaz Ahmed and Saeed Ahmed, as the score dipped to a 116-6 from which the Pakistanis did not recover.

Although the West Indians overwhelmed India by three matches to nil in 1958/59, they did not start the series too well at Bombay. Collie Smith and Rohan Kanhai pulled them through some initial embarrassment against leg-spinner Subhash Gupte. Smith scored another half-century in the second innings when Sobers lashed the bowlers into submission. His services were not required in the next three games, which the tourists won by one-sided margins. Then in the fifth Test at New Delhi he came into his own again when the fast bowlers were injured. Collie ended Chandrakant Borde's fine innings, which was the Indians' only century of the rubber. Openers Holt and Hunte broke up the bowling with efficient rather than entertaining methods when the West Indies went in. Smith and Solomon reached their own hundreds by a more direct approach. In the second innings the Jamaican bowled a long stint in taking 5 wickets for 90. He worked hard for his results, but swung the match his way in dismissing Pankaj Roy, Dattu Gaekwad, Hemu Adhikari, Vinoo Mankad and wicket-keeper Narendra Tamhane. Borde was still there, and hung on to deny the tourists victory. He hit his wicket for 96 in the last over possible. That was the last important thing Smith achieved in Test Matches. He played League cricket in England during the summer. In the last week of the 1959 season he suffered fatal injuries in a car accident while travelling home from a charity match.

Denis Atkinson had been on the edge of regular selection since the first tour to India. He was a sound batsman, and bowled at a lively medium-fast pace. Atkinson was called to the captaincy in circumstances that were bound to be controversial and did not leave adequate time for his own development. After he had made three half-centuries against England in 1953/54—which included valuable support for Clyde Walcott at Bridgetown—he was appointed vice-captain for the next rubber against Australia. Jeff Stollmeyer's injury projected him into the leadership for three games before he had made his place secure, and when there were other, more experienced cricketers in the side. To make matters worse the West Indians were no match for their opponents. Denis Atkinson began badly, but confirmed his standing in front of his home crowd in the fourth Test Match at Bridgetown. The Australians ran up a massive 668, and took 6 wickets for 146. Another overwhelming defeat was a near-certainty. Wicket-keeper Clairmont Depeiza, who had had little previous batting success, joined his new captain. The two Barbadians stood up to everything bowled at them. Atkinson led the way with 219 in a seventh-wicket stand of 347 runs, a record for any type of first-class cricket. Although the West Indians did not score enough to ensure that the Australians would have to bat again, they extended the enemy bowlers so much that they could not risk another session in the field immediately. There was still a danger as the visiting batsmen looked for quick runs which would put the West Indies under pressure on the final day. Atkinson gave them a powerful jolt by bowling Bill Watson for 0 and taking four other wickets. Because Ian Johnson could not declare with any confidence, the game was left drawn.

As captain of the 1956 touring team to New Zealand Denis Atkinson excelled in batting and bowling. He made a duck at Dunedin, but did not look back after that. His aggressive 85 in partnership with John Goddard at Christchurch prevented the New Zealanders from capitalizing on a minor breakdown of the middle batting. Atkinson made another 60 in supporting Everton Weekes at Wellington. The opposing batsmen came unstuck against his medium

The Fifties

pace in the second innings. The West Indies won by 9 wickets and clinched the rubber. Then they lost the next game at Auckland by 190 runs. It was a one-off defeat, but it unfairly cost Atkinson the captaincy.

Denis did his best to avert the result, and threw himself into the attack when the New Zealanders batted a second time 110 runs ahead. He had McGregor taken at the wicket, and Lawrie Miller and MacGibbon caught by Weekes. John Reid, whose first-innings 84 was crucial in a low-scoring contest, and Taylor were also caught. In all Atkinson took 7 wickets for 53. It was all in vain. The conditions which he had used so skilfully also helped the New Zealand seam bowlers. They bustled the West Indians out for a meagre 77. Atkinson was stripped of the leadership, which was especially harsh now that Stollmeyer had retired. Instead the selectors recalled John Goddard, who had been away for five years for the 1957 tour to England.

The opening weeks of that season flattered to deceive in more ways than one. Atkinson took an instant liking to those green wickets, and scythed his way through a succession of county sides. At Lord's he could have been an effective counter to Bailey's seam bowling, the determining factor of the match, but he had been over-bowled already to compensate for the shortcomings of others. Not surprisingly Atkinson's batting did not attain its earlier standard, though his defensive backing of Collie Smith helped to save the third Test Match at Nottingham. His brother Eric replaced him as the team's medium-paced bowler at the end of the year.

Clairmont Depeiza alternated with Alfie Binns in 1955. He scored 122 in the record seventh-wicket stand with Denis Atkinson at Bridgetown. Both wicket-keepers were taken to New Zealand. Depeiza's quick work behind the stumps contributed much to the success of spinners Ramadhin and Valentine at Christchurch. There were three West Indian 'keepers in that game, because New Zealand's Guillen was the former Trinidad player who had moved there after the 1952 tour. Binns, Depeiza and McWatt were favourites for selection in 1957. They were rejected for Gerry Alexander, who ranked below Binns and Jackie Hendricks in Jamaica. There is a rumour that some of the selectors thought that Depeiza had been chosen, but was not taken because he could not be found. The lack of an experienced wicket-keeper in England was a root cause of the poor field-work, missed catches and the all-round frustration of the bowlers. Because Alexander did not come up to expectations, young

Caribbean Cricketers

Rohan Kanhai was made stumper for the first three matches.

Tom Dewdney was one of a whole lineage of Jamaican fast bowlers who had some passing success. He replaced Frank King against Australia at Bridgetown. Dewdney's 4 wickets in the innings cost him over a hundred runs. In the next game he had Arthur Morris lbw in the opening overs before Neil Harvey and Keith Miller enjoyed a huge third-wicket partnership of 295. Tom gave his best performance at Auckland. He had opening batsman McGregor caught, and came back at the tail when New Zealand were in a strong position. The Jamaican made John Reid hit his wicket 16 runs away from his century. Then he dismissed the last three batsmen in his 5 wickets for 21. He did not make the progress expected of him in England. Dewdney lacked the extra fire, lift and inspiration which distinguishes a great fast bowler from a good one.

Although his genius was obvious even then, Gary Sobers took some time to settle into the team. He came in for spin bowler Alfred Valentine at Kingston in 1953/54, where he had his side's best analysis of 4 wickets for 75. Trevor Bailey was his first victim. Sobers batted at number nine in that game, but he moved up the order with 47 against Australia at Port of Spain and, opening the innings with Holt, put on 52 for the first wicket at Bridgetown. In his more familiar role in the middle order the Barbadian left-hander added 179 runs with Clyde Walcott at Kingston. His share was 64. The uncertainty of his batting position was reflected in a temporary loss of form in New Zealand. When Valentine came back as the first choice left-arm spinner Sobers's selection became more precarious.

He played solely as a batsman in 1957 and began the tour with a string of good scores against the counties. Gary made a commendable 53 in the first Test Match at Birmingham and a heroic 66 in facing the fast bowlers on that vicious wicket at Lord's. This innings underlined his outstanding ability more than anything else. When he had to go in first again at Nottingham, Sobers and Worrell scored 87 together, the tourists' best opening stand of the entire series. Tony Lock's aggressive spin was too much for the West Indians on an unpredictable pitch at the Oval. Sobers alone stood apart from the general débâcle with a fighting 39 out of 89 in the first innings and 42 out of 86 in the second. Here obviously was a batsman around whom the side could be built anew.

Rohan Kanhai gave tantalizing glimpses of his future skill, but it was remarkable that his career was not ruined before it had begun.

The Fifties

Although he had made his name for Guyana as a middle-order batsman, he was sent in first against the best fast bowlers in the world. On top of that he had to take over as stop-gap wicket-keeper. He was not helped by ragged fielding and sub-standard bowling. Fortunately, neither of these experiments were continued long after this series. Kanhai was not a very good opening batsman because he tried to force the pace too quickly. His time was yet to come.

The very successful team from 1947 to 1951 disintegrated because the reserve resources to support the main batsmen and bowlers dried up. When the 1957 tour ended it was apparent that the batting fulcrum of Walcott, Weekes and Worrell could not continue for much longer, and that Ramadhin and Valentine were not the bowling force they once were. Collie Smith and Gary Sobers were the probable nucleus of the new side. If the West Indies were to regain their former status, some new players would have to develop very quickly ... and they did.

CHAPTER NINE
Professional Captaincy

There was a lot of fresh thinking to do before the Pakistanis arrived at the end of 1957. The bowling needed a complete overhaul. The first-wicket pairing had to be straightened out. There was no wicket-keeper. John Goddard retired again with no undisputed successor as captain. Above all, the West Indies needed a new sense of direction. The very extent of the task forced the selectors to take decisions they would not have contemplated otherwise. By starting again almost from scratch they put together a side which had little responsibility for the past humiliations. The young players still had their hopes and confidence for the future. Collie Smith, Rohan Kanhai and Gary Sobers were retained as expected. Fast bowlers Roy Gilchrist and, later, Wesley Hall were kept, even though they had not taken advantage of their previous chances. Opening batsman Conrad Hunte and off-spinner Lance Gibbs were two obvious new selections. As Everton Weekes and Clyde Walcott agreed to stay for one more season until the team found its feet, there were only two other places to fill. Frank Worrell, the designated captain, could not play because of his studies. In his place the selectors appointed Gerry Alexander, who was not even sure of getting into the side as a wicket-keeper.

At first sight this decision smacked of the tradition of reserving the captaincy for a white West Indian with an English university background. Alexander did not have the experience of Walcott, the vice-captain in England, or even the individual promise of his own contemporaries Smith and Sobers. Former captain Denis Atkinson was also waiting in the wings. In the thirty years of Test Match cricket only Jeff Stollmeyer had become leader on his record as a player. In

Professional Captaincy

retrospect, however, Alexander's appointment was a master-stroke. He provided the nursery conditions for the harvest of talent in the 1960s. As with Jackie Grant, his own performance rose to the responsibility. Because the captain was not a dominating personality the other players had the freedom to develop their own skills. Overnight the batting, the fast bowling and spin, the chief weaknesses against England, made spectacular progress. However unfortunate it was for the individuals concerned, the by-passing of an entire generation was an irrevocable vote of faith in the future. From the senior members of the outgoing team only Worrell survived into the new era for more than a couple of years. He had sufficient time away from the game to start his career all over again.

Alexander's automatic inclusion also solved the problem of wicket-keeping. His previous performance was so much down on expectation that he ought to have been replaced by Jackie Hendriks, another Jamaican. West Indian wicket-keeping has usually had a chequered history. It was a major weakness in Aucher Warner's party. Before the war Cyril Christiani, Derek Sealy and Barrow were chopped and changed. Clyde Walcott had been the only one to hold his place as a certainty. After his injury Guillen, Legall, McWatt, Binns, Depeiza, Kanhai and Alexander followed each other turn and turn about. Gerry's retention gave some semblance of continuity, even if it was only temporary. He quickly showed himself better keeping to the fast bowlers in the Caribbean than he had to the spinners in England's capricious conditions.

The errors of the early selection were put right more easily than expected. Hunte gave the start of the innings a touch of assuredness from the moment he took his first guard. The departure of Binns and Depeiza relieved some of the pressure from Alexander behind the stumps. The fiery Gilchrist was trusted to shake the fast bowling into shape, and the mercurial matching of Ramadhin and Valentine gave way to a more orthodox approach. None of these moves could have come off if the batting trio of Sobers, Kanhai and Smith did not make good. These young men had been shepherded for several years; now they had to stand on their own feet. They did so with unforeseen results.

The West Indies overwhelmed Pakistan by three games to one in an orgy of batting records. The first innings of each side at Bridgetown showed that there was something different in the air. Old-stager Weekes and newcomer Hunte led a welter of runs in taking the West Indian score to 579–9 dec. Then Gilchrist managed to keep his direction steady as the tourists succumbed for 106 against some of the best fast bowling seen for years. Hanif Mohammad saved his team on that occasion by batting over sixteen hours for his 337. Nothing could avail them in the next three games. Gary Sobers scored almost at will, and the other batsmen followed closely after him. The West Indians made 790–3 dec at Kingston, and included four centuries at Georgetown. This was run-scoring with a vengeance. As Hanif Mohammad became more and more ineffective against the fast bowlers the Pakistanis could not get going to the same extent. They won the fifth Test Match at Port of Spain through one good innings by Wazir Mohammad, and, more decisively, by the bowling of Fazal Mahmood and Nasimul Ghani.

The same core of players went to India in 1958/59. They emulated the example of John Goddard's side a decade earlier in winning the series. This time they did not so much beat the Indians as annihilate them. Fast bowlers Roy Gilchrist, Wesley Hall and Jaswick Taylor brushed aside the batsmen, several of whom were well past the first flush of youth. The first two put greater fear into their opponents than anyone since the heyday of Ray Lindwall and Keith Miller. The Indian bowling, which had deteriorated alarmingly, depended solely on Subhash Gupte. Well though he bowled, the leg-spinner could not stop the flow of runs from batsmen who knew that they had nothing to fear. The West Indians won the second, third and fourth games at a canter, and came very close in the fifth. They were held up only at Bombay before settling into their match-winning stride.

Alexander increased his value as a batsman and a wicket-keeper. The West Indians did not look very convincing in playing Gupte on the first day of the second Test Match at Kanpur. He took 9 wickets in the innings. Sobers and Kanhai made only 4 runs between them, as the first 6 wickets went down for 88. Never was a captain's example more needed. Alexander counter-attacked with a score of 70 which showed that the leg-spinner could be played. The other batsmen responded well enough to make totals of 443–7 dec, 614–5 dec, 500 and 644–8 dec in their next five innings. Alexander's safe hands helped the fast bowlers with five catches at Calcutta and at Madras.

The following three-match visit to Pakistan was an anticlimax played on pitches of varying nature. The tourists showed their real ability only at Lahore. By then they had already lost the extremely low-scoring matches at Karachi and Dacca. The batsmen could not

Professional Captaincy

go through with their strokes on slower wickets which assisted cut and spin. The patient grafting which was necessary to survive here was out of tune with the thrilling hitting of the past few weeks. Three of the first five batsmen made ducks at Karachi. So did the last six batsmen at Dacca, where the total plunged from 65–3 to 76 all out. The bowling did not fail as only Hanif Mohammad scored a century against them.

The home series against England in 1959/60 was one of the most frustrating. The West Indies had the better of at least three of the five matches, but didn't win any. England took the rubber through their victory in the second Test Match at Port of Spain. Freddie Trueman bowled the West Indians out for 112. Otherwise batsman Gary Sobers and Wesley Hall took the eye with their individual brilliance. The rest of Alexander's team was very much a rag-time band. They were ahead on first innings by 81 runs at Bridgetown, by 76 at Kingston and by 107 at Georgetown. Still they couldn't turn this advantage into positive results. Colin Cowdrey stood between the fast bowlers and victory in Jamaica, where he made 114 and 97. Jim Parks and Mike Smith rescued England with a century stand in the evenly balanced fifth Test Match at Port of Spain. Three vulnerable spots had developed in the side which had been triumphant in India. Gilchrist had been sent home as a disciplinary measure and was not reinstated. Hunte had no steady partner, and there was too much tampering with the middle batting.

Frank Worrell returned to the team at Bridgetown after an absence of two years in which he missed 13 matches. He played himself in with a painstaking and painful 197 not out. Although the innings was woefully out of character with his usual fluency, he took the opportunity to find his former touch. As such it was as valuable for the future as Don Bradman's knock at Brisbane in 1946/47. Worrell and Sobers blunted the edge of the English bowling and scored 399 runs for the fourth wicket. The older man took 4 wickets for 49 at Georgetown, and made 61 in the unsuccessful race against the clock in the fifth Test Match. The selectors were sufficiently impressed to invite him to be captain for the next tour to Australia. Alexander, who had been made the scapegoat for the failure to beat England, was vice-captain.

The wicket-keeper was under general attack from the West Indian press throughout the season. In spite of his leadership in India he was held personally responsible for falling morale and the apparent psychological deflation. Gerry had difficulty in dealing with the volatile Gilchrist, and could not shore up the decline in confidence which followed defeat at Port of Spain. His position was imperilled by the reappearance of Worrell, whom many people considered more qualified for the captaincy. C. L. R. James, the distinguished writer who spearheaded the newspaper campaign, has a fund of stories from the pioneer days in Trinidad and the other centres of the Eastern Caribbean. He does not always divorce his journalism from his socialist commitment, and that philosophy's tendency to see every issue in a set schedule of clearly defined heroes and villains. Alexander kept to his task even though he knew that his job was forfeit. As wicket-keeper he made the then record 23 dismissals in a series.

The West Indian visit to Australia in 1960/61 has become the yardstick for exciting cricket and sportsmanship. All other tours are judged against it, and necessarily are found wanting. Nobody knew quite what to expect in advance. Both countries had fought boring battles with England. The emphasis had been on not losing rather than on winning. For their part Australia relied on Colin McDonald's obdurate batting and Alan Davidson's left-arm fast bowling as much as the West Indies depended on Sobers and Hall. Yet there was an undercurrent of talent in both sides which required only moderate encouragement to blossom. Frank Worrell gave that encouragement by his positive approach, the development of all skills, a sense of responsibility, and, above all, joy in the game itself. Richie Benaud, his opposite number, responded with a similar attitude. In addition to the spirit in which the game was played, the series gave rise to some exciting cricket which was quite without precedent.

The first Test Match at Brisbane was tied, with each team striving for victory until the very last ball. The next two games resulted in sweeping wins either way, and then came the nail-biting finishes at Adelaide and Melbourne. In the first Ken Mackay and Lindsay Kline, the last Australian pair, batted through the final session for a draw. Australia scraped home by two wickets in the confusion and controversy of the last match. The West Indian performance seemed more in keeping with the romp through India than the war of attrition in the last year. Rohan Kanhai became a world-class batsman. Sobers was as great as he always was. The enthusiastic fielding and catching, plus an improvement in spin bowling, took some of the work-load off

Professional Captaincy

Hall. There seemed to be a new player or two pushing for each position.

Frank Worrell introduced more professionalism and discipline than any of his predecessors because of his own personal example, and the younger players' respect for his experience and his record. His word carried greater weight because he spoke rarely, but when he spoke he meant what he said. When Sobers showed dissent with an umpiring decision Worrell reprimanded him, irrespective of his prestige and his closeness to his captain. The all-rounder was man enough to accept the rebuke, and did not transgress again. Chester Watson, the young fast bowler who had succeeded Gilchrist, ignored previous warnings by pitching repeatedly short in the second Test Match at Melbourne. He played no more after that.

The series opened at Brisbane with the most famous Test Match of all time. The tourists were worried by Alan Davidson, who slanted the ball across the right-hander's body towards the slips. Left-hander Gary Sobers took him on with a century which was the first step towards some remarkable cricket. For once the Barbadian was not alone. Frank Worrell, Joe Solomon, Gerry Alexander and even Wesley Hall made half-centuries at an attractive rate. Norman O'Neill replied with a dominating 181 which, well supported by opening batsmen Colin McDonald and Bobby Simpson, put Australia in a commanding position. Davidson took 6 wickets for 87 as Worrell—who made his second score of 65 in the match—fought hard to keep the tourists in contention. Australia were set to make 233 runs to win, and right away Hall blasted them apart with 5 wickets for 63.

The advantage switched from one side to the other on the last day. The score slumped to 92–6 under Hall's assault. Benaud and Davidson picked up the pieces in turning the game Australia's way with 134 runs for the seventh wicket. With defeat staring the tourists in the face, Solomon ran out Davidson before Hall began what had to be the final over. Benaud tried to hook a bouncer and was caught at the wicket with the score at 228. In the excitement Hall dropped a caught and bowled chance by Grout. Two singles were taken. Then Ian Meckiff hit firmly to square-leg for the winning run. Hunte fielded just inside the boundary, and with a hard, straight throw ran out Grout with the scores level. The batsmen, who might have remembered their opponents' inaccurate fielding in the similar tension at Melbourne on the previous tour, tried to scamper another single. Solomon swooped, fielded and, with only one stump to aim at, produced his second superlative piece of fielding. The stump went over, and the game was tied ... the only tied Test Match ever.

The Australians won so easily at Melbourne that it seemed the West Indies would repeat their tradition of falling away after initial success. Davidson destroyed the tourists with 6 wickets in the first innings, which revolved entirely around the stand between Nurse and Kanhai. Conrad Hunte made 110 and Alexander 72 in the closing stages, when it was too late to change the result. The former captain again gave vent to his new-found batting talent with 108 at Sydney. Sobers had already shown that this West Indian team was better disciplined than before with a brilliant 168. Worrell made 82, his third half-century in as many games. On this tour he batted at number six to protect the tail and to give greater freedom to the younger batsmen. In this match the tourists twice topped 300 against first-class bowling by Davidson and leg-spinner Benaud. The Australians—for whom O'Neill made seventy in each innings—were bowled out by Gibbs and Valentine to let the West Indians draw level in the series in winning by 222 runs.

The fourth Test Match at Adelaide was drawn on a knife's edge. The West Indies won all along the line, but did not complete the knockout. Rohan Kanhai took the honours with a century in each innings, and Alexander was not far behind with 63 not out and 87 not out. The wicket-keeper had his best series in heading the batting averages ahead of Sobers, Hunte, Kanhai and Worrell. He had improved beyond recognition from his unfortunate beginning in England. Regrettably, this was his last season. Worrell made his now customary two half-centuries which prevented the Australian bowlers from sweeping away the tail. The runs scored by the late-order batsmen told greatly in the West Indians' favour. Although they were only 27 runs behind on the first innings, the Australians lost important wickets early on the final day. Kline, the number eleven, joined Mackay with victory impossible and the closing over a long way away. The dour left-handed Queenslander loved this type of situation. He denied the bowlers his wicket by taking the bumpers on his body. The fieldsmen crowded round the bat, but could not dislodge him. Australia finished 186 runs behind with only one wicket in hand.

The rubber was decided in another tense finish at Melbourne. The West Indians batted unevenly against Davidson and new fast bowler

Professional Captaincy

Frank Misson. Simpson and McDonald got Australia under way with a cluster of boundaries, before the spin bowling of Gibbs and Sobers narrowed the difference between the teams. The script was very much as before. Davidson took 5 wickets and Alexander made the top score of 73. Australia batted last on a turning wicket. They had to score 258 to win. It was still anybody's game, with all the makings of another tie. Simpson cut loose on the fast bowlers once again. When he was out for 92 the West Indian spinners came back at the middle batting. Peter Burge was the chief obstacle, with his fourth successive score of over 45. Shortly after he was out the next batsman, Wally Grout, gave up his wicket after the umpires had judged him not out to a ball which apparently removed his bail. Australia won on byes from a ball which brushed the stumps. The West Indians lost the series, but they won the moral victory. The crowds thronged the streets for their departure. No other event in this period has caused such emotion. Cricket itself was the real winner.

After such a tough struggle against the strongest team in the world the West Indians had a much easier work-out against India. They won all five Test Matches. The visitors crumpled yet again to the fast bowlers. This time off-spinner Lance Gibbs was equally destructive, especially at Bridgetown. The Indians couldn't do anything right. The bowling had not recovered from its trouncing in the 1950s, and now it did not even have Gupte to fall back on. Apart from Polly Umrigar's great personal success in the fourth Test Match at Port of Spain, they were outplayed at every turn. Frank Worrell could take most credit for turning a party of gifted individuals into a winning combination. He made half-centuries in each of the last four matches, including 98 not out in the fifth Test Match at Kingston when he deserved a hundred. There were others to hit the really big scores now.

The greatest contemporary cricketer was not above helping somebody at the start of their career. Due to the proximity of our seating positions, he took me under his wing at Lord's in 1961. He was covering the England/Australia series for the world press, and I was just a messenger with Hayter's Agency. During the game's natural intervals he asked me about my ambitions as a writer, and inspired me to try to build a bridge between the English community and the embryonic West Indian press. Those words changed the whole course of my professional, social and married life. Many stars of sport and entertainment lose some of their appeal on closer acquaintance;

Worrell's humanity gave an added dimension to his public image.

I saw him next when we arrived together at the Oval's press-box door for the first morning of the fifth Test Match. The doorman (whose memories must have stopped at Jack Hobbs and Andy Sandham) refused him entry because his pass applied only to the annexe. Recognizing me from an earlier county game, the old man eventually let the West Indian captain go in only on the condition that I would be held responsible for any damage he caused. He accompanied this remark with an unsavoury epithet about the cricketer's race. Perhaps sensing that he did not really know what he was saying, Worrell accepted this without rancour or the official complaint to which he would have been entitled, and which he would have made if he had considered the slight intentional.

Several times Worrell complained about climbing the pavilion or press-room steps and, later still, nodded off while awaiting his turn to bat. Many of us put it down to acquired kidology, a veneer of unflappability, or some minor concession to advancing age. There was no need to worry; after all, Colin Cowdrey and Geoff Pullar were known respectively as 'Kipper' and 'Noddy' because of a similar disposition to sleep. Few guessed that it might have been the first signs of the leukaemia which brought his life to such a tragic and premature end in 1967. Frank had so much more to give as team mentor, Jamaican senator and folk hero.

The tour to England in 1963 came close to engendering the same excitement as the West Indians had raised in Australia. There was some sporting tension as the tourists sought to wipe out the bitter memories of their last visit, and England wanted to recover from their own double defeat by Australia. It was a very good year's cricket. The issue was not settled until the last innings of the fifth Test Match. In spite of their impressive batting line-up, the West Indies won primarily because they had the better bowling. Fast bowlers Hall and Griffith or spinners Gibbs and Sobers could deal with any pitch conditions, and not one English batsman scored a century. After three matches the teams stood level with a one-sided victory each and a draw at Lord's which, if anything, rivalled the Brisbane tie in interest. Then the West Indies went ahead by winning convincingly at Leeds. England seemed about to catch up when they led by 29 runs at the Oval. They faltered in the closing stages and went down by 8 wickets. Frank Worrell's team were the most popular tourists ever to visit England.

Professional Captaincy

Worrell carried an aura of effortless grace, giving the impression that he was part of the action but also above it. Like a benevolent duppy, he proceeded with the certainty of a sleepwalker. The old charm never left him. He was as sound as ever, while the boyish Butcher punished the bowling at Lord's. What did it matter if he did not score many runs? His composure in a crisis was almost lethargic. He was portly now, though his mental energy could not be denied. With his velvet touch, he put the screws on his opponents, and they succumbed with a smile.

Worrell's grip on the captaincy was so secure that he did not need to come off with the bat or to bowl. His talented team beat England on every front, in contrast to the tour in 1957 when he had to plug so many gaps. He batted well enough on a good wicket at Manchester to be sure of a hundred, but team considerations took over from individual ambition. He had to declare with his score at 74 to give his bowlers the chance to bowl England out twice. The West Indians won by 10 wickets.

The Lord's Test Match is regarded by many as more exciting than the game at Brisbane because it was contested so evenly throughout. Conrad Hunte began the match with boundaries off the first three deliveries from Freddie Trueman. Thereafter the rate of scoring slowed as the initiative passed to the bowlers. Trueman showed that he was still far from a spent force by taking 6 wickets for 100. Ted Dexter, the England captain, met the fast bowlers with a string of strong drives which sent the scoreboard rotating at a run a minute. He was lbw for 70 before he could put his side ahead. 'He gave us Jessop when we wanted Bradman' the local press declared. The rest of the innings was a sparring match between fast bowler Charlie Griffith and batsmen Barrington and Titmus. The Barbadian, who took 5 wickets for 91, was especially effective with his slower yorker. The West Indies led by a mere 4 runs. Then Basil Butcher rescued them from the loss of early wickets with a superb demonstration of driving and cutting. When he was out for 133 the innings capitulated to Trueman and Derek Shackleton, who bowled at medium-pace at and around the off-stump.

The final innings was played out against a blackcloth of poor light, rain and the accident to Colin Cowdrey. Wickets and runs came in equal proportions as the two teams grappled for a decisive opening. The initial advantage was with the West Indian fast bowlers. It was nullified by Brian Close, who moved out of his crease to attack them.

All four results were possible going into the last over. Eight wickets were down and 8 runs needed. Shackleton went for a single. Worrell, the fielder, kept cool. A wild throw at the stumps could give away precious overthrows. He outran the batsman and broke the wicket. It was the same consideration by which he let Hall bowl the over with the old ball. A new ball, which was due, might have beaten the batsmen more easily, but it could have eluded the wicket-keeper as well and gone for byes. Cowdrey, his injured arm in a sling, came out and watched David Allen play the last two deliveries for a draw. It was one of the few times I have known the Lord's press-room full and the bar empty.

The team Frank Worrell moulded stayed intact for another three successful series. The captaincy passed to Gary Sobers instead of vice-captain Hunte. Under his leadership the West Indies achieved their ultimate ambition of beating Australia. Now they were indeed undisputed world champions. All three games which were decided were determined by the bowlers. Paceman Wesley Hall and spinner Lance Gibbs were instrumental in winning at Kingston and Georgetown. The rubber was already decided when Graham McKenzie and Neil Hawke, the Australian seamers, gained some revenge at Port of Spain. The batting showed to better advantage in the two drawn games where Australia built very strong totals of 516 and 650-6 dec. On the latter occasion both touring openers, Bill Lawry and Bobby Simpson, scored double centuries. As several new players had come forward to replace those already established, the team's prospects seemed good.

The West Indians confirmed their superiority by winning the next rubber in England in 1966 with big victories in three of the first four games. Defeat by an innings in the fifth Test Match at the Oval did not seem to matter in the overall context. A closer analysis shows that this triumph was not so comprehensive as the similar success three years beforehand. The West Indies came close to defeat at Lord's and at Nottingham. They won at Manchester only because they won the toss on a below-standard pitch and the English fielders dropped their catches. The tourists were indebted throughout to Sobers's superlative all-round achievements. He hit three centuries and a 90 in the first four matches, and bowled just as effectively. Seymour Nurse was reliable in the middle order. Butcher, Hunte and Holford had only one major innings each. The fast bowlers were past their best, and it required the spin of Gibbs and Sobers to win the three games which went their way. The home selectors did not help their own cause by making repeated team changes and having three different captains.

At the end of the year the West Indians went to India. They won two out of the three games with one drawn. Once more too much depended on a few key players. Batting at number six, Sobers helped the batting to its feet several times. Hunte scored the only century of the season, and Gibbs had to make up for the failure of the fast bowlers.

The Indians were outclassed at Calcutta, but came nearer to winning at Bombay than the scoreline indicates. With greater confidence they could have won at Madras. The batting of Borde and Engineer showed greater enterprise than had their predecessors. Spin bowlers Chandrasekhar and Prasanna showed a new aspect of Indian cricket which is still with us. The West Indians were tired from eight Test Matches in a year, but with so many talented individual players they were still favoured to beat Colin Cowdrey's side twelve months later.

CHAPTER TEN
Gary Sobers

By the end of the 1957 tour to England Sobers had been playing international cricket for four years without scoring a single century in his three full series. He had shown often that he had the necessary ability, and at last against the luckless Pakistanis he got the runs that his talent deserved. In one season Sobers matured from a promising youngster into the greatest batsman of the era. He began his run of high scores with 183 not out for Barbados in the first match of the tour and did not let up. Gary made half-centuries in each of his first three Test Match innings, then a triple century and two hundreds in the same game in his total of 824 runs in the rubber. A new blossoming of batting sprang up under his protection.

Sobers wrote his name indelibly in the record books in the third Test Match at Kingston. Pakistan started the game with a competent 328. Wicketkeeper-batsman Imtiaz Ahmed made a century. The West Indian openers, Conrad Hunte and Kanhai, began with 87 for the first wicket. Another 446 runs were scored before the next man was out. The fielding side suffered injuries and became demoralized as they chased the ball to all parts of the ground. Nine bowlers were tried in all, including the great Fazal Mahmood who sent down over 500 deliveries after his partner, Mahmood Hussain, had pulled out in the first over. Hunte seemed certain to overtake Len Hutton's record individual Test Match score of 364, but he was run out for 260. Nothing stopped Sobers from going on towards the same goal. Clyde Walcott's 88 not out was almost forgotten as the young left-hander moved towards the record. When he eventually reached 365 not out the West Indies declared with 790–3. It was still only his first Test

Match century. Pakistan scored almost 300 runs in their second innings, and yet lost by an innings and 174 runs. Now that he had got the taste for high scoring, Sobers did not relent easily. The tourists began well at Georgetown by making 408, which included 150 from Saeed Ahmed. Sobers opened the batting this time, and took part in a second-wicket stand with Walcott which was full of brilliant strokes. Both batsmen passed three figures before teenaged Nasimul bowled Sobers for 125. The West Indians had to score 317 to win, a difficult proposition batting last. Sobers made 109 not out in century partnerships with Rohan Kanhai and Conrad Hunte. His last three innings had brought him 599 runs for once out.

The Barbadian carried on in just the same way in India. He hit further centuries in each of the first three Test Matches, twice not out, two of which swung the entire course of the game. His clear superiority over the slow bowlers encouraged the growing landslide of runs from the other batsmen as their confidence increased accordingly. He was also the next most successful bowler after pacemen Roy Gilchrist and Wesley Hall. Sobers failed with the other batsmen in the first two games in Pakistan, though making the top score of 29 in the deplorable 76 runs total at Dacca. He recovered to hit an attractive 72 in his stand with Kanhai at Lahore.

The West Indian fast bowlers blasted the Indian batting aside for a lead of 75 runs in the first Test Match at Bombay. Their own batsmen fared disastrously against Subhash Gupte. Sobers had to subdue the leg-spinner if the tourists were to have any chance in the match and the series. He did it in the best way possible with 142 not out. The bowler was hit for over a hundred runs. The West Indies declared well ahead, but were held to a draw by some unexpectedly stubborn Indian batting.

Gupte had the better of the next immediate argument by taking 9 wickets for 102 in confounding all the West Indians at Kanpur. As the teams finished level on the first innings victory would go to whoever first destroyed their opponents' bowling power. The West Indies started their second innings badly with opening batsmen Hunte and Holt out without a run on the board. Sobers was even more commanding in this crisis than he had been in the preceding game. He ended Gupte's moral ascendancy once and for all by hitting 198 before he was run out. The Indians made no further headway in the rubber which became a one-way annihilation. The tourists' juggernaut steamrollered over them by an innings and 336 runs at Calcutta as well. Yet again they stumbled before ending at a staggering 614-5 dec. Sobers, the third man to make a hundred, reached 106 not out in a bright unbroken partnership with Joe Solomon in exactly even time.

The West Indians looked forward to renewing their rivalry with England in 1959/60. The fortunes of their erstwhile conquerors had declined while their own had improved since the last meeting. Gary Sobers was considered to be the decisive difference between the two sides. England had nobody who could compare with him. He did more than could be expected of any man in making three scores of over 140, but it was not enough to compensate for failures elsewhere in the team. The West Indies were lucky to have him at all. At one time it was not even certain that he would play. Sobers and Dewdney were in the car crash which killed Collie Smith just over three months before the series began. It had been feared that the mental wounds would take a long while to heal.

Ken Barrington and Ted Dexter gave England a comfortable total of 482 in the first Test Match at Bridgetown. There was little life in the wicket, and the West Indians could only play for a draw and compile a sufficiently large score to give them the psychological edge for the rest of the season. Sobers and Frank Worrell, who was returning to international competition after a lay-off, put on 399 for the fourth wicket in a harmonious blend of the generations. Gary was no longer the junior partner as he had been the last time these two batted together. He was the more entertaining in his innings of 226 against several of the same bowlers who had given them so much heartache in 1957. Competitive interest in the match petered out once the West Indians passed their opponents' total.

The third Test Match at Kingston rose and fell in the course of some fine individual achievements mixed with below-standard cricket. Sobers appeared to have set the West Indies on the way to a match-winning score as he monopolized partnerships with Easton McMorris and Seymour Nurse. Yet when Trueman dismissed him for 147, the other wickets tumbled so quickly that they led by only 76 runs. The margin was so close that when Cowdrey and Pullar stayed at the crease long enough in their second innings the West Indians had to take risks in their pursuit of runs. The match ended all square with the home side 55 runs short of their target with 4 wickets in hand. The next game at Georgetown went much the same way without the same exciting finish. Batsman Cowdrey and bowler Hall were once more the outstanding personalities of the English first innings. Off-spinner David Allen's half-century, though, was more important in gaining time for the tourists. Sobers hit another 145 as the West Indies went ahead by 107 runs, but he had very little support. Dexter and Raman Subba Row scored hundreds as England got the draw which retained their narrow lead in the rubber.

The West Indies had to win the fifth Test Match at Port of Spain. Sobers scored 92 but was bowled by Alan Moss only 8 runs short of making a century on each Test Match ground in the same series. Alexander declared, in spite of being behind on the first innings, in order to force the pace. Cowdrey, whose century on the first day had put England in a strong position, was out cheaply this time. Jim Parks, brought into the team as wicket-keeper from a coaching assignment elsewhere in the Caribbean, and Mike Smith repaired that early breakdown and quashed any prospect of a surprise result.

Gary Sobers was universally acknowledged as the world's outstanding all-rounder after his performances on the Australian tour of 1960/61. Until then he had been merely the world's best batsman. As a left-hander he was favoured to counter the prospective menace of Alan Davidson and leg-spinner Richie Benaud. He went much further than that in playing two fine innings which inspired his team to heights which they had not attempted before. Gary also held several breathtaking catches, and, when Chester Watson did not come up to expectations, he shared the new ball with Hall. He was already a left-arm spinner backing up Valentine. The Barbadian southpaw went after the bowlers from the moment that he came in at Brisbane. The attack which had beaten South Africa, England, India and Pakistan was treated in such a cavalier manner that he reached his century at not far off a run a minute. The bowlers included Ian Meckiff, whose bent-arm delivery had caused such controversy in the series with England. Sobers was finally caught for 132 in setting the scene for the most thrilling finish ever. Davidson, now at his peak, took 11 wickets in the match, but nobody else suffered the assault without wilting.

Sobers made an even more important appearance on the first day of the third Test Match at Sydney. The West Indians by then desperately needed a boost after the thrashing at Melbourne. To them Davidson was as much of a bogeyman as the combined talents of Lindwall and Miller in former years, but Sobers took the attack to the Australian all-rounder with a superb 168 which is often considered his best innings of all. He demonstrated the rare gift of almost nominating where he would place each ball, and how. Gary rendered the fielders helpless, and treated Davidson and Benaud, respectively the best left-arm fast bowler and the best leg-spinner in the world, as if they were club cricketers. No other batsman reached 50, but his innings put the West Indies on their way to victory by 222 runs. They were now level in the rubber.

The fifth Test Match at Melbourne decided the issue. Sobers made the top score of 64 in a far from stable first innings total of 292. The tourists seemed to have thrown away their chance. Their position seemed even less secure when opening batsmen Simpson and McDonald hit out for 146. Bowling at first change, Sobers dismissed Simpson and then had his partner lbw for 91. He induced left-handers Harvey and Davidson to snick catches to the ever alert Alexander and finished with 5 wickets for 120. Australia were only 64 runs ahead and needed a disputed umpiring decision and a fluke extra to win. Gary Sobers, Wesley Hall and Rohan Kanhai, the most popular members of a very popular side, were invited back to play in Australia's Sheffield Shield domestic competition.

The Indians were so outclassed the next year that all the leading West Indian batsmen—and several not even that advanced—boosted their personal aggregates. Sobers's highest innings was 153 in the second Test Match at Kingston, where he shared a double-century stand with Kanhai. His best was probably the 104 in the fifth Test Match on the same ground. All the seam bowlers found some early movement off the pitch, but Gary kept out medium-fast Ranjane and then scored another 50 in the second innings. In addition to these knocks he took 5 wickets for 63—he had bowled well all season. India lost by 123 runs, to complete their unenviable performance of five consecutive defeats in the series.

Gary Sobers had been so successful since 1957 that by the law of averages he had to fail some time. He did not do so yet. All the same, his batting on the 1963 tour to England wasn't quite up to his usual standard. However, he could afford to relax; other batsmen were now available to get the runs, and the bowling was more than adequate for the task in hand. After a promising 64 in the first Test Match at Manchester he made 50 in only one other game. Nevertheless, his bowling was particularly useful on the wilful wicket at Birmingham. He took 5 wickets for 60, in restricting England's lead to 30 runs. The conditions were tailor-made for Freddie Trueman. Bowling at reduced speed, he returned 7 wickets for 44 in putting the West Indies out for only 91 in their second innings. Sobers made his one century of the summer with 102 in the next match at Leeds. He batted with a damaged finger, and scored most of his runs in partnership with Rohan Kanhai. Because the bowling got on top of the batting so often that year these runs were vital in a total of 397. England collapsed to fast bowler Charlie Griffith, and trailed by 223 runs. Gary scored another 52 in making the victory certain.

When Frank Worrell retired from the international game at the end of this tour Sobers was made captain for the next series against Australia. Now he could prove his gift for leadership as well as being the world's best batsman, best left-arm bowler in two styles, and a top fieldsman. Under his direction the West Indies avenged their past defeats in beating Australia by two games to one. The real margin of superiority was more decisive than that one-match difference. They won twice in the first three Test Matches, and though behind on the first innings at Port of Spain and Bridgetown they were not in danger of defeat until the batting breakdown in the very last innings of the season. Sobers himself had an unusually quiet time in spite of his success as captain. He made fifties in only the second and fourth games. The first helped Butcher and Hunte reach a total which denied Australia any hope of winning, and the second was made in the shadow of Seymour Nurse's double hundred. Since they had lost in 1960/61—a result which could have gone either way—the West Indies had beaten India, England and Australia with ten matches won and only two lost. Three successive captains had shown that West Indian confidence and enthusiasm need not necessarily evaporate. It could be retained from one year to the next. This team was the equal of Don Bradman's Australians and Peter May's Englishmen among the great sides of the post-war period.

The West Indies crushed England again in 1966. That is not quite correct. Rather, Gary Sobers crushed them with an all-round excellence which has been rarely approached by any of the sport's great players. It more than made up for his shortage of runs over the past two series. He scored hundreds in three Test Matches and half-centuries in the other two. In their spinning role, Sobers and Gibbs shared the responsibility of the attack when the fast bowlers lost their earlier vitality. In addition to all that Sobers was an inspiration with his catching and fielding. No captain has ever given his side a better example of leading from the front. The Barbadian by himself provided a popular counter-attraction to the football

World Cup, which took place in England during the same summer.

The tourists lost 2 quick wickets in the first Test Match at Manchester. Sobers went for his strokes and, helped by several dropped catches, scored 161. He opened a season of high aggregates in which, contrary to the experience of Frank Worrell's team, the bowlers took excessive and increasing punishment. With Trueman finally retired England turned to the steady seam bowling of Ken Higgs and off-spinner Freddie Titmus, who took 5 wickets in this innings. Neither of them were attacking bowlers, and they were no competition for this batting genius. The initial blitz by the visiting batsmen panicked the English selectors into massive team changes. Mike Smith, the captain, was the first victim.

The second Test Match at Lord's is as memorable (though in a different way) as the equivalent game in 1963. For much of the match England were ahead by virtue of dismissing their opponents for a moderate 269. They led by 86 runs on the first innings. The West Indians could not get their play together, and lost 5 wickets for 95 when they batted again. England's new skipper, Colin Cowdrey, could be forgiven for anticipating a successful start to his new term of office. It was not to be. Sobers, the last recognized batsman, and leg-spinner David Holford, his cousin, played themselves in while the bowlers and fielders were still lulled by the foregoing events. By the time the Englishmen threw themselves into the battle more vigorously the two Barbadians were scoring with embarrassing ease, and could not be checked. They put on 274 without being parted. Sobers declared with the total at 369–5 and his own score on 163 not out. His boldness was rewarded by 4 quick wickets and the outside prospect of winning. Colin Milburn, the tubby, hard-hitting opener, saved England with an unbeaten hundred.

The West Indies won by 139 runs at Nottingham, from being 90 runs behind on the first innings. Butcher broke England's hold with a dogged double century. Sobers's own faster 94 gave him enough leeway to declare and take full advantage of the changed circumstances. England crashed to defeat on the dismissal of Tom Graveney and Colin Cowdrey, around whom the earlier lead had been built. Then Sobers improved even on himself in the fourth Test Match at Leeds. He hammered 174 from bowlers already dispirited from his previous attention. His stand with Seymour Nurse raised 265 runs on the first day. The speed with which the 500–9 dec total was accumulated gave England no chance of averting another heavy

Gary Sobers

defeat. They went down by an innings and 55 runs. Not satisfied with his carnage as a batsman, Gary bowled them out with 5 wickets for 41.

Sobers stood as high in renown as any cricketer before or since. He attempted all strokes, and mastered each of them with a whippy, wristy action which sent the ball straight, square or fine with unexpected speed and precision. His genius was such that he could play with his bat further from the body than is normally recommended. When he was sure of his batting Gary gave his bowling greater attention. With his greater control and use of the seam he was more effective than the fast bowlers in the opening overs. In addition he bowled tight left-arm spin, and had such telepathic anticipation in the close field that he was outstanding in an age of great slip fielders such as Colin Cowdrey and Bobby Simpson. No one player has had so many talents at his command. In spite of his professional dexterity—or perhaps because of it—Sobers did not have the same human rapport with the public as did Worrell, Constantine or Lloyd. He suffered in comparison to his predecessor, against whose reputation anyone would have fallen short. To be honest, the 1966 series was a little more bad-tempered and the county matches were taken less seriously. At any other time Gary's record as captain would have been incomparable, but in the ensuing years his free-ranging talents seemed to be unduly restricted by the responsibility of leadership.

England's eventual runaway victory at the Oval was achieved only after intense competition in the early stages. For once that summer, runs were hard to score. Brian Close, his country's third captain in the season, maintained great pressure with aggressive field placings. Kanhai's century and Sobers's 81 were the only significant contributions to the first-innings total of 268. The tide turned the tourists' way when England slumped to 166–7. Tom Graveney, who was batting better than ever in the twilight of his career, and wicket-keeper John Murray picked them up by scoring 217 for the next wicket. While the bowlers were still stunned John Snow and Ken Higgs rounded off the performance with another hundred for the last wicket. Showing that he was human after all, Gary made a duck in the second innings.

Sobers scored over 50 each time he went to the wicket in the three matches against India in 1966/67. Since taking over the captaincy he had batted at number six, and therefore had no opportunity to attain his former high scoring due to the shortage of partners. He was still the most competent batsman in dealing with the new breed of Indian spinners who gave the West Indians more trouble than they had faced in that country before. There was little really wrong with the batting, but the fast bowling failed totally. India's fight-back from a dreadful start at Bombay owed most to mystery bowler Chandrasekhar. He took 7 wickets in the first innings, and the only 4 wickets which fell in the second. He posed the same problem for the West Indies as their own Ramadhin had set to others. With one 50 behind him already, Sobers made 53 not out in partnership with young Clive Lloyd as his side won by 6 wickets.

Crowd riots overshadowed the innings win at Calcutta. The result was more in keeping with the traditional West Indian supremacy. Sobers made 70, and took 4 wickets for 56 as the Indians were hustled out on a pitch which started to break up far too early.

The match at Madras, in contrast, was in balance until the last delivery. Sobers scored 95 in eking out a narrow lead of 2 runs. It was hardly enough on a wicket already responding to spin. Chasing 322 runs to win, the tourists slipped up against off-spinner Erapalli Prasanna and left-arm spinner Bishen Bedi. They stuttered to 193–7. Sobers came through the crisis with 74 not out, and steered his team to within sight of victory at 270–7 by the close. The West Indies were now undefeated in five consecutive rubbers. Gary Sobers was worth a whole team on his own, but he could not always carry his country with him in his six remaining years in international cricket.

CHAPTER ELEVEN
Rohan Kanhai

Rohan Babulal Kanhai has been one of my favourite batsmen since he stepped into the Test Match arena as a boyish twenty-one-year-old in 1957. He seemed so fresh and untried, but his subsequent achievements have shown him to be one of the greatest cricketers of the modern age. His looks and his attitude reflect the effects of experience and the benefits of acquired technique. The jutting black hair, the instantly recognizable trademark of his youth, turned gradually grey. The cheeky enthusiasm and the temptation to try to score off every ball gave way to a mature discretion by which, according to the state of the game, he could defend, play a secondary role, or still attack with his old vigour. There was never anything negative about his approach. Even when he concentrated solely on keeping the bowling out, he did so purposefully. Something was bound to happen all the while he was at the crease. Kanhai's fielding had to be seen to be believed. He was especially agile in close-in positions on the leg-side, whether at leg-slip or catching the ball barely inches off the turf at square-leg. He failed only as a bowler and, having seen him in the nets, I can quite understand why.

Kanhai was thrown into international cricket at the deep end as an opening batsman, and by keeping wicket to Roy Gilchrist's thunderbolts and Frank Worrell's guileful seam. It was hard not to feel sorry for him. He took the first wicket to fall in the series by catching Brian Close, but he was never really comfortable. On the evening of the same day he had to face Freddie Trueman, Brian Statham and Trevor Bailey. Young Rohan survived that session, but he was lbw for 42 to Statham immediately play commenced the next morning. He made the top score in the first innings at Lord's, and batted well lower in the order at Nottingham. Relieved of the wicket-keeping responsibilities, he put his head down for a sound 47 in the next game at Leeds. Jim Laker had him lbw in terrible light. The selectors could not leave well alone, and Kanhai was asked to open again in the last innings of the series. His adventurous spirit was out of place here. He whacked Trueman for two fours. Trying to repeat the stroke before his eye was in, he sliced a catch to Godfrey Evans. It is a wonder that his enthusiasm was not extinguished there and then. It was not: his exuberance and willingness to succeed endeared him to the public.

Clyde Walcott, who guided him from minor cricket in Berbice, Guyana, to the pinnacle of world fame, has explained the young man's fear of letting down the people who believed in his ability. In many ways his overt desire to push the score along too quickly—especially in England, where the contrary nature of the pitch and the elements require an innings to be built soberly—harped back to Clifford Roach. He seemed more likely to prosper on better batting wickets; it was impossible to foresee that the prime performances in the latter half of Kanhai's long international and county career would take place in England. In those days the air of exoticism was heightened by writing his name always in full as Rohan Kanhai in a pseudo-Muslim fashion.

He was retained as opening batsman for the first Test Match against Pakistan, but showed his appreciation better when he was moved down the order at Port of Spain. The young Guyanese was caught by Wallis Mathias off Mahmood Hussain for 96, his side's best effort in their first victory of the rubber. He could not maintain that promise in the other games. He came into his own on the following tour to India and Pakistan. The batting of Kanhai and Sobers was as devastating in its own way as the fast bowling of Hall and Gilchrist. Rohan disconcerted the Indians by the power of his shots against slow bowling which came through at an even pace and height. Significantly, it was wrist-spinner Subhash Gupte who tied him in most knots. Kanhai and Collie Smith pulled the first innings round at Bombay with sound if uncharacteristic batting. Then they went to Kanpur, where the leg-spinner bowled Kanhai for a duck. The young batsman was well into his third series, and still did not have a century to his name. Sobers and Smith were pulling away from him in the terms of runs scored. Basil Butcher, his Guyanese compatriot—

whom some observers considered should have had his berth in England—was pressing his claims for priority.

Rohan came in to bat in the third Test Match at Calcutta when Holt was caught cheaply off medium-paced Surendranath. From that moment his place in the side was not really in doubt until his final departure 15 years later. He savaged the bowling with relish. When his first two partners were out Butcher helped him put on another 217 runs for the fourth wicket. The veteran Phadkar was blasted unhappily into retirement with no wicket for 173. More significantly, Gupte's lone success cost him 119 runs. Kanhai was eventually caught for 256 off Surendranath, whose delivery off the wrong foot complicated what was really a modest pace. If Gary Sobers had taken over Worrell's mantle, Rohan Kanhai was now compared to Weekes and Walcott. He had shaped so well previously with little result. This one big innings made all the difference. In the years ahead he batted even better against superior bowling, but it is doubtful if anything else had such a beneficial effect on his career.

The Indians strengthened their spin section for the next match at Madras. It did them no good. Kanhai tore into the attack with his new-found confidence. Gupte was the chief victim, yielding another 166 runs, and the innocuous new-ball pairing of Ramchand and Surendranath gave away 122 runs for their one wicket. Even now the batsman was his own worst enemy: Kanhai's impetuosity and optimistic judgment of a run had caused his colleagues concern before now, and would do so again. Poor running between the wickets may well be akin to genius. Denis Compton was an especially bad runner, and George Headley had enough trouble in this respect. When Kanhai was tantalizingly run out for 99 the game was already well within the visitors' grasp.

The second leg of the tour to Pakistan went sadly for the West Indians. The batsmen whose stroke-play had been so fluent in India came adrift against good-class medium-fast bowling on matting pitches. Although the first defeat at Karachi could be attributed partially to acclimatization problems, the even worse failure at Dacca derived solely from Fazal Mahmood's skill. The last 7 wickets went down for 11 runs. Kanhai, who had been moved up the order again, could not get going. When he was restored to first-wicket down at Lahore it made all the difference. Fazal Mahmood quickly dismissed temporary openers Gerry Alexander and Robin Bynoe, but there his success ended. Kanhai and Sobers had suffered enough. They put on

162 runs, chiefly from Fazal, who conceded his bowler's 'century'. Kanhai pressed on relentlessly even while his partners fell by the wayside. He was caught and bowled by Shujauddin for 217. That score exceeded the combined aggregate of any other batsman for the whole three-match series. Now that the West Indians were sure that the Pakistani jinx had left them they bowled and fielded with greater alacrity, and won by an innings and 156 runs.

The transition between the two generations of West Indian players was complete by the time Peter May's side arrived in the Caribbean in 1959. Only Ramadhin had appeared regularly since the start of the decade. Worrell's return from a two-year lay-off made up for the loss of Smith. England had dropped Trevor Bailey and Tony Lock, two of their most competitive cricketers, following their defeat in Australia. Not that it seemed to make too much difference at first. Freddie Trueman and Brian Statham had only too obviously retained their old fire. With the first Test Match at Bridgetown drawn inconclusively, these fast bowlers whipped out the West Indians for 112 in the first innings at Port of Spain. Kanhai was lbw to Trueman before he had really got going. May set his opponents the near-impossible task of getting 501 to win. As with Smith at Nottingham, it was the allegedly most spontaneous batsman—this time Kanhai—who showed most successfully the virtues of restraint and application. He kept his end up for well over six hours, but nobody stayed with him. Rohan was out for 110, and defeat was already inevitable.

The third Test Match at Kingston was the most evenly contested. After many swings of fortune the West Indies had to score 230 to win in just over four hours. Hunte got them away speedily before he was bowled by Trueman, who hit the stumps four times in all. Everything depended on Kanhai, who was suffering from a muscle injury which restricted his mobility. The English captain—who apologized afterwards for an inadvertent misinterpretation of the rules—refused him permission for a runner. The umpires upheld the decision, even though it was found to be wrong afterwards. All West Indian hopes of victory disappeared then. The game ended in a draw with no clear advantage to either side.

The team which had come through its baptism of fire against India with some credit proved its real mettle in Australia. In spite of their variable form in the initial matches against state sides, they fought the current world champions to a standstill. They only just came off second best. Kanhai was encouraged by his double century against

Victoria on the way to the first Test Match at Brisbane, but the bowling he faced there was several classes higher than anything he had met in India. His 54 in the second innings picked up the tourists from their half-way deficit and helped them put the pressure on the Australians which brought about the remarkable finish.

The next game at Melbourne was heartbreaking. Facing a score of 348, the tourists lost their two opening batsmen for only one run. Seymour Nurse and Rohan Kanhai counter-attacked so well with a range of scintillating strokes that the bowlers were thrown temporarily off course. They hit out with their own unorthodox panache, but there is always an element of risk in such stroke-play. With Davidson bowling to his slip fielders, that danger was soon realized. Harvey caught Kanhai for 84 when the batsman was going at full throttle. Nurse and Kanhai were the only West Indians to reach double figures in the 181 runs total. The surrender of the later batsmen was so abject that one prominent newspaper altered the name of the team in its headline from 'W. Indies' to 'Windies'. It was a curious feature of this time that Sobers and Kanhai could not do well together. When one succeeded the other failed, and so it continued in Australia. Sobers hit the match-winning innings at Sydney when the latter was out cheaply. Bill Ponsford and Don Bradman fared similarly in the early 1930s, but they combined with a vengeance in their last international series. The time would come when Sobers and Kanhai would also decimate an attack in partnership.

Rohan returned to the forefront at Adelaide. The tourists did not score as many as they hoped in Davidson's absence through injury. Three batsmen were soon out. Kanhai steadied the innings in a century stand with his captain, Worrell. He leapt into the hook shot, sometimes falling over in the process, but still sending the ball to the boundary. Opposing bowlers realized by now that if they did not get him out early the Guyanese stroke-maker would make them pay with a big score. This time was no exception. He made 117, and even that wasn't the end. As not too much separated the two sides at the halfway stage the outcome depended on how well the batsmen fared against the Australian spinners. Hunte and Kanhai added 163 for the second wicket. They were in such command that centuries were there for the asking. Then there was a muddle, in which the Barbadian opener was run out for 79. Shortly afterwards Sobers followed him to the pavilion, out the same way. Kanhai, whose concentration had been broken by such an incident in his first series, had progressed enough to play through these crises, even though he was distressed. He was lbw to Benaud for 115, his second century of the match. The West Indies were now so far ahead that only Ken Mackay's long and at times lucky resistance prevented them from winning.

Little stress is usually put on the players' achievements in 1962 because the Indians were so much out of their depth. With wicket-keepers Jackie Hendriks and Ivor Mendonca and tailender Wesley Hall scoring fifties the specialist batsmen ran wild. Kanhai was one of the three century-makers at Kingston where he shared a stand of 255 runs with Sobers and the visitors lost by an innings in spite of scoring 395. He led the way with 139 in the fourth Test Match at Port of Spain. Although India lost that match by 7 wickets, old campaigner Polly Umrigar enjoyed a rare personal triumph by taking 5 wickets for 107 and scoring 56 and 172 not out.

Kanhai's powerful range of strokes was an important factor in the 1963 series against England, where he did not reach a hundred at all. He came very close indeed to that target by making 90 in the opening engagement at Manchester and 92 later at Leeds.

The diffident debutant of six years ago was now the most feared batsman in the world. However, whereas Sobers was sure of a good score whenever he batted, and Hunte's reliability was accepted, Kanhai was more unpredictable. Because his bursts of scoring could not be anticipated they were more likely to turn the course of the match. His hitting was particularly disheartening for the bowlers. He set the pace on the first morning of the series with an innings of delightful aggression until he was characteristically run out. His 73 on the opening day at Lord's was more restrained, but caution was needed. The pitch at headquarters had favoured seam bowling for several years, and was well exploited by Freddie Trueman and Derek Shackleton. By the time of the fourth Test Match at Leeds the home country had drawn level in the rubber, due to Trueman's manipulation of a dusty pitch at Birmingham. For a brief instant the West Indians seemed in danger of losing their momentum and the initiative. Kanhai and Sobers took charge in hitting up a total of 397 runs which was far in excess of anything their opponents achieved all summer. It finished England.

And so to the final game at the Oval, and one of the greatest innings I have seen. England had to win here to square the series. They put themselves in a strong position in leading by 29 runs on the first innings, with the tourists to bat last. Although Trueman was out of action through injury, spin bowling would be the bigger danger the longer the match continued. The dismissal of temporary opening batsman Willie Rodriguez gave Kanhai the chance to turn the proceedings upside down. While Hunte remained steadfast, the Guyanese batsman murdered the bowling. In a remarkable spate of scoring he won the game before the bowlers either knew what had hit them or could use the conditions to their advantage. When he was out for 77—made at well over a run a minute—the West Indies were home and dry. The effect and the execution were very much in line with Alvin Kallicharran's mugging of Dennis Lillee on the same ground in the Prudential World Cup tournament of 1975.

The 'world championship' series between the West Indies and Australia in 1965 was patchy, with some excellent cricket, especially by the home bowlers, mixed with controversy and boring batting in the drawn games. The West Indians began the season better than they had really expected. Although the recent performances had been a source of growing optimism, the players themselves, and also the spectators, were still smarting under the memory of the past indignities put on them by these very opponents. It was almost too good to be true when they won the first Test Match at Kingston, forced a draw at Port of Spain, and then had first use of a bowling wicket at Georgetown which was lethal to the side batting last. Kanhai was the only batsman to score more than 50. He was batting really well when Neil Hawke—who made up in guile what he lacked in speed—clipped his off-stump for 89. No other batsman came to terms with the conditions. The West Indies won by 212 runs, and emphasized their right to be considered world champions.

In the context of the match and the pitch, Rohan's innings in Guyana here was worth more than the 129 he made at Bridgetown. Australia took a heavy toll of the bowling in running up 650-6 dec, but the wicket was so docile that a double-century stand between Kanhai and Nurse cancelled out that advantage and led to a tame draw. The Australians improved from their poor start to the tour, and when the West Indians relaxed their concentration now that the rubber was won they sprang a surprise in the fifth Test Match at Port of Spain. Graham McKenzie and Neil Hawke bowling at medium-fast achieved the same effect as Pakistan's Fazal Mahmood had produced in similar circumstances in 1957/58. The West Indian batting disintegrated entirely. Kanhai was the one exception. By now he had developed two gears, depending on the circumstances. He was no longer just a brilliant stroke-player; he could battle with the uncompromising determination of Trevor Bailey or Geoffrey Boycott. This time he scored 121 out of 224, but Australia still won by 10 wickets.

Something wasn't quite right with the one-sided triumph in 1966. Although it was not obvious at the time, Frank Worrell's all-conquering side had started to come apart at the seams. Sobers's personal omnipotence covered up frailties in almost every other department. While the rubber was sewn up as quickly as possible, with victories in three of the first four games, the West Indies were on the losing end of three matches for much of their duration. England lacked the finishing power to put a sound professional side away. The tourists won at Manchester, where they had first use of a short-lived wicket, and otherwise played as invincible world champions only at Leeds. The heroic fight-back in the second Test Match at Lord's has been already described.

The see-saw balance was repeated in the following game at Nottingham. England gained a first-innings lead of 90 runs through the batting of Tom Graveney, Colin Cowdrey and Basil D'Oliveira. The West Indian effort seemed almost anaemic in comparison. They were in trouble with the further dismissal of Conrad Hunte and Peter Lashley before the arrears were cleared. Then the prospects of victory for England disappeared as surely as West Indian hopes had been vanquished at Birmingham in 1957. Rohan Kanhai and Butcher, usually two of the most attractive batsmen in modern cricket, just stayed put, keeping the bowlers at bay. Neither the crowd's disapproval nor the precarious situation deterred them. Kanhai was out for an unusually dull 63, but he had paved the way for the middle-order batsmen to flog the tired bowlers. The West Indies won by 139 runs to set up an unbeatable lead.

For the second time in successive series the West Indies lost the fifth Test Match after the rubber had been decided. They put up a real fight when Kanhai and Sobers added over 100 runs. The former reached his first century in fifteen Test Matches in England. He was caught by Graveney off Illingworth for 104, but the rest of the batting fell away, and the side was all out for 268. England were 102 runs behind even that modest total when the seventh wicket fell. Now it was the West Indians who couldn't finish off a stricken opponent. The batsmen recovered remarkably throughout that sunny Saturday afternoon, and trapped the jaded tourists into a totally unexpected defeat.

The same tiredness showed on the three-match tour of India at the end of the year. Once more the West Indians seemed disappointing in spite of winning the first two games handsomely. Perhaps too much was expected of them now. Kanhai was so much out of touch in the second Test Match at Calcutta that it was no surprise when Pataudi caught him off Surti for 90. Even so, it was the highest individual score of the match and enough to win by an innings. He was in much better form in hitting 77 at Madras, and, with a whole year's rest, he would obviously still be a formidable proposition when England next visited the Caribbean.

CHAPTER TWELVE
Wesley Hall

Fast bowlers come in all shapes, styles and temperaments. Few have been as near to the ideal image as Wesley Hall. Everything about his physique, his delivery and his conduct was just as it should be. The Barbadian fitted the description of Alfred Mynn, the Kent all-rounder of the early nineteenth century: 'With his tall and stately presence, with his nobly moulded form,/His broad hand was ever open, his brave heart was ever warm'. Even Hall's optimistic opinion of his own batting, which was good enough for two Test Match fifties, fitted the general conception of the genial paceman. He bowled his heart out for a decade from 1958 in which he terrorized the Indians, overwhelmed the English and startled the Australians. Perhaps if he had not put his heart into everything he attempted, he might have lasted a year or two longer in the highest company, but then that would not have been Wesley Hall. The picture of him trudging back, shirt-tail out over his trousers, mopping the sweat from his brow, for just one more over when others would have given up long ago, whether it was in Adelaide, Kingston or Lord's, is one of cricket's most abiding memories.

Hall almost missed his date with destiny. He came into junior cricket as a wicket-keeper, set a batting record in his first serious trial, and was selected in 1957 as a fast bowler. His enthusiasm was much greater than his performance. He couldn't pitch the ball anywhere near the wicket. He was so bad that he wasn't considered for the home series against Pakistan, and was left out of the side to tour India. Frank Worrell's withdrawal from that party created vacancies for an extra batsman and bowler. Wesley got a few wickets for Barbados, and was taken along as deputy to Jaswick Taylor. After a particularly hostile and successful spell against the Baroda state side he replaced the Trinidadian as Gilchrist's first-choice partner, with results which are only too well known.

Human nature is inclined to see public figures as wholly good, bad or ugly. Just as there was no doubt about Hall being in the first category, the two bowlers associated with him most closely, Roy Gilchrist and Charlie Griffith, were definitely in the others. Gilchrist, a comparatively small Jamaican with unusually long arms, bowled as fast as anyone has ever bowled. Unfortunately, he did not always control either himself or his temper. After the first leg of the double tour to India and Pakistan he was sent home for a disagreement with his captain, allegedly over the use of bumpers in minor matches, and he did not play Test Match cricket again. If Gilchrist had been available to link up with Hall the rubbers against England and Australia between 1959 and 1961, which were lost so narrowly, would almost certainly have been won.

Charlie Griffith was not a 'bad boy' in this respect. He has no record of indiscipline, and he never gave less than his best. Charlie was affected too deeply by criticism of the legality of his action, much of which was unfair, and he gave the impression of moodiness. For one season he was a very good bowler, and he might have remained so much longer if the circumstances had been different. Jaswick Taylor, who took 5 wickets for 109 against Pakistan at Port of Spain, Chester Watson and Lester King were all overshadowed by Hall, Gilchrist and Griffith. After twenty years without any consistent fast bowler the West Indies now had almost too many.

Gilchrist was kept in the team in 1957/58 because there was no alternative. He had had one burst of alarming pace on a balmy summer evening at Lord's—the ball which bowled Peter Richardson sent the stump reeling viciously. Otherwise his direction and control were wayward. In the Caribbean his speed shocked the Pakistanis from the moment he dismissed Imtiaz Ahmed and Alim-ud-din at the start of their first innings of the series. The Jamaican wrecked their opening partnership by causing even the great Hanif Mohammad to move down the batting order to avoid the worst of his assault and by cramping Alim-ud-din's hitherto attractive style.

There is no instrument accurate enough to measure the degree of terror which Gilchrist and Hall spread among the Indian batsmen in 1958/59. The Indians had already acquired a reputation of weakness against true pace since their surrender to Freddie Trueman at Manchester in 1952. Now they were faced with a really quick bowler at either end. Gilchrist was most effective in short bursts. Hall could bowl for seemingly endless spells even under the hot tropical sun. The batsmen made the mistake of trying to duck under the bumpers—Ramchand suffered a nasty injury by estimating the line wrongly—or moving away from them and thus exposing their stumps. They did not have the experience or the physical capability to stand up, to drive or to hook. The selectors tried 24 players in an attempt to find somebody to resist the fast bowlers.

Hall began the season ominously at Bombay by having Nariman Contractor caught for a duck. With the score at 37, he dismissed both Roy and Manjrekar. Gilchrist then took over and captured 4 wickets for 39 in the rout. Taylor came in for the injured Gilchrist in the second Test Match at Kanpur. That game, however, belonged to Wesley Hall. India started quite well in reaching 182–2 before Hall had top-scorer Umrigar caught by Holt. He ended the innings just 40 runs later with 6 wickets for 50. First-wicket pair Roy and Contractor put on 99 the second time round, but once they were separated Hall struck again. He brushed aside Ramchand—who had scored a century against Lindwall and Miller just two years previously—and ran through the tail for 5 wickets for 76. Wesley hit the stumps three times and Taylor twice as the batsmen dived for cover. To be fair to the Indians, who had four different captains in the series, the changes of fortune and team-selection over a decade had given the side an unfair blend of old-timers and raw youngsters. The West Indians revelled in their superiority after their own humiliation by England and Australia, and their confidence increased with each encounter.

The landslide victory by an innings and 336 runs at Calcutta eclipsed all that had gone before. The desire to fight went out of the Indians when their visitors scored 614–5 dec. Surprisingly, the first wicket fell to spinner Ramadhin, but after that Hall and Gilchrist had everything very much their own way. Umrigar made 44 not out as he watched 5 wickets go down with the score in the fifties. When they followed on 490 runs behind Hall had Pankaj Roy caught at the wicket for a duck, and sent back two more batsmen, including Umrigar. Vijay Manjrekar tried to rally his side with an undefeated 58. Even he could not protect his colleagues from Gilchrist's late attack, which was as destructive as anything ever seen in Test Matches. He clean bowled five batsmen in taking 6 wickets for 55, three with the total at 131. Whenever the Indians did succeed in getting the bat to the ball they were often caught by Alexander or the slips. The wicketkeeper-captain was outstanding again at Madras. His four catches to the fast bowlers sent the home side reeling to their third successive heavy defeat. Although both main bowlers were injured during the fifth Test Match at New Delhi, Roy Gilchrist had a final fling whereby he wrapped up the Indian second innings by having Chandrakant Borde hit his wicket only 4 runs short of what would have been his second century in the match, and bowling two tail-enders as 3 wickets fell for 1 run. That was it. He received his marching orders, and did not play again.

Moving the ball through the air, rather than striving for pace, Hall took 4 wickets at Dacca as Pakistan tumbled to 22–5. The more accommodating style of Eric Atkinson, who shared the new ball instead of Taylor, could not keep the batsmen under the same pressure. Hall finished off the Pakistani second innings by taking the last 4 wickets in the course of 14 runs. The West Indians themselves could not cope with Fazal Mahmood and lost a match in which none of the four totals reached 200. The Barbadian broke the home batting with a hat-trick in his 5 wickets for 87 at Lahore. His victims were Mustaq Mohammad, who was making his international debut at the age of 15 years and 125 days, the youngest cricketer to play in a Test Match, Nasimul Ghani, who held that record previously, and Fazal Mahmood.

It was one thing to terrify the Indians, who had no experience of pace, and quite another to bowl out England, with its own recent fine record in this respect. Hall's performances at Kingston and Georgetown in 1959/60 rank among the great fast-bowling feats of the last hundred years. He almost won the third Test at Kingston as soon as it started. Colin Cowdrey, battered and bruised, stood in his way with an equally magnificent innings. Whenever the bowler pitched short the Kentish batsman picked up the line early and hooked to the boundary. The other batsmen were not so quick, and sprayed a variety of catches to the wicket-keeper and close field. Wesley was most impressive in knocking over the stumps of Mike Smith and Roy Swetman before they had scored. The West Indian crowd had not seen such consistently hostile bowling since the halcyon days of Martindale and Constantine. England, who survived that match solely through Cowdrey's efforts, carried with them the memory of Hall's frightening talent and his 7 wickets for 69.

Chester Watson, a Jamaican, also bowled well in his homeland by taking 4 wickets for 62 in the second innings. He seemed to be the perfect replacement for Gilchrist. Unfortunately, he was too much like his predecessor, in that he could not discipline either his direction or his penchant for short-pitched bowling. Watson went with Worrell's team to Australia, where he bowled with much fire and little success. Hall demonstrated time and again that although he could bowl a bumper as well as anyone, that delivery was only a part of his repertoire. He did not become bouncer-happy, and depended for his success on the virtues of speed, length and direction.

Hall produced another great effort at Georgetown. England weathered his opening attack on a pitch deadened by rain. When he had Cowdrey caught by Alexander early on the second day, however, the middle batting caved in under the force of his bowling. Although most of the batsmen were out to catches close to the wicket, Hall bowled Mike Smith for a duck for the second successive match. He put the West Indies right back into the match, but the batsmen squandered this opportunity with some excessively slow scoring. Wesley had burned himself out by the approach of the fifth Test Match at Port of Spain, where Charlie Griffith partnered him for the first time. The latter was the fast-bowling find of the season. The selectors considered him too inexperienced for the arduous tour of Australia, sending Watson and Dewdney instead.

The Australians, who are connoisseurs of good fast bowling, took an instant liking to Wesley Hall. He plodded wearily back to his mark for over after over, shook the perspiration out of his eyes, fingered the crucifix around his neck, and bounded in for the next delivery with the same energy and concentration. He didn't do too much after the first two Test Matches, but his performances in those two games were good enough for him to be invited to play for Queensland in the Sheffield Shield competition. Wesley's attitude to the game was well received everywhere.

Hall was a key contributor to the Brisbane tie. He started the game by scoring his first international half-century before, becoming too ambitious, he was stumped by Wally Grout off slow bowler Kline. The Barbadian's own bowling was handled disrespectfully at first by Colin McDonald, Bobby Simpson and Norman O'Neill. Later he hit a better length and had O'Neill caught by Valentine as part of the surge which brought Australia down from 469–5 to 505 all out. Their second innings began sensationally. Hall had Simpson and Harvey caught before the score was in double figures, and also dismissed O'Neill and Favell before it reached a hundred. The decision to exclude another fast bowler in favour of an additional batsman might well have cost the tourists the game at this crucial point.

Hall bowled the last over which brought the match to its historic climax. After Grout stole a run from a delivery which struck him in the stomach, Wesley tempted Benaud with a bouncer. The Australian captain waved his bat at it, got a thin touch and Gerry Alexander completed the catch. The excitement was turned to despair as the bowler, carried away by the euphoria of the moment, next went for and dropped a catch that should have been left to Kanhai. Nevertheless, his tight bowling contributed as much as the fielders to the conclusion. There are many stories about Worrell's good-natured warnings of what would happen to him back home if he bowled a no-ball or a long-hop. Unable to hit the ball to the boundary, the Australians were forced to take risks, and they paid the penalty.

Wesley Hall bowled well on the first morning of the second Test Match at Melbourne. He was stimulated by Watson's return as new-ball bowler in place of Worrell's easier pace. Although he had some outstanding performances when bowling alone, Hall was usually at his best when there was somebody just as fast at the other end to keep the batsmen hopping. He dismissed both openers before they got going and clean bowled both Davidson and Benaud, the heroes of Brisbane, in his 4 wickets for 51. When Australia batted a second time needing only a few runs to win he maintained the tension by dismissing McDonald and Harvey at the same score. Hall and Watson gave the batsmen a very uncomfortable few overs. The pitches later in the series favoured slow bowling. As Gibbs and Valentine were in the team Hall was not called upon as much as his opposite number, Davidson.

The Indians' existing fear of Hall's bowling was deepened in 1962. Assisted by sound batting throughout the order rather than by any spectacular individual efforts, the tourists seemed to have ensured a draw in the second Test at Kingston. They scored 395, and watched the West Indies similarly play out time with 631–8 dec. Hall wasn't satisfied with any such tame ending to the game. He blasted the innings wide open with 6 wickets for 49, and his team won without having to bat again. For their part India had to live through a revival of the nightmare of the last series between these two countries, and they did not have any confidence for the remaining matches.

Caribbean Cricketers

The situation was made worse when the captain, Nariman Contractor, suffered a severe blow by a ball from Charlie Griffith in the game against Barbados. His life was saved only by substantial blood transfusion. The wicket for the fourth Test Match at Port of Spain was sufficiently suitable for batting for Hall himself to make 50 not out in a West Indian run spree. The Indians were still not convinced that their fears were groundless. Wesley cut deep into their ranks with 5 wickets for 20, which doomed their batting effort from the start and made Umrigar's lone stand all the more admirable. Hitherto West Indian fast bowlers had a reputation for fading after a meteoric rise. Hall seemed to get better the more often he played.

The scars of the ordeal were such that the Indians could not benefit from the absence of the regular new ball bowlers in the fifth Test Match at Kingston. Newcomer Lester King broke through the top of their innings with 5 swift wickets for 46. He found some of the same lift Bailey had discovered in 1954. King was unlucky to be at his best at the same time as Wesley Hall and Charlie Griffith, to whom, after this, he was the regular understudy for four years. He bowled well against the counties in England in 1963 and was one of the first players to be selected for the next touring team three years later. Injury caused King to withdraw before the party left the Caribbean.

The first arrival of Hall and Griffith in England was greeted with the public awe and press build-up formerly accorded to Ted McDonald and Jack Gregory or Ray Lindwall and Keith Miller. Their deliveries in the practice nets were photographed and timed in miles per hour. The one was a model fast bowler with a fine physique and flowing action. The other was similar in stature but more introverted, which became more pronounced in later years when he was accused of throwing his faster ball. Sonny Liston was world boxing champion then, and Charlie seemed to be made from the same menacing stock. At least, that was the image the media projected. The English batsmen were so mesmerized by the allegedly illegal bouncer that they did not guard against his more lethal slow yorker with which he reaped a rich harvest in wickets. Though they worked well as partners, Griffith more than Hall dominated this particular summer.

The opening exchanges between Ted Dexter and the two fast bowlers at Lord's were among the most thrilling in post-war cricket. The England captain's dismissal brought back the usual tense confrontation which Griffith won with 5 wickets for 91. He operated mainly from the Nursery End, the least favoured end for fast bowling.

Wesley Hall

Hall bowled faster, but Griffith's style, accuracy and the intensity of his whole approach were the more successful because they were unexpected. The final day brought a challenge of a different kind from Brian Close to the pacemen. It had been preceded by a lively kicker from Hall which exploded like a grenade close to Cowdrey's body and broke a bone in his arm. The batsman bore no grudge; he admired the effort the bowler put into his work. Close, a left-hander from Yorkshire, moved swiftly down the pitch to put the fast bowlers off. Hall and Griffith did not falter in their duty throughout that whole miserable afternoon of rain and poor light. Close sustained a terrific battering about the body through his foolhardy tactics, but he brought his side to the verge of victory. Hall bowled the last over of that now legendary match, as he had done at Brisbane. He kept going all day from the pavilion end, and knew now that one error, a wide which eluded the wicket-keeper for byes or a no-ball which could be hit freely, would give victory to England. As before Hall put the ball exactly on the right spot, and made the batsmen take the risks. The match was a draw.

Griffith was again the more effective at Leeds, where he took 6 wickets for 36. The Englishmen did not have a clue what to do about him. During this season Charlie showed a variation of pace and style which he did not repeat. Later he worried as much as his opponents about the controversy which marred his career. It seemed as if he was in two minds as to whether he resented the accusations or whether he was determined to live up to his role as 'big, bad Charlie'. There was only one thought in his mind in 1963, however. The bowlers were so much in command that Phil Sharpe's 85 not out at Birmingham was the best score against them in the whole series. The struggle between Sharpe, who made two more half-centuries, and Griffith was renewed at the Oval. Although the pitch had favoured spin in the time of Jim Laker and Tony Lock, the West Indian fast bowlers were as effective here as they had been all year.

Griffith thwarted England's attempt to build a big score by taking 6 wickets for 71, and Hall did better in the second innings with 4 wickets for 39. Batsmen are usually more likely to hit the headlines than bowlers, but in 1963 Hall and Griffith were the centre of attraction and the key to victory. England had not been tested so severely before by West Indian fast bowlers, and were not so again until they came up against Andy Roberts, Michael Holding and Wayne Daniel in 1976.

England's worries about these two bowlers were minor compared to the Australians' advance fears in 1965. They appeared to yield the initiative even before the cricket began. The tourists were overawed in the first three Test Matches, during which time the rubber was irrevocably lost, and they were obsessed with the dispute about Griffith's delivery. Ironically the bowler himself—perhaps affected by the argument—suffered a setback after his success in England. They had no qualms about Wesley Hall, and as usual he hit them right at the start of the proceedings.

The battle of wills was effectively settled in the first Test Match at Kingston. Hall tore through the first three batsmen and finished with 5 wickets for 60. Not one of the tourists reached 50. Because their own earlier batting effort had been so paltry, the West Indies led by only 22 runs. They did not fail a second time. Australia were set to score almost 400 runs in their final innings, and their slim chance was reduced even further when Wesley sent back skipper Bobby Simpson and Cowper. He took 4 wickets for 45 in a victory which confirmed the tourists' phobia about fast bowling, and preyed on their minds afterwards. Strangely enough, the quicker bowlers were not so successful again until the fifth Test Match at Port of Spain. Griffith had been frustrated by his inability to get wickets, but he took a reasonable revenge for his traumas on and off the field. Although the West Indies were destined to defeat after their poor batting on the first day, Charlie had left-hander Lawry caught with only 2 runs scored, and ended the century stand between Simpson and Bob Cowper by bowling the former. Then he dismissed three middle-order batsmen to finish with 6 wickets for 46.

The English press worried unduly about Hall and Griffith before the 1966 series began. Once play had got under way, however, it was apparent that the new-ball bowlers had lost much of their spirit and energy. Griffith brooded, and achieved little. His best bowling was 4 wickets for 34 in the closing stages of the third Test Match at Nottingham. That was the game in which he moved down to first change to let Sobers open the bowling. Hall had his moments of success, but could not rekindle the inspiration over any length of time. His stamina had been as remarkable as his speed and accuracy. His most memorable achievements were the three quick wickets at the start of the English innings at Leeds and his part in their initial discomfort at the Oval. His action was as poetic as ever and his commitment was just as great, but something was missing. The

Wesley Hall

English batsmen made three centuries and three scores of 90 where previously they had made none in 1963.

In India Wesley Hall was a shell of the great bowler who had swept through the sub-continent with Gilchrist. The pitches reduced his pace and sapped his inspiration. Griffith perked up a little by taking 4 wickets in an innings at Madras, and perhaps surprised even himself by staying with Sobers in scoring 40 not out to save the game. The great fast-bowling partnership was obviously coming to an end, but the prestige and psychological influence of this pair was such that the selectors dared not replace them even if there had been anyone else available. Griffith took 5 wickets for 69 against England in the first Test Match at Port of Spain in 1967/68, and Hall bowled with his old enthusiasm at Kingston. It was an illusion. They suffered heavily as the season progressed, and resembled exhausted volcanoes on the following tour to Australia.

The picture of Wesley Hall in full flow as he ran towards the wicket is still treasured in the memories of all but the opposing batsmen—and maybe in theirs as well—and the thought of Griffith's bouncers mixed with the yorker can yet disturb his former opponents' sleep. That is how it should be with fast bowlers.

CHAPTER THIRTEEN
Lance Gibbs

Lance Gibbs was the quiet killer. Orthodox off-spinners are hardly the most exciting bowlers, even at their most destructive. They do not arouse the passions as much as the faster men, and are less interestingly unpredictable than the leg-spinners and 'mystery' bowlers like Sonny Ramadhin, Jack Iverson, B. S. Chandrasekhar and John Gleeson. Many long hours of my youth were spent in watching Jim Laker and Hughie Tayfield wheeling away for overs on end with little apparent result. When conditions were against them they shut down the game by adopting a defensive pitch, length and trajectory. If things turned in their favour their mastery was so complete that the match became one-sided. Few spinners have the extrovert characters to compare with Freddie Trueman, Keith Miller or Roy Gilchrist. (Left-arm spinners are less conventional. For example, Bobby Peel is reported to have collapsed through the after-effects of overnight drinking on his approach to the wicket in a Test Match in Australia. His captain helped Peel to his feet and out of international cricket.) And yet where would any team be without these most classical of bowlers?

Gibbs was never boring. He was too positive for that. Lance bounded in like a spring hare bobbing in a morning field, and he turned the ball a very long way. He approached the kill with the professional, almost clinically scientific, certainty of a good pugilist who has a stricken opponent against the ropes from which there is no escape. At least once every season, and often more than that, Gibbs had one devastating spell which settled the rubber. Hall and Griffith gave the batsmen a chance to hit or edge runs before they were out.

Lance Gibbs

There was no possibility of that happening with Gibbs. The Guyanese off-spinner took a temporary rest from Test Matches at the end of the 1960s, and, after and during his very successful service with Warwickshire in the county championship, he came back better than ever to set a new record for the highest number of victims at international level.

The West Indies have had only three really good spin bowlers. Ramadhin was a law to himself. Valentine bowled left-arm. Gibbs had the only straightforward delivery in the game's most orthodox style. Throughout his career he was helped and encouraged by the competence of the wicket-keepers and the fielders. Some slow bowlers can perform well only on certain surfaces: the Indian and English spinners are vulnerable in this respect, but Gibbs maintained a consistent standard of excellence in all four countries in which he played for any length of time. If he did not figure in the same kind of nail-biting finishes as the fast bowlers, it was because when he found any help at all in the pitch there was never any doubt about the result. Few anecdotes are told of him, because it is difficult to invent stories about a man who does his job so efficiently and undemonstratively. Sobers was another whose concentrated effort on the field left little scope for embellishment.

Lance Gibbs flourished at a time when the emphasis in world cricket was on speed. The value of slow bowlers has decreased since the new ball became so much more readily available. He succeeded through being the best attacking right-arm finger-spinner in Test Match competition, certainly since the Second World War. Many batsmen failed against him just because he was at his best in those circumstances in which spinners were not expected to do well. In spite of the fine array of seam bowling at his disposal, the captain frequently brought Gibbs into the attack early with the view to dismissing a particular opponent or exploiting a known weakness. As he was not used in a defensive role—or hardly ever so—Gibbs gave the batsmen no time to relax and fortify their confidence. Anyone who tried to take liberties or momentarily broke his concentration was caught with the certainty of a mouse-trap. The West Indies did not need another specialist spinner all the while he was around.

Gibbs made his first important mark in the fourth Test Match against Pakistan at Georgetown in 1957/58. He bowled well in the early matches of that series, and was trusted to share with Collie Smith the responsibility of breaking down the tourists' second innings after only two runs separated the teams. The young man struck at once by bowling Imtiaz Ahmed, but his real value was towards the end after a stubborn stand between Wazir Mohammad and A. H. Kardar. Lance dismissed the latter and spun out the tail in his 5 wickets for 80. He took another 4 wickets in the next game at Port of Spain. This time he gave away over 100 runs as Wazir Mohammad—who had been stranded on 97 not out in Guyana—hit 189. Wazir was the eldest of the five famous Mohammad brothers, four of whom played in Test Matches. Gibbs bowled only moderately in India, and was replaced by Reg Scarlett for the series against England in 1959/60. His qualities had been noted, however, and he was taken to Australia as the third spinner to Ramadhin and Valentine.

Australia is known as the graveyard of off-spinners, and with good reason. Jim Laker took a record haul of wickets against the Australians in 1956, but when he went Down Under two years later he had to struggle. No rubber there in living memory had been settled by finger-spin alone. For the first two Test Matches Frank Worrell (who may have been guided by these precedents) included in the side both Ramadhin and Valentine. They had the greater experience and the styles most likely to succeed. Gibbs sat on the sidelines and watched the fast bowlers take the headlines. When the teams moved on to Sydney there was nothing to lose in giving him a chance in Ramadhin's place.

Gibbs and Valentine shouldered most of the bowling in the Australian first innings. Although the bowlers were always on top, the end of the innings came with a startling suddenness. Gibbs had taken some time to get into his stride. When he persuaded the stubborn Mackay to edge a catch to Joe Solomon, Lance struck the 'killer' mood that would become so well known in the years ahead. The young man from Guyana took 3 wickets in four balls as John Martin and Wally Grout were out for 'no score'. The more mature Valentine had the better figures with 4 wickets for 67. The prospect of these two bowlers operating on the final day was a daunting one for the home side. Neil Harvey, a small, stylish left-hander, and Norman O'Neill, more powerful with very strong arms, boosted the second innings by taking the score to 191–2. Then they were out in identical fashion—caught Sobers bowled Gibbs. Once they had gone Benaud was the only batsman to reach double figures. The off-spinner cracked what remained of the batting by dismissing Favell

Lance Gibbs

and Mackay straight after each other in his 5 wickets for 66. Valentine was not outclassed in taking 4 wickets for 86. The Australians, who had expected an artillery battle between rival batteries of fast bowlers, were caught napping on a different front and went down by over 200 runs.

The batsmen regained their composure in the early stages of the fourth Test Match at Adelaide. With Bobby Simpson and Richie Benaud playing well, Australia reached 213-3. Shortly afterwards they were 281-5 when Gibbs thrust home his three deadly blows. Mackay went back on his stumps and was lbw. Grout was caught by Sobers for his third successive duck to the same bowler. Frank Misson was clean bowled . . . a 'hat-trick'. Lance was the first bowler to take 3 wickets in three balls in a Test Match in Australia since Hugh Trumble in 1903/04. The Australians had batted badly against spin in England, but they did not expect this treatment in their own country. In view of this success, it is surprising that Gibbs did not get a single wicket in the second innings as Mackay played out time. This enigmatic left-hander had shown many times that he was uneasy against any ball which did not keep a straight line. The fielders crowded him close, but Mackay survived. Gibbs was back to his best with 4 wickets for 74 in the final match at Melbourne. Although he missed two games, the off-spinner headed the averages by taking each of his wickets at over 8 runs cheaper than Wesley Hall, the next best. Arthur Mailey was said to bowl like a millionaire because he bought his wickets by giving away runs: on that assessment Lance Gibbs bowled like a miser.

The explosive impact of the West Indian fast bowlers against the Indians in 1962 has distracted attention from their most devastating breakdown of all, which occurred against Gibbs at Bridgetown. Although the Indians have a traditional fear of pace, they have usually played above themselves against even the most penetrative spin. Over the last thirty years visiting slow bowlers have had a tough time in India. Wilfred Ferguson comes easiest to mind. Even Valentine's success against them at home in 1953 was expensive. With Sobers and the fast bowlers sharing the early honours in 1962, Gibbs did not get a proper look-in until halfway through the season. The third Test Match at Bridgetown was the least exciting of the five in many ways. After Rohan Kanhai's sparkling 89 had put the West Indies ahead the later batsmen laboured to increase that lead. It was as if they were bored with the one-sided competition. Dilip Sardesai and veteran Vijay Manjrekar took the tourists into lunch at 158-2 on the last day. Some time during that adjournment Gibbs discovered again the 'bite' he had in Australia. The batsmen made the mistake of going on to the defensive, and snicked a cluster of catches to the eager fielders. The stalemate became a slide which developed immediately into a procession. In one session Gibbs took 8 wickets for 6 runs, and had only 38 scored against him in the entire innings.

The side that went to England in 1963 had the best balanced and most economic West Indian attack of all time. Hall and Griffith took the new ball. Gibbs was the only specialist spinner, and Sobers helped out wherever he was needed: no other bowler was really required. With the minimum number of bowlers, the West Indies kept England in check and beat them on a variety of pitches. Frank Worrell's team (which was short of only a second reliable opening batsman) and Clive Lloyd's party in 1976 (where only spin was under-represented) are considered to be the best of all West Indian sides. I would not like to judge between them.

The tourists stamped their authority on the rubber from the first Test Match at Manchester. The batsmen knocked up 501-6 dec while the pitch lasted. Afterwards Lance Gibbs ran through the home batting with 5 wickets for 59, and then 6 wickets for 98. Although winning the toss was all-important because the pitch responded early to spin, England had been considered better equipped in these conditions. The strategy of holding Hall and Griffith on the faster tracks and going out to win whenever the ball turned had to be thought through again. The English batsmen had their backs to the wall whatever happened. Gibbs took 4 wickets for 49 on the curious pitch at Birmingham, where England won by 217 runs after scoring less than that in their first innings. He returned another 4 wickets for 76 in their own victory by an almost identical margin at Leeds. Gibbs was a very competitive bowler. Many off-spinners come off only when the wicket is right and batsmen commit errors. Lance welcomed the attention of his opponents. He altered the line of flight, tossed the ball further up or spun it more. Whether playing back or coming forward, the batsman ended by feeding a catch to the expectant fielders or missing the ball completely.

The Australians renewed their acquaintance with Gibbs in 1965. He had his side's highest aggregate of wickets with 18, half of which came in the third Test Match at Georgetown. This was his first international game in his homeland since he had become a world-

Lance Gibbs

class bowler. In the first innings he had top-scorer Bob Cowper caught at the wicket and sent back Brian Booth, who had made a hundred in the previous game. As it had against India, the real destruction came on the last day. Australia proceeded cautiously to 88–1. Then Gibbs struck. Jackie Hendriks stumped Cowper and caught Booth for a duck off him. (The wicket-keeper also held two more catches off other bowlers.) Lance bowled Bill Lawry, and had O'Neill and Philpott caught by the acrobatic Sobers. He ended the match by bowling McKenzie. Gibbs and his captain sent down over 40 overs, while Wesley Hall had only two. The West Indies beat Australia comprehensively and went on to take the rubber which made them world champions without a doubt.

The decline of the fast-bowling partnership put a lot more work on Gibbs in 1966. He bowled almost a hundred more overs than Hall in the series, and headed both the bowling aggregates and the analysis. Yet again he started with a personal triumph in the first Test at Manchester. The game was very similar to the equivalent match in 1963, except that the margin was even larger. When Colin Milburn, the promising new opener, was run out without scoring England virtually gave up the match with an inept display of batting. They were 85–6 at one stage, but improved to 167. Gibbs had 5 wickets for 37. The second innings started on a different key as Milburn made amends for his earlier shortcoming, but although he was a beefy hitter of fast bowling, he was less convincing against spin, and Gibbs bowled him for 94. The rest of the innings was a fight for survival against the odds. Gibbs's further 5 wickets for 69 included the last three batsmen as well as the opener. He was helped again by the effective work of the new wicket-keeper, David Allan.

The off-spinner played his part in the win-from-behind at Nottingham, and he had another deadly spell at Leeds. England were cast as the ideal sacrificial lambs. They followed on 260 runs behind, without a hope of reprieve. Bob Barber hit out boldly for 55, and then Gibbs moved in for the kill. He bowled Milburn, Graveney and Titmus in his 6 wickets for 39. Gibbs had delivered the decisive thrust at the critical moment in each of the four consecutive Test Match rubbers which the West Indies had won. Even the most talented sportsmen are subject to the occasional failure, and he was hit for 115 runs without taking a wicket at the Oval. He was entitled to at least one poor game.

Gibbs took more wickets than Hall and Griffith together on the short tour of India. He shared the limelight of the series with Chandrasekhar. Lance won the first Test Match at Bombay with his 4 wickets for 67 in the second innings. The below-standard pitch for the next match at Calcutta was made to measure for him. The West Indian total of 390 did not accurately reflect the travail which they too had to endure. Kunderan and Jaisimha began confidently with 60 for the Indians' first wicket. Against them Gibbs spun the ball viciously and Sobers moved it sharply either way. When the Guyanese bowled Jaisimha the last 9 wickets folded up for only 107 more runs. Gibbs took 5 wickets for 51, and started the break-up of the second innings by catching Jaisimha off his own bowling. Sobers, however, was the chief wicket-taker on that day. In the third Test at Madras Gibbs had 7 wickets in the game, including 4 for 96 in the second innings.

The West Indies rallied from a hesitant start against England in 1967/68 and seemed to be closing on their rivals when Sobers's surprise declaration in the fourth Test at Port of Spain gave the tourists the chance to win against the run of play. There was a batting breakdown from a supposedly stable position in each match that year. It was nowhere more striking than in the second Test at Kingston. Sobers rescued the West Indies, who followed on 233 runs behind. England still held the advantage when the crowd rioted on Butcher's dismissal, but the interruption unsettled their concentration. Their batting collapsed on a terrible pitch on the last day. The fast bowlers had the first four batsmen in the pavilion for only 19 runs. Gibbs added to the torment by dismissing Graveney, Parks and Titmus. A surprise ending was on the books. England held out, however, and closed at 68–8.

England appeared to have a firm grip on the next match at Bridgetown, where John Edrich and Geoff Boycott put on 172 for the first wicket. They were only 30 runs behind the West Indies' 349 when Gibbs dismissed Graveney and Parks at the same score. After that both sides were too cautious to bring about a definite result. There was no such stalemate in the fifth Test at Georgetown. The West Indies had to win to offset their defeat at Port of Spain. They were ahead throughout the whole match. England had to survive the final day to draw. It was no easy task. Within an hour and a half they were 41–5, and Gibbs was their chief destroyer. Colin Cowdrey and Alan Knott fought back with courage and determination. At 168 the off-spinner had Cowdrey lbw. Two more batsmen were out. Then when

Lance Gibbs

Gibbs had Pat Pocock caught by Lloyd, fast bowler Jeff Jones, the number eleven, was required to play out the final over. He survived in spite of first-class bowling and a tight field. Lance finished with 6 wickets for 60.

The West Indians had high hopes of regaining their winning ways on the 1968/69 tour to Australia. Their hosts were midway through changing their team, and had been outplayed, if not beaten, by England. Man for man the tourists seemed the more talented combination. That assessment was apparently confirmed by the first Test Match at Brisbane. The batsmen coped adequately enough with mystery spinner Johnny Gleeson, and the manner in which Ian Chappell and Bill Lawry sailed into the bowling showed little concern for the pitch. And yet when they were separated Gibbs bowled right through the rest of the innings. Sobers partnered him with left-arm spin in the style of Valentine. The West Indies won by 125 runs, and were ahead for the first time in Australia. That was the cruel deception. The bowling was massacred in the remaining four games. Lawry, Ian Chappell, Ian Redpath and especially Doug Walters carved out a sequence of centuries in running up totals of 510, 547, 533 and 619. It was 1955 all over again. The sharp catching which had spurred the bowlers in earlier series broke down. Maybe the fielders were just getting too old. Gibbs was the only bowler to keep his form, but even he lost his cutting edge. He could not be a shock and stock bowler at the same time. The great West Indian side of the 1960s was dismantled at the end of this tour. Gibbs, who did not do himself justice on his third visit to England in 1969, took a short rest before coming back for a second, record-breaking career.

CHAPTER FOURTEEN
The Sixties

The team led by Frank Worrell and Gary Sobers was remarkably well balanced and stable, so that there was scarcely any need of change except through injury and retirement. Conrad Hunte, Rohan Kanhai, Gary Sobers, Basil Butcher, Joe Solomon, Frank Worrell (later Seymour Nurse), Deryck Murray when he was available, Wesley Hall, Charlie Griffith and Lance Gibbs were an almost permanent line-up. Their ability to complement each other was a key factor in that success. The only areas of variation were in the permutations of first-wicket partners for Hunte and the hereditary fluctuations concerning the choice of wicket-keeper.

Conrad Hunte commenced his Test Match career as a quick-scoring opener with a cluster of really high scores interspersed by some spectacular failures. Later in the light of experience and necessity he tightened his defence and became an anchor-man in the style of Allan Rae. As such he was adept on most pitch surfaces, and scored hundreds in four continents. It was Hunte's misfortune, and his team's, that there was nobody with comparable skill to accompany him. Generally he provided the solid background on which the stylists painted their pictures.

The circumstances in which Hunte was omitted from the 1957 tour to England have still not been fully explained. He was playing League cricket in Lancashire when the party was announced, and would have been an ideal selection. The West Indies didn't even call on him when things started to go wrong, especially concerning the opening partnership. Nevertheless Conrad was an automatic choice for the home series against Pakistan. On his debut he showed how wrong the

The Sixties

selectors had been in overlooking him before. Hunte raced to 142 in the first Test Match at Bridgetown. The touring bowlers were already aware that here was a new star batsman, and they were made even more conscious of his ability in the ensuing games. Runs streamed from the bat in the third Test at Kingston. Hunte's purposeful aggression put Len Hutton's record individual score under pressure. The bowlers seemed powerless to arrest his advance, but he was run out with his personal contribution at 260. His partner at the time, Gary Sobers, went on to break the same record later in the innings: they put on 446 runs for the second wicket. There but for a fielder's intervention cricket history might have been quite different. Hunte's thirst for runs had not been quenched, and he passed three figures for the third time in the season with 114 at Georgetown.

The Barbadian opener missed out on the run harvest in India. He made a duck in each of the first two matches, and struggled to find his form for the rest of the rubber. While the middle-order batsmen were scoring very much as they pleased, Hunte was lucky to keep his place in the side. Eventually Holt and Hunte came good with a stand of 159 in the fifth Test Match at New Delhi. Hemu Adhikari had the latter lbw for 92. He was caught at the wicket in the first over of the subsequent series in Pakistan, and was dropped immediately. For the moment it seemed that Hunte's promising career was over.

He was chosen to play against England in 1959/60, primarily because there was no suitable replacement. Conrad shaped well enough in the first four games without reaching 50. He was injured by a bumper from Trueman in the fifth Test at Port of Spain, but rallied to hit 72 not out, and was picked for the Australian tour. Hunte's career took a turn for the better in the second innings of the second Test at Melbourne. The West Indies followed on 167 runs behind and were heading for ignominy. Hunte's innings of 110 in near-impossible conditions stamped him as a batsman of rare quality. About this time he changed away from his eye-catching brilliance towards a more defensive attitude. Even so, his partnership with Rohan Kanhai at Adelaide was still spectacular. A century seemed well within his grasp when he was run out for 79 after they had added 163 runs. Although his colleague's impetuosity was the direct cause of the dismissal, Hunte had advised him a few balls earlier that they could push some short runs against apparently lax fielding. He walked over to comfort the sorrowful Kanhai. Then he lost his way trying to find the gate, much to the merriment of the crowd. He scored another half-century in the final fixture at Melbourne, which put the West Indies in a challenging position after they had been behind.

Conrad contributed only two 50s to the 'whitewash' of the Indians in 1962. He seemed to relish better the challenge of more worthy opponents. When Frank Worrell's side arrived in England his vital part in the batting line-up was immediately evident. Hunte wore down the bowlers while the other batsmen went for their strokes. His metamorphosis was now complete. He was at his best in the first and fifth Test Matches. The opening batsman took control from the start with 182 at Manchester. That score was not exceeded throughout the rest of the summer. He showed a flash of his former aggression by dispatching to the boundary the first three balls bowled by Trueman in the next game at Lord's. Hunte got over that rush of blood, and soon reverted to his more sober role.

The Barbadian's first-innings 80 was essential in the final victory at the Oval. Without him the early exchanges would have gone very much England's way. Thanks to Hunte and the fast bowlers, the West Indies still had a good chance of winning when they went in a second time. Conrad and his temporary partner, Willie Rodriguez, gave them a much better start than they dared to hope with 78 for the first wicket. The former batted stoically while Kanhai and Butcher belaboured the bowling. He had time to collect his century and take his score to 108 not out before Butcher hit the winning run. As well as his batting, Hunte had been a sound vice-captain on the tour. The decision to appoint Gary Sobers as Worrell's successor must have been a severe disappointment to him.

Since Holt was dropped on the return from India and Pakistan there had been no regular second opener. Easton McMorris had a disastrous and bizarre Test Match debut when as the non-striker he was run out off a no-ball against England at Pakistan in 1959/60. He did not even face a ball. In spite of suffering an injury, he looked more secure with 73 on his home ground in Jamaica. Surprisingly, McMorris was not in the touring party of Australia. Easton looked good with 125 against India at Kingston, and made two half-centuries at Port of Spain. He failed on both of his visits to England, where the ball moved more appreciably, and could not reproduce his prolific inter-territorial form on any of his future Test Match appearances.

Cameron Smith, a noted hitter of sixes, was taken to Australia. He startled spectators, the opposing side and some of his own team by attacking the fast bowlers, including Alan Davidson, from the first delivery of the game. Smith did not believe in playing himself in. His innings were entertaining, and very seldom lasted long. Cammie rattled a hasty 55 at Sydney, but was considered too risky after that. Joey Carew, an enterprising left-hander, went to England in 1963. He also tried to score runs too quickly, and was frequently caught before he had judged the pace of the pitch. Carew failed several times before he lived up to his potential with some powerful scores at the end of the decade.

Hunte shook off any hangover from his frustrated ambitions of leadership with great consistency against Australia in 1965. In heading the batting averages he made the top score of 81 in the important victory at Kingston, 89 and 53 in ensuring a draw at Port of Spain and 75 and 81 in the high-scoring draw at Bridgetown. The Australian seam bowlers had the best of nearly all the arguments in the fifth Test at Port of Spain. Hunte, however, carried his bat for 60 not out as the second innings crashed to Graham McKenzie and Neil Hawke for 131 runs. For once he had some support in left-hander Bryan Davis, who had county championship experience with Glamorgan, and the change was significant. At one point they put together four successive stands of over 50, adding 116 at Port of Spain and 145 at Bridgetown. Davis himself scored three half-centuries.

The first Test Match at Manchester in 1966 had many features in common with that on the same ground three years previously, not the least being Hunte's 135 on the first day. His contribution was more valuable than before because medium-fast bowler Ken Higgs took two early wickets. He steadied the innings before Sobers made all further speculation pointless. The English bowlers must have feared another long, fruitless summer, but that threat did not materialize from Hunte. He did not make 50 in any of his 7 other innings. With his captain scoring so many runs, Conrad's own falling-off was hardly noticed.

Hunte's 101 in the first Test Match at Bombay was the only West Indian hundred in the three matches against India. He put on 110 with Clive Lloyd for the fourth wicket, which went a long way to offsetting Chandrasekhar's initial break-through. Hunte passed 40 in each of his next 3 innings. He was obviously back to his best, and should have been a regular player for several more years. Yet there were other claims on his loyalty. Conrad Hunte did not play in another Test Match. He was attracted to the Moral Re-armament movement while watching the film *The Crowning Experience* in

Australia. As an enthusiastic student in these years I saw the same film a dozen times with less long-lasting effects. Hunte was more constant, and gave the rest of his life to the movement. He missed by only one season the chance of playing with Roy Fredericks. Now that would have been a first-wicket pairing!

Basil Butcher was the quiet, self-effacing, methodical run-scorer in the great team. He was not flamboyant, either as player or as man, but opponents rated him the most difficult batsman to get out. Butcher gave bowlers little hope of taking his wicket, except that he tended to bring the bat across his body and was out lbw more often than most. He came to attention in the upsurge of batting talent in Guyana on Clyde Walcott's arrival in the mid-fifties, and was considered unlucky to miss selection for England in 1957. Basil had to wait for his opportunity until both Weekes and Walcott had retired.

Butcher was an immediate success on the Indian tour in 1958/59. He settled easily into the batting array, and scored at least 50 in each of the five Test Matches. After scores of 60 in Sobers's shadow in the first two games Basil made his first century at Calcutta, where he shared a fourth-wicket stand of 217 with compatriot Rohan Kanhai. Nobody else shared the attention when he struck 142, the only hundred, at Madras. The Guyanese batsman closed the season with 71 at New Delhi. The change of batting surface in Pakistan upset his composure as much as that of any of his colleagues. Butcher did better than most in the disappointing first Test Match at Karachi, where he scored 45 not out and 61. He missed the revenge run-feast at Lahore by being run out early in the innings. Basil was dropped after a bad start to the next series with England, and he did not go to Australia.

The West Indies lost 5 quick wickets in their second innings at Lord's in 1963. Basil Butcher then played one of the most enjoyable knocks I have ever seen. While Worrell defended his wicket with mature authority, the young Guyanese drove and cut with growing confidence. His enterprise was never rash, and he waited for the bad ball. He drove the fast bowlers straight into the shadows of the pavilion as the Saturday evening sun went down. This was cricket as it should be, hard but entertaining. Butcher was lbw to persistent medium-pacer Derek Shackleton early on Monday morning, and the innings folded up with him. He had earned his place alongside the best in the team, and confirmed his promise with 78 at Leeds and 53 at the Oval, where he also hit the winning run.

Butcher disappointed after starting well in the rubber against

The Sixties

Australia in 1965. He was Hunte's principal partner with 71 at Kingston, and was batting in complete command at Port of Spain before Brian Booth's sharp fielding ran out both him and Sobers, with whom he had put on 160 for the fourth wicket. This form of dismissal seems to be an occupational hazard for West Indian batsmen; Basil was out the same way at Georgetown, when he wanted only one more run for his 50. Although he fell away after that, he was behind only Kanhai and the superbly consistent Hunte in the averages.

Different times bring different tactics. The West Indian approach to the series in England in 1966 was patchy. Following a good start at Manchester, they came within an ace of losing at Lord's, and trailed by 90 runs at Nottingham. The situation was made worse when Basil D'Oliveira sent back both opening batsmen before the leeway had been made up. Butcher came in at 65–2 with defeat likely, and took out his bat for 209 not out at 482–5 dec when victory was almost certain. It was a hard and painful innings, far out of character with his neat driving in 1963. He ground onwards relentlessly, aided by dropped catches. Basil gave the innings stability while Kanhai, Nurse and Sobers helped him put on 110, 107 and 173 respectively. He made up in efficiency what he lacked in glamour, and later scored 60 in the modest second innings at the Oval.

Butcher was less successful in India and against England in 1967/68. He made the top score of 52 in the fight-back from the brink of defeat in the first Test Match at Port of Spain, and hit half-centuries in each innings at Bridgetown. Otherwise his chief claim to fame was his bowling in the fourth Test at Port of Spain. England were well set with Colin Cowdrey in full flow when Sobers, in desperation, called on Butcher as an occasional leg-spinner. Straight away he had Cowdrey caught at the wicket for 148, sped through the rest of the batting and finished with 5 wickets for 34. Superficially it was comparable to Ramadhin at his best. In fact, and paradoxically, Butcher's success went a long way towards the West Indies losing the match. Even with his front-line bowlers injured, Sobers was sufficiently impressed to make a suicidal second declaration. Basil couldn't work the trick twice.

Old as they were, the batsmen did not let the side down in Australia. Butcher made two hundreds in the series. The first was a lone 101 as the innings collapsed around him in the third Test Match at Sydney. His century in the next game at Adelaide was even more effective. With all their batsmen scoring runs, Australia were 257 runs ahead on the first innings, then the West Indies retaliated as surely as they had at Nottingham. Butcher led the way with 118 in a total of 616. Their hosts were snared with the necessity to score against the clock. They panicked in the last hour, lost several men through run-outs and came within one wicket of defeat.

Butcher scored three consecutive half-centuries in New Zealand, and was senior batsman to Gary Sobers on the tour to England in 1969. He saved his best batting for the last innings of the three-match series at Leeds. With the West Indies chasing 303 to win, Butcher rolled back the years with some of his best stroke-play. At 219–3 the target seemed just around the corner. Butcher was caught at 91 by Alan Knott off Underwood. He deserved a hundred in this his last international innings. The decision was hotly disputed, but the batsman himself didn't argue. Barry Knight bowled Sobers immediately afterwards for no score, and the dreams of victory crashed into defeat by 30 runs. Over the weekend before that innings I met Basil Butcher and Lance Gibbs at a social reception for Guyanese nationals at the Café Royal in London. That was two hundred miles away from the cricket ground. On hearing that he had got out so close to his century I wondered if the social obligations on contemporary cricketers affected their playing ability.

Joe Solomon is sometimes forgotten when one remembers great West Indian sportsmen. He came in at number six, where he could help out either the batting or the bowling. His support enabled the specialist batsmen to score at their own pace, and his few overs with the ball rested the main-line bowlers without weakening the quality of the attack. Solomon's pinpoint fielding in a crisis has become proverbial, as have some of his more curious methods of getting out. He could do a little of everything well.

Solomon was the third string of the Guyanese triangle which formed the backbone of West Indian batting on the double tour of India and Pakistan in 1958/59. He scored 86 on his debut at Kanpur, where he shared a substantial partnership with Sobers, and followed with 69 not out in a run-a-minute century partnership with the same player at Calcutta. Joe finished the series with a lively 100 not out at New Delhi. By virtue of his several undefeated innings, he headed the batting averages. He made 66 in an attempt to save something from the defeat at Karachi, and hit 56 in easier circumstances at Lahore, but his development was hindered by the unsuccessful attempt to turn him into an opening batsman against England in 1959/60.

The Sixties

The name of Joe Solomon will always be associated with the tied Test Match at Brisbane. In the first innings he trod on his wicket for 65 when he stepped back to play the off-spinner. (Curiously enough, he was dismissed in a like manner at Melbourne, where his cap fell on the wicket.) His fielding in the final climax was decisive. Alan Davidson and Richie Benaud were heading for victory with a stand of 134. They risked a tight single, as Solomon had only one stump at which to aim. He threw, that stump went over and Davidson was on his way back to the pavilion. And so it was on the last ball of the game. With the scores level, Lindsay Kline hit out and ran for the winning run like lightning. Solomon did not have enough time to field cleanly and to throw with studied aim. If he had missed or even hesitated Australia would have been home. Joe swooped, fielded and threw all in one action. Ian Meckiff dived for the crease, but the ball got there first. He had hit the stumps from almost impossible angles twice in two overs, and a Test Match had been tied for the first and only time.

Although the rest of his career was played in the shadow of that achievement, Solomon continued to be a steady middle-order batsman and change spin bowler who was always in the team as long as he cared to play. He made his highest Test Match score with 96 against India, and hit a steady 56 at Lord's and 62 at Leeds in 1963. They did not make the headlines, but the team would have been badly placed without them. Joe scored a useful 76 against Australia at Kingston in 1965, which pushed the target too far beyond them. His retirement at the end of the season took away some of the team's batting stability.

For several years Seymour Nurse was considered too unorthodox for his own good. He had a pressing desire to chase runs that seemed almost primeval, but his unharnessed enthusiasm derived from his general participation in sports—he was also a very good footballer. Nurse was kept out of the side by more conventional batsmen like Butcher and Solomon, and the cultured stroke-players Kanhai and Sobers. When he was given a permanent position on Worrell's retirement Seymour showed himself to be second to none. His brisk batting was the outstanding feature of the tours to England, Australia and New Zealand, but while he was still improving his performance yet further he retired.

Nurse made his debut as long ago as the third Test Match at Kingston in 1959/60. He came in when McMorris was temporarily out of action after being struck on the chest, and he batted confidently with Sobers. The innings closed swiftly after Nurse was out for 70. He was dropped for the rest of the series to allow Walcott to come back into the side. Something similar happened in Australia. Nurse, who made another 70, and Kanhai put on 123 runs out of 181 in the second Test Match at Melbourne, but he played only once more. Clearly his time had not yet come. He was not helped by an injury which kept him lame for the greater part of the 1963 tour.

Nurse failed as an opening batsman at Kingston two years later. Then he was switched back to the middle order for the rest of the season. The West Indies faced an uphill task at Bridgetown from the moment both opening batsmen, Lawry and Simpson, scored over 200 each in compiling 650-6 dec. Bryan Davis and Butcher were soon out, and Hunte was injured by glancing the ball into his own face. Nurse got out of trouble the only way he knew how, by hitting. He and Kanhai scored exactly 200 runs for the third wicket. The Barbadian was caught eventually for 201. Although he was lbw without scoring in the second innings, he had made his future selection sure, and given the West Indies the prospect of a surprise victory which they almost brought off.

Nurse was the soul of the side in 1966. He began with a modest 49 at Manchester, and made at least one 50 in each of the next four games. He was second in the averages to Gary Sobers in his phenomenal year, and he scored runs at Lord's and the Oval where others laboured, besides relieving the tedium of Butcher's long double century at Nottingham with a dashing 53. He had already scored 93 in the first innings when John Snow and Ken Higgs broke through the early batting and could have taken his century if he had been prepared to moderate his aggression. That opportunity came again in the fourth Test Match at Leeds. For a change there were already 100 runs on the board when he came in to bat. Nurse and Sobers applied themselves to knocking all the fight out of the bowlers with some of the most scintillating strokes ever seen in England. They hit a whirlwind 265 for the fifth wicket which left the opposition sagging, limp in spirit and set up for the inevitable innings defeat. Seymour showed his customary variability by getting out for a duck at the Oval, but in the second innings he resisted almost alone as the West Indies went down to defeat.

With Hunte's premature retirement Nurse was tried again as an opener against England in 1967/68. He was not really cut out for the position. The Barbadian helped his captain, Sobers, save the second Test Match at Kingston. Batting at first-wicket down, he and Kanhai put on 273 runs for the third wicket in establishing what seemed to be a winning position in the fourth Test at Port of Spain. He opened the batting again at Georgetown, and failed once more. It is interesting, though useless, to speculate how many more runs he might have scored if he had not been asked repeatedly to face the new-ball bowlers so early.

Nurse didn't find his best form in Australia immediately. The batsmen were generally troubled by John Gleeson's unorthodox spin and McKenzie's ability to move the ball in the opening overs. He hit a typical stroke-lined 74 at Melbourne, and a more dynamic 137 at Sydney in the closing moments of the tour. Following Doug Walters's achievement of the first double century and century in the same Test Match, Nurse and Sobers showed some of the sparkle which had been missing from too much of the play that season. If the batting had to be rebuilt from these disappointments, as it had after the other débâcle in 1951/52, they were the two batsmen to do it.

Seymour Nurse closed the double tour with a crescendo of scoring in New Zealand. He made 95 in the first innings at Auckland, and with Joey Carew took the total to 195-1. The subsequent collapse was so great that New Zealand led by 47 runs on the strength of Bruce Taylor's dynamic century. Then Nurse brought the West Indies from behind to win by 5 wickets with a brilliantly sustained exhibition of stroke-play in which he scored 168. He went even better at Christchurch in scoring 258 and sharing a stand of 231 with Carew. The score was 247-1 at one point, but fell away again so sharply that the tourists could only draw the match. Nurse was on the threshold of a really great career when he retired suddenly from international cricket. In him the West Indies lost a run-maker who could have taken them unscathed into the 1970s.

When Gerry Alexander retired after the 1960/61 Australian tour the position of wicket-keeper was in the melting-pot once more. Jackie Hendriks, the tall, lean Jamaican, was the leading contender, but throughout his long cricketing life he was prone to injury. Both he and Guyana's Ivor Mendonca scored 50s against India in 1962. David Allan of Barbados took over from them for the 1963 tour. In turn Allan missed the Test Match series because his understudy, Deryck Murray of Trinidad, kept so well in the opening game at Manchester when he himself was ill. Murray retained the position for the season, and took a record number of victims for a West Indian wicket-keeper in an international series. When he stayed in England to study, Hendriks and Allan alternated in the role. Murray came back for the 1967/68 rubber, but did not strike his usual form. Hendriks went to Australia and New Zealand, where he scored 54 not out at Wellington. Apart from Murray's performance in 1963, there was little between the rivals. Probably Hendriks would have been chosen more often if he had suffered less injuries.

Eric Atkinson replaced brother Denis against Pakistan in 1957/58. With an accurate medium-fast pace as a foil to Gilchrist's speed, he took 5 wickets for 42 at Kingston. Atkinson was not needed in India, where Hall, Gilchrist and Taylor handled all the quick bowling. He responded better to the matting pitches in Pakistan by taking 4 wickets for 42 at Dacca. Willie Rodriguez of Trinidad was another utility player who could bowl leg-breaks and keep up an end batting. He made 50 against India at Port of Spain without giving any indication of winning permanent inclusion in the side. Tony White of Barbados was in a similar situation. He went in to bat in the first Test Match at Kingston in 1965, when Australian seam bowler Laurie Mayne was causing problems. He laid about him to robust purpose, and made the top score of 57 not out in securing a vital lead of 22 runs, but he managed nothing of comparable quality after that.

Leg-spinner David Holford was the surprise selection of the 1966 side to England. He was known best as Gary Sobers's cousin, and had little experience when he went into the first Test Match at Manchester. The two kinsmen put on over a hundred runs for the sixth wicket, but as Sobers was so much the dominant partner nobody paid attention to the younger man. Then came the second Test Match at Lord's. With a deficit of 86 runs, the West Indies lost another 5 wickets for 95. Defeat was within touching distance. Sobers, who was again batting at the other end, took the important decision not to shield the youngster from the bowling: they had to sink or swim together. The pressure on Holford let his captain pick up runs. David became increasingly confident in knowing that he had received no favours and was soon matching strokes with the great man. He helped spread the field with some well-placed hits. When his cousin was 105 not out Sobers declared the innings closed, with their undefeated stand at 274.

The surprising success of Holford's development was matched by his subsequent failure to live up to his promise. He was quite ill in

The Sixties

India, where he hit 80 at Bombay, and could not take up a regular place in the side. He continued on the edge of Test Match cricket for another ten years, did not disgrace himself in Australia and bowled so well against New Zealand in 1972 that he was considered as a possible captain in England the following year. Just when it seemed that he had finally faded from the scene, he took a match-winning 5 wickets against India at Bridgetown in 1976.

CHAPTER FIFTEEN
Years of Transition

The successful side of the sixties disintegrated much more quickly than anyone could have anticipated, and not one of the next seven series was won. There was no apparent reason for the decline in performance; the basic ability and framework of the team was maintained. Gary Sobers and Rohan Kanhai were there nearly all the time. Basil Butcher and Seymour Nurse stayed for a while, and were succeeded by Clive Lloyd, Lawrence Rowe, Alvin Kallicharran and Roy Fredericks, all world-class batsmen. The overall competence of the batting was in itself a large part of the problem. It was the bowling which bent, buckled and collapsed while the batting fought on without inspiration.

Four of the rubbers were at home, including the three most frustrating between 1971 and 1973, where the side was subject to territorial tensions and political pressures. The attitude taken by some authorities, particularly Guyana and Jamaica, against those who had played in southern Africa or against teams from that part of the world threatened to rend Caribbean cricket asunder several years before Kerry Packer arrived on the scene. Politicians took a hand in team-selection, and a difference of generations opened up within the ranks of the players.

Sobers bore the brunt of the criticism. Any losing captain must expect to be blamed for his team's defeats, but there was more to it than that. He had ceased to be a purely West Indian cricketer and had become an international celebrity to a greater extent than any of his predecessors. Gary played more cricket in Nottinghamshire and South Australia and for miscellaneous itinerant parties than he did for Barbados. With this wider view he could not have the same rapport with the changes of fortune of his compatriots. The critics made great play with his addiction for golf and his love of gambling, but that was unfair, since he never gave less than his best as batsman, bowler or fieldsman. Maybe he should have withdrawn from the captaincy much earlier.

It was his leadership which was chiefly under fire. He became increasingly negative, and did not respond with sufficient urgency to tactical opportunities on the field. There was a general lack of determination and concentration, especially in the disappointing home series against India and New Zealand. No doubt the Barbadian would point to the hostile public reaction to his bold declaration at Port of Spain in 1967/68 which backfired in defeat by 7 wickets. Once bitten, he was several times shy.

A change did come over Sobers after that rubber, though he dominated it with the bat in his accustomed manner. The left-hander saved the first Test Match at Port of Spain with a defiant 33 not out after his side had followed on 205 runs behind, and he made an even greater contribution to the next encounter at Kingston. Fast bowler John Snow zipped through the West Indian first innings with 7 wickets for 49 on a pitch which was cracked from the first day. Following on for the second successive match, the home team were 204–5, still 29 runs behind, when the crowd rioted on Butcher's dismissal. After order was restored Sobers upturned the balance with an undefeated 113 in masterly technical control. He received such good support from the tail that he could afford to declare, and then he had England in danger of imminent defeat by himself sending back Boycott and Cowdrey without a run on the board.

Sobers made 68 in the stalemate at Bridgetown followed by his calamitous declaration in the fourth Test Match at Port of Spain. He gambled extravagantly on his under-strength bowling, and paid the penalty. Popular opinion swung so violently against the former hero that he ran the risk of physical abuse in the final fixture at Georgetown. However, he replied to this outcry with a superb all-round performance, outstanding even by his own standards. He scored 152 in the first innings, in which Rohan Kanhai helped him put on 250 for the fourth wicket, and was stranded on 95 not out in the second. He also took 3 wickets in each innings. It was not enough either to win the match—which England saved with their last two batsmen together—or to regain the adoration of his countrymen.

The story was repeated in Australia. With Wesley Hall and Charlie Griffith well over the hill, Sobers and Lance Gibbs carried the bowling against a battery of batting talent. The captain also finished the rubber strongly as a batsman. The first Test Match at Brisbane had seemed to point towards a revival of West Indian fortunes, but both sides experienced setbacks after some good performances by their early batsmen. Finally Sobers applied the *coup de grâce* by taking 6 wickets for 73 as Australia went under by 125 runs. Contrary to the initial indications, this was the beginning of the end for the tourists. They could not recapture that form in the rest of the season, and Gary was blamed for an absence of purpose or direction in his leadership.

Sobers had the best bowling return in the second Test Match at Melbourne, but the game had been lost on the first morning when pace bowler Graham McKenzie took 8 wickets. Bill Lawry, the tall, thin left-handed opener, made a double century, and young Ian Chappell scored 165 as the visiting attack was pasted to an innings defeat. The West Indies then went down by a further 10 wickets at Sydney. They fought back well at Adelaide, where a first-innings breakdown had thrown them on to the defensive. Only Sobers, who hit 110, batted with anything like his true fluency. He hit another century in the closing stages of the forlorn fifth Test at Sydney. There Doug Walters made a double century and a century, and both Lawry and Ian Redpath passed 100.

The strain of so much responsibility was beginning to show. Sobers did little worth mentioning in the three-match rubber against England in 1969. After a one-sided defeat at Manchester—where the luck of the toss was decisive—a sub-standard West Indian side which was short of good bowling and an attacking batsman did well to bring England to the brink of defeat at Lord's and come within 30 runs of winning from behind at Leeds. Sobers himself was stale, and his attention seemed to wander at important times. He was lame when bowling at Lord's, but scored 50 not out in the second innings. England were 61–5 at one point, before they recovered to share the honours through the batting of John Hampshire and Ray Illingworth. The touring captain did much to restore the balance at Leeds, where he took 5 wickets for 42 after England were 62 runs ahead. The West Indies began their final innings so well that they seemed set to win. Then Butcher was out controversially, and Barry Knight bowled Sobers immediately for a duck. It was the difference between victory and a narrow defeat.

Years of Transition

Towards the end of the decade the English championship opened its gates to professionals from overseas, and within a few years almost every county had its star West Indian. The practice has been as old as the century, since C. A. Ollivierre joined Derbyshire after the very first tour, but it increased greatly in extent. Test Match replacement players, or those who were just below international standard, sought a more secure career with the counties. Australian spinners George Tribe, Bruce Dooland and Colin McCool came after the Second World War, and were soon followed by West Indians Roy Marshall, Peter Wight, Laurie Johnson, Danny Livingstone, Carlton Forbes, Harry Latchman and Rudi Webster. The relaxation of the rule of residential qualification caused a considerable influx of front-line cricketers who could still represent their country and their Caribbean territory. The practice became so widespread that Michael Holding was the only member of the 1976 Test Match side who has not had experience with an English county at some time or other.

The new opportunities had many advantages over League competition, where earlier generations had matured. Three-day matches were a better training-ground for Test Match cricket, on the same grounds on which the international games were played. There each cricketer played alongside and against the men they would oppose for their countries. The leading West Indians were introduced as well to Sheffield Shield matches in Australia, and appeared for the Cavaliers or other composite teams which carried the willow to every part of the known cricketing world. Far from having too little action at the highest level, as in the time of Martindale and Challenor, the current generation faced the prospect of staleness and diminished motivation from having too much. And nobody had as much as the world's leading cricketer, Gary Sobers.

The Indian tour of the Caribbean in 1971 showed some similarities to the previous visit by England. The West Indians had the edge over their opponents in many important respects, but lost the rubber by the one game decided. Sobers failed to score at least 90 only in the second Test Match at Port of Spain, where Erapalli Prasanna and Srinivas Venkataraghavan spun the tourists to victory. Gary had already scored 93 in a match-saving stand with Kanhai at Kingston, and finished the season with hundreds in three consecutive games. He hit 108 not out in the evenly contested match at Georgetown, a huge 178 not out at Bridgetown and 132 in the return fixture at Port of Spain. It was no good. Sunil Gavaskar, who accumulated 774 runs in his first international series, and Dilip Sardesai prevented the West Indians from coming back on level terms.

New Zealand's visit the next year was even worse. All five matches were drawn in one long bore. Sobers's leadership lacked imagination, which showed most clearly in the two games at Port of Spain when the West Indies had an early advantage. In the fifth Test Match he failed to enforce the follow-on, which might have added some interest to the proceedings. The despondency was reflected in dropped catches and a lowering of morale. The captain himself played just one important innings. He saved the game at Bridgetown with 142 in a double-century stand with Charlie Davis after his side had trailed by almost 300 runs.

The rubber against Ian Chappell's Australians in 1973 began with a dispute about Sobers's position generally, and the captaincy in particular. He missed the opening fixture at his own request, and when he asked to come back into the team the authorities told him to prove his fitness first. That was too much for the greatest West Indian all-rounder of this or any other age. Gary missed all five Test Matches, where his presence could have altered the result, and returned to Nottinghamshire in the English county championship. Although his deeds there are really beyond the scope of this book, I cannot mention Sobers and Nottinghamshire without reference to his hitting Malcolm Nash of Glamorgan for six off every ball of a regular over at Swansea in 1968. Every delivery was despatched with a different yet precisely executed stroke.

Rohan Kanhai, the senior professional (if such a term still existed), was the ideal successor as captain. He had achieved universal respect for his conduct and admiration for his attacking batting. Rohan delighted thousands upon thousands of spectators in England, India, Australia and the Caribbean with the power of his stroke-play, yet he developed into one of the most defensive of modern West Indian leaders. Kanhai was the first Guyanese to hold the office permanently, apart from the successful one-match tenure of Fernandes in 1929/30, and he brought the team back from the lower reaches of despair to renewed triumphs.

In the late 1960s Kanhai was the only batsman to match Sobers in brilliance and consistency. He enjoyed a good series against England in 1967/68, which he commenced with 85 in the first Test Match at Port of Spain, reaching a peak in the final two games. He scored 153 in a massive third-wicket stand of 273 with Nurse in the fourth Test,

Years of Transition

as the West Indies raced to an apparently safe total of 526-7 declared. At Georgetown he made 150 in another substantial stand with Sobers. There had been some doubt concerning his ability against outright pace, but he was nearly irresistible wherever the ball came off the pitch with time to hit.

But Kanhai was a disappointment in Australia. He started well enough, but was often out before he could convert a sound score into a good one. His best effort was 94 in the first innings of the series at Brisbane. With Joey Carew he took the total to 217-1, before he was caught by Gleeson off McKenzie, starting a batting breakdown. Kanhai had only two more half-centuries, and was clearly out of touch. He asked to be left out of the 1969 side in England, where his batting and experience would have been useful in the close second and third Test Matches. At the time it seemed that his international career was over.

He was back in the side for the 1971 rubber against India ... and how! When the West Indies were made surprisingly to follow on in the first Test Match at Kingston, Kanhai, who had top-scored in the first innings, slammed 158 not out to put the game beyond the tourists' reach. The pendulum of fortune swung erratically in this match. India improved from 75-5 to 387 all out, with Sardesai making 212, and the West Indies slipped from 202-4 to 217. Rohan made only one other 50 that year, and missed the series against New Zealand.

Kanhai's career seemed to be so much on the ebb-tide that his eventual elevation to the captaincy in 1973, though welcome, was hardly considered in advance. Old territorial rivalries had reopened, and the team had shown temperamental fragility. They met an enthusiastic young Australian side whose morale was rising quickly following their good showing in England. Although the Aussies won by two clear victories, the West Indies improved on recent results and lost twice on batting breakdowns when the outcome seemed to be going their way. The new captain had his best batting season in six years, scoring 84 in the first Test Match at Kingston, where the teams finished level on first innings and 105 in putting his side ahead at Bridgetown. Age had not dimmed his agility as he caught top-line batsmen Keith Stackpole, Doug Walters and Ian Redpath.

Rohan made further half-centuries in the lost games at Port of Spain and Georgetown, so that he was confirmed in the captaincy for the following tour of England. It was something of a homecoming: Kanhai had settled to English championship cricket as well as anyone.

Caribbean Cricketers

He developed a second career with Warwickshire as a versatile batsman who could meet the requirements of both the three-day and the limited-over codes. While he was with the county he put on a world record 465 runs in an undefeated second-wicket stand with John Jameson against Gloucestershire at Birmingham in 1974.

After some debate on his status as an allegedly self-imposed exile, Gary Sobers joined the team in England. There the old firm of Kanhai and Sobers, who had first come together on the disastrous tour sixteen years previously, shared their last and greatest triumph. From the start of their itinerary the party showed a more positive attitude than any West Indian team for a long time. Cricket was once more a sport to be enjoyed, at least as far as the Oval and Lord's were concerned. The second Test Match at Birmingham, in contrast, was marred by bad temper following a disagreement between umpire Arthur Fagg and some of the tourists over the former's refusal to uphold an appeal. As captain Kanhai was seen as a chief participant in the dissension. Whether this was right or wrong he exhibited less tact and diplomacy than had some of his predecessors. The match became a stalemate, ruined by slow scoring and an even slower bowling rate.

The run avalanche in the third Test Match at Lord's erased the memory of all that had gone before. The West Indies scored 652-8 declared, and won by an innings and 226 runs. Kanhai and Sobers vied with each other by making 157 and 150 respectively in a systematic massacre of the bowling. The parallel with Bradman and Ponsford in their last partnership in England was now complete. Sobers, who retired temporarily through illness, had the satisfaction of closing his international career on a sequence of two 50s and a century. Kanhai led the West Indies out of the wilderness and back to the paths of victory; his short reign was the springboard for the triumphs in the years ahead.

The record books show that both of them played against England in the Caribbean later that year without distinction, and at the end of that series Kanhai was removed from the captaincy with little ceremony and even less excuse. In public recollection and sympathy, however, they went out in a blaze of glory at Lord's. There was one happy epilogue. Rohan Kanhai made one further appearance by playing in the first Prudential Cup Final against Australia in June 1975. He made a half-century in an innings of great restraint which held the West Indian batting together while Clive Lloyd unleashed his

Years of Transition

famous hundred. It was a fitting end to one era and the start of another.

If these two batsmen dominated these years of transition—as indeed they did— they were not the only ones who prospered. The selectors solved the opening batsman question by including two left-handers, newcomer Roy Fredericks and Joey Carew who had not done too well in the past, in the team which toured Australasia in 1968/69. The Trinidadian was inclined to rush into his shots too soon in his innings. Even so, he was the surprise success of the season where so many others failed. Carew and Kanhai got the tourists away to an exciting start at Brisbane with 165 runs for the second wicket. They thrived on an Australian attack which for once did not have a really fast bowler. The two batsmen were out to successive balls, Carew being run out for 83. His attacking qualities were seen best in the fourth Test Match at Adelaide, where the West Indies trailed by 257 runs. The left-hander threw his bat about to great effect until he was caught by Ian Chappell off Alan Connolly for 90. It was the inspiration and prelude to the team's best batting of the summer.

The first and third Tests in New Zealand revolved almost entirely around the batting of Carew and Seymour Nurse. The former scored his only international century with 109 at Auckland, including some typical robust hitting. He was more circumspect in scoring 91 and sharing another double-century stand with the Barbadian at Christchurch. Although the other batsmen did little, the tourists ran up a lead of exactly 200, and New Zealand were rescued only by Brian Hastings's unbeaten century. After the many years of trial and tribulation Carew seemed to have played himself into form at last, but as with so many other strange occurrences during this year, his fall from grace came hard on the heels of his greatest triumph.

Carew played in the first Test Match at Manchester in 1969. He failed in the first innings, but helped Fredericks put on 92 in the second. After that he was replaced by bespectacled Steve Camacho from Guyana, who bore some passing physical resemblance to Bruce Pairaudeau. He settled into the side at once with half-centuries at both Lord's and Leeds, in a series where runs were not so abundant as they had been previously. On the first occasion the first-wicket pair raised 106 and 73, the best for the West Indies in England since the heyday of Allan Rae and Jeff Stollmeyer. Camacho was Butcher's main support in the fight-back which almost brought about an unlikely win at Leeds.

Camacho had appeared already in the previous home series against England. He seemed to stake his claim as Conrad Hunte's successor with a competent 57 at Bridgetown and an even better 87 at Port of Spain. In Trinidad he and Carew scored 119 for the opening wicket. With Fredericks taking over Joey's role as left-hander the problem ought to have been solved. Camacho did not make the progress expected, however. Although several others were called, nobody could fill the position adequately. Perhaps the biggest disappointment was Geoff Greenidge, who made 50 against New Zealand at Georgetown. He failed, but the surname would be heard again soon enough.

Charlie Davis, the brother of Hunte's partner in 1965, was the only West Indian to score a century in 1969. He was a fluent stroke-maker in inter-territorial matches. At Lord's he was involved in the mix-up from which Sobers was run out, and consequently concentrated on defence in a marathon 103 which gave a good idea of his value to the side but a wrong impression of his ability to entertain. His patience was rewarded when England slumped to 61–5. Unfortunately, they rallied so well that only 36 runs and three wickets separated the teams at the close.

The Trinidadian was the leading run-scorer in the disappointing rubber against India. In spite of his left-handed stance, which was considered particularly open to the slant of the Indian spin bowling, Davis alone faced Prasanna and Venkataraghavan with any confidence in scoring 71 not out and 74 not out in the defeat at Port of Spain. He made 125 not out at Georgetown, when the West Indies were in danger of slipping again, and 105 in the fifth Test Match, also at Port of Spain.

Davis took some of the few highlights against the New Zealanders. He scored 90 in the second Test Match at Port of Spain, where so many of his colleagues were out to injudicious strokes, and compiled a marathon innings of 183 at Bridgetown in the style of his careful hundred at Lord's. The West Indies failed against Bruce Taylor's lively medium-pace on the first morning and began the second innings 289 runs behind. For a moment it was touch and go as some early wickets were lost. Davis's sober battle of attrition avoided any further prospect of a breakdown. In view of his fine batting over the past three years, Davis was a surprising omission from the next series against Australia and the next tour to England.

Desmond Lewis, the Jamaican wicket-keeper, was one of the more

Years of Transition

consistent batsmen against India in 1971. He played so well that he was moved from the middle order to open the batting. Lewis made the top score of 81 not out at Georgetown, hit 88 and held four catches at Bridgetown, and scored 72 at Port of Spain. In spite of his success, Desmond was replaced by Mike Findlay, his predecessor, for the games against New Zealand. Jamaica has had a good tradition of wicket-keeping from the time of Ivan Barrow and Karl Nunes, through Gerry Alexander and Alfie Binns, to Jackie Hendriks and Lewis.

Findlay, the first prominent West Indian cricketer from Saint Vincent since Charles Ollivierre, first took over from Hendriks for the 1969 tour, on which representatives from the smaller islands were included for the first time since the turn of the century. He was a competent batsman and wicket-keeper. However, having regained his position from Lewis, Findlay himself was replaced by Deryck Murray in 1973. The latter showed greater maturity than before, and secured his selection by hitting 90 against Australia at Bridgetown. Murray became the first wicket-keeper to be sure of automatic inclusion since Clyde Walcott in his early days and, as vice-captain, was a key member of Clive Lloyd's world-beating team. Findlay's greatest defect was to be around at the same time.

While there was little weakening of the batting, the bowling could not regain any of its former glory. This drawback was especially true in the failure to find adequate successors to Hall and Griffith. Richard Edwards took 5 wickets for 84 against New Zealand at Wellington, but he was not chosen to visit England. His replacement, John Shepherd, returned 5 wickets for 104 at Manchester in 1969. He was over-bowled, and later found the Caribbean pitches less suited to his style. Shepherd is still a hard-hitting batsman and a deadly swing and seam bowler in English conditions. His story belongs to the achievements of Kent in the county championship.

Vanburn Holder was introduced to the attack in 1969 as well. At that time he tried to bowl faster than really suited him, but he could bowl effectively for long stints. Holder limited his opponents' scoring capabilities without really threatening to break through. Usually he had one effective spell in each series. Fiery Uton Dowe whipped out four Indian batsmen at Bridgetown in 1971. The tourists stood at 70–6, but Dowe wasted the new ball as Dilip Sardesai hit 150 in putting India right back in the fight. Keith Stackpole, the beefy Australian opening batsman, set out to knock the erratic Jamaican out of the firing-line, and, with the bowler pitching short and wide, he succeeded conclusively.

Previously retired off-spinner Jack Noreiga had an amazing game in the second Test Match at Port of Spain in 1971. In spite of the Indians' deserved reputation for playing spin well, Noreiga took 9 wickets for 95, the best innings analysis ever returned by a West Indian bowler. All of his victims were caught, including two caught and bowled. Even that record-breaking feat was not enough to prevent India from winning by 7 wickets. After diminutive Gavaskar had scored 220 in the second innings of the fifth Test in the same city Noreiga put a check on the batting with 5 wickets for 129 in bringing their score from 374–4 to 427 all out. He did not play again. Another Trinidadian, left-arm spinner Inshan Ali, took 5 wickets for 59 against New Zealand on his home ground the next year. Because of his effort the West Indies led by over 200 runs on the first innings. Inshan Ali was in and out of the team over several years, but did not do as well as promised.

CHAPTER SIXTEEN
Batsmen of the Seventies

Clive Lloyd has been the captain who had most in common with the majority of West Indian cricket followers. The earlier leaders were drawn from an exclusive section of society, and even the detached Frank Worrell seemed remote from the hurly-burly of everyday emotion. Lloyd, however, has apparently stepped straight from the crowds on the terraces on to the field of play and shares the public's hopes, their fears and their sentiments. He has opened up the game when they would, closed it down when they would and has made mistakes when they would. For that reason alone the gangling Guyanese left-hander has been rightly called the people's captain.

There is never any two minds about his batting. Clive hits every ball as hard as possible, excelling in all strokes with a preference for the drive through mid-off and sweep to leg. He is capable also of pulling a ball from outside the off-stump to high over square-leg for six. In the field he moves with the stealth of a panther and the speed of a cheetah to cut off runs in the deep and hold blinding catches close-in. His early work in the covers ranked with that of Colin Bland, the phenomenal South African. Clive's shrugging shoulders, hearty laugh and occasional look of crestfallen sorrow are instantly recognizable, so that people everywhere have taken him to their heart.

Lloyd was the one important new member of the party which Gary Sobers took to India at the end of 1966. He must have been very good even then to get into that efficient batting line-up, and he showed his potential in the first Test Match at Bombay. The tourists were puzzled by 'mystery' spinner Chandrasekhar, who dismissed seven batsmen. Three wickets were down before the newcomer, and Conrad Hunte rescued the situation with 110 for the fourth wicket. Clive survived some initial unease to score 82. Chandrasekhar took another 4 quick wickets on the last day, but Lloyd, who made 78 not out, and Sobers put on over 100 in knocking off the runs required, to win by 6 wickets.

His exciting 118 in the first Test Match at Port of Spain in 1967/68 impressed the English visitors, even though the West Indies failed to save the follow-on. Lloyd showed different qualities in registering a top score of 34 not out against John Snow in the first innings at Kingston, and hit freely to make 113 not out in drawing the game at Bridgetown. Here obviously was a young man of rare ability who hit the ball tremendously hard off either foot. His speed and enthusiasm in the field cut off many more runs.

Clive began the Australian series with a thunderous 129 at Brisbane on a dangerous pitch where Johnny Gleeson turned the ball awkwardly. His knock was decisive in a match which otherwise was determined by slow bowling. He performed badly in the rest of the series, and exceeded 50 again only in the fifth Test Match at Sydney, where the West Indies faced the massive Australian total of 619. Lloyd's attacking play was capable, but he was suspect in defence. His presence in England in 1969 was even more important once Rohan Kanhai and Seymour Nurse stated that they did not want to be considered for the tour.

Lloyd did not do himself justice in that strange summer which began in torrential rain and blossomed into a heatwave by the time the Test Matches came around. When the West Indian bowling and fielding let England off the hook at Lord's the Guyanese southpaw regained the initiative by blasting a quick 70. The match ended with England only 36 runs behind with 3 wickets in hand. Clive had the opportunity of three consecutive home series to disprove the rumour that he could not bat as well in the Caribbean as overseas. He did not help his case by being run out with embarrassing frequency. (Admittedly, it was rarely his own fault.) The Indian spinners caused the West Indian left-handers a great deal of trouble. In spite of being run out twice, Lloyd helped Kanhai save the first Test Match at Kingston. His best innings was 60 in the even third Test Match at Georgetown. He was out in a rare manner. He and Sobers went through for their run without looking at each other, crashed in mid-pitch, and got up dazed, to find the younger man beaten to the stumps

Batsmen of the Seventies

by the ball yet again. At this time he could do little right, and missed out entirely against New Zealand.

Because of this poor run of form Lloyd's inclusion in the side to meet Ian Chappell's Australians was disputed, and fraught with political overtones. There was only one way and one place to prove his point ... in the middle. He did so in a most convincing fashion. Lloyd hammered the bowling at Georgetown for a mighty 178, which seemed to be a formidable foundation for a match-winning total. Alas, he and Kanhai scored all but 31 runs in the score of 366. The batting plunged from 307-4 against the mild pace of Doug Walters, and when it failed a second time the game was lost. That one innings secured Clive's position, for the immediate future at least.

His batting against England in 1973 showed that he was here to stay. The batsman was on familiar terrain as he had played a major part in Lancashire's revival of fortune, and was undoubtedly the county's most popular batsman since Cyril Washbrook. Lloyd was the 'king' of the Gillette Cup, which Lancashire won in three successive years from 1970. His brilliance was again obvious from the moment he hit 132 in a stand of over 200 with Kallicharran in the first Test Match at the Oval. The English bowling reeled under his attack. Clive's second-innings 94 was the one entertaining feature of the dreary and bickering draw at Birmingham. His 63 at Lord's was almost overlooked in the overall rush of runs. Meanwhile his fielding still drew as much attention as that of anyone since Constantine. By now Lloyd could move out of the covers and became adept at point or in the slips where his height was an advantage. As the cricketers who had served the Caribbean well in the 1960s began to drop out of the side Clive was clearly the focus of the necessary rebuilding. Those plans seemed to go awry when he made only one fifty in the 1973/74 series. There was a change in the air, and a new broom was needed. Kanhai was dismissed from the captaincy in circumstances that are still not entirely clear. An inexperienced side including Roberts, Richards and Gordon Greenidge, three young men who had played most of their cricket in England, was sent to India under Clive Lloyd's command.

A good captain leads by example, and Lloyd had a hand in each of the three West Indian victories. He massacred the fragile bowling with 163 in almost as many minutes in the first Test at Bangalore, adding 207 for the fourth wicket with Greenidge. That must have been a stand to remember. Through him the younger batsmen were encouraged to go for the runs, and Viv Richards led the way at New Delhi. The captain made the second highest score of 71. After that the team lost its way against the Indian spinners and suffered defeat in the next two games, but they made full amends for their shortcomings in the fifth Test at Bombay. Lloyd himself hit a massive 242 not out, and put on 250 runs with wicket-keeper Deryck Murray for the sixth wicket. In spite of making 406 in their first innings, India were crushed by over 200 runs.

Moving to Pakistan, the West Indian leader hit 83 in support of the more staid Baichan at Lahore, but by then there was little likelihood of getting a definite result. His 73 was part of an all-round batting performance at Karachi which put the tourists 87 runs ahead. They were foiled by dapper left-handed opening batsman Sadiq Mohammad, carrying his bat for 98 not out. Clive Lloyd had followed John Goddard and Gerry Alexander in moulding a new side through victory in India. He had gone one better than the latter in that his team remained unbeaten in Pakistan.

Although they had been inconsistent against both England and India, the West Indies were favourites to win the Prudential Cup in 1975. The conditions suited their temperament. Lloyd's own reputation in one-day cricket must have gone a long way towards that assessment. He saved his team in the tense battle with Pakistan at Birmingham. After Sarfraz Nawaz—a particularly dangerous seamer in England—had taken 4 early wickets Clive retrieved the position with 53 in preparation for the hectic scramble home by one wicket. It was surely the most exciting of all limited-over matches. The Guyanese giant did better than that in the Final at Lord's. The West Indians again lost cheap wickets to Lillee, Thomson and Gilmour. Lloyd appreciated that the only way to halt these bowlers was to knock them out of the attack. He smothered them with a welter of strokes and power, while his predecessor, Kanhai, kept up his end with commendable restraint. Clive was out for 102 to a disputed catch at the wicket. It was more than enough to sink the Australians. He was the hero of the hour, and his team were world champions.

The pendulum of fortune lurched the other way almost immediately. Australia has long been the graveyard of West Indian ambitions, and 1975/76 was true to the pattern of 1951/52 and 1968/69. A very talented team, the same side which won the Prudential Cup, broke under the impact of the fast bowling of Dennis Lillee and Jeff Thomson and the batting of the Chappell brothers.

Batsmen of the Seventies

Like Sobers before him, Lloyd as captain came in for much of the criticism, for allegedly cutting himself off from a crisis by mere brooding and for leaving the players too much to their own devices. All this may or may not have been true, but these were the very same tactics which had taken the West Indies to the pinnacle of success and would do so again. The real reason for the breakdown was probably immaturity, as any side with Fredericks, Richards, Murray, Roberts, Gibbs, Lloyd, Holder and Kallicharran cannot be accused of any lack of resolve or application.

Lloyd scored more runs than any other tourist, but it was not enough. Following Fredericks's scintillating example, he scored a bright 149 in the second Test Match at Perth, where the West Indies went ahead by 256 runs and won by an innings. They could do nothing after that, as Lillee and Thomson made inroads into the batting and their own bowling, dependent almost entirely on Andy Roberts, could not reply in kind. Clive's 102 in the third Test Match at Melbourne came too late, and his batting at Sydney was cancelled out by a second-innings collapse to Thomson, who took 6 wickets for 50. Lloyd ended a frustrating series with 91 not out in the sixth Test at Melbourne. The first-innings débâcle against Lillee and Gilmour—each of whom took 5 wickets—made the situation impossible, but Viv Richards and his captain showed with some of the best batting that the future was not without hope.

As had happened more than once before, the visiting Indians provided the stepping-stones for the West Indies to find their feet again. There was one major surprise in this rubber before the home team won convincingly but controversially. The victory by an innings and 97 runs in the first Test at Bridgetown fitted the tradition of earlier games between these two sides. Lloyd himself scored 102 in an encouraging West Indian batting performance. The Indians fared much better in the second and third matches, both of which were played at Port of Spain. In the first of these Clive saved the day with 70, after Sunil Gavaskar and Brijesh Patel put the tourists 161 ahead. Worried again by the Indian spinners, the West Indies owed their lead of 131 in the next match to Richards and Lloyd. Inspired by Gavaskar and Viswanath, the Indians surprised everyone by scoring over 400 in their second innings to win by 6 wickets. Bishen Bedi's captaincy was not without incident, as when he appeared to be less than helpful in respect of Richards's injury in Trinidad. It was a source of heated dispute amid the bumpers at Kingston. Chandrasekhar's 5 wickets, including that of Lloyd without scoring, gave India a good chance of victory. Only 85 runs separated the teams. The tourists began their second innings comparatively well, but when 5 wickets went down quickly the remaining batsmen failed to come to the crease on the grounds that they were 'absent hurt'. As a result the West Indians had to score only a farcical 13 runs to win what could have been an exciting match and the rubber.

The sweeping success against England in 1976 crowned Lloyd's captaincy. The home country called up their old-timers to hold the young tourists and stood all square after two drawn games. Then Clive unleashed his fast bowlers at Manchester, and the contest was all over. The West Indies ran out winners by three victories to nil. With Richards, Greenidge and Fredericks scoring so heavily, Lloyd's own batting prowess was not so essential. He made 50 in the second Test Match at Lord's when it mattered—this was the only time the run-machine faltered—and 84 in a very fast 174 runs fourth-wicket stand with Richards at the Oval. The captain handled his bowlers well and showed tactical wisdom in not enforcing the follow-on in the final match, thus saving his players from any unnecessary exhaustion.

Lloyd thrashed 157 against Pakistan in the first Test Match at Bridgetown in 1977. The West Indies recovered from 183–5 to 421 through a 151-runs sixth-wicket partnership between Clive and vice-captain Deryck Murray in which the former did most of the scoring. Now he was ready to meet the Australians again, and to exact revenge for the humiliations of the recent past.

Alvin Kallicharran, also of Guyana, was the other regular middle-order batsman throughout the greater part of the decade. He was the almost complete antithesis of his captain in physical appearance and in style. Short and with an oriental appearance, he scored freely with nudges, deflections, glances, and, more surprisingly, full-blooded hooks, drives and cuts. The more hostile the bowling the more vigorous was his response. The scoreboard was always ticking over while he was at the wicket. Later on he slowed up, and provided the foil to his more extrovert partners. Kallicharran's strength has been his timing of strokes, and like all touch players his entertainment value has risen and fallen with his fitness.

Kallicharran brought a breath of fresh air into the extremely dull match against New Zealand at Georgetown in 1972 by making 100 not out on his debut. The huge but unenterprising first-wicket partnership of 387 between Glenn Turner (who compiled his second

Batsmen of the Seventies

double century of the series) and Terry Jarvis robbed the game of any competitive interest. The young Guyanese followed this with 101 in the following game at Port of Spain, where Sobers did not enforce the follow-on after Inshan Ali had bowled the tourists out over 200 runs behind. Alvin's batting was the one bright spot of a not very memorable year.

Twelve months later the Australians came to the Caribbean with every intention of avenging their loss in 1965. The first two matches showed the batting of both sides to be stronger than the bowling; Kallicharran made 50 in the opening game at Kingston. The overs just after lunch on the last day of the third Test Match at Port of Spain were decisive to the eventual outcome. The West Indies went into the adjournment well placed at 268–4, needing only another 66 runs to win. Kallicharran, already with one half-century in the game, was on 91 not out. The little left-hander had met the spin of Jenner and O'Keeffe with textbook defence, but immediately on the resumption he waved his bat at a ball from Max Walker and was caught at the wicket. That was the end of any effective resistance and the Australians recovered from the brink of defeat to win by 44 runs.

Kallicharran was instrumental in the victory over England in 1973. His major partnership with Lloyd on the opening day of the first Test Match at the Oval showed the limitations of some moderate English bowling and pointed the way for the very high scoring which followed. Alvin scored 80 in each innings. He put his team ahead in the first game of the return rubber in the West Indies. His superb innings of 158 when all the other specialist batsmen failed against off-spinner Pat Pocock set up the 7 wickets win at Port of Spain. Towards the end of that knock he was involved in the most controversial incident of the entire tour. His partner played the last ball of the day, wicket-keeper Alan Knott pulled up the stumps to signify the end of proceedings, and Kallicharran started to go to the pavilion. Tony Greig, the over-enthusiastic fielder, broke the bowler's wicket and, as the umpire had not signalled the close, he was given the decision. The action was allowed by the letter if not the spirit of the law. Overnight the appeal was withdrawn diplomatically and the batsman continued his innings the next morning. He could not settle, and was dismissed shortly afterwards. Alvin scored another 93 in the high-scoring game at Kingston, and made 119 in a record second-wicket stand of 249 with Lawrence Rowe at Bridgetown.

Caribbean Cricketers

The little man passed 50 in six of the seven Test Matches on the double-tour to India and Pakistan in 1974/75. His performance was important in encouraging the untried batting. He thrived against both India's spin quartet and the new generation of pace bowlers in Pakistan. Kallicharran began the rubber with 124 in the runaway victory at Bangalore, where he and newcomer Gordon Greenidge made all but 65 of the runs which came from the bat. He was in complete command of the later part of the innings. He missed his half-century by 6 runs at New Delhi, and, in spite of falling to Madanlal for no score in the first innings, made 57 in the losing fight against Bedi and Chandrasekhar at Calcutta. The tourists went down by 100 runs at Madras after leading at the halfway stage. Kallicharran alone had the technical skill to counter Prasanna and Bedi, but he was run out for 51. Having thrown away their 2–0 lead in the series, the West Indians chased runs with renewed determination at Bombay. Alvin took part in three-figure stands with Fredericks and Lloyd before he was caught by Viswanath off Ghavri for 98. There was no way in which the anaemic Indian batting could match that kind of scoring.

While other batsmen made the running in the games that were won, Kallicharran's value was greatest in a crisis, and he emphasized this aspect against Pakistan at Lahore. Sarfraz Nawaz sorely troubled the West Indies with 6 wickets for 89—excellent bowling for those pitches. The Guyanese left-hander was equal to the responsibility with 92 not out in a total of 214. Neither side could win from that stalemate. It was the same at Karachi. Pakistan built up a strong score through hundreds by Majid Khan and the unorthodox southpaw Wasim Raja. Kallicharran hit back with 115, and shared another century stand with Lloyd which put the visitors ahead on first innings. The Lloyd-Kallicharran link was the axis of the entire batting.

Alvin Kallicharran's most memorable innings was played in a preliminary round of the Prudential World Cup competition in 1975. The West Indies, who had barely survived against Pakistan earlier in the week, came up against the powerful Australian bowling at the Oval. In the afternoon Kallicharran launched a determined assault on the much-feared Dennis Lillee and battered him with a succession of boundaries. His hooking was as good as anything seen on even that historic ground. Kallicharran was out for 78 with victory almost achieved. He also hit the top-score of 72 in the semi-final against New Zealand at the same venue. His second-wicket stand with Gordon

Batsmen of the Seventies

Greenidge gave the Kiwis no chance to come back into the contest.

The fast bowling of Lillee, Thomson, Gilmour and Walker which destroyed the West Indian batting in 1975/76 did not suffer the indignity of such cavalier treatment over the full extent of a four-innings Test Match. Too often Kallicharran was called upon to repair the breach in the early batting, and could not attack with his usual flair. He made his only century with 101 in the second innings at Brisbane in adding 198 with Lawrence Rowe for the fourth wicket. Once they were out the batting flagged, and the game was lost. Alvin scored a fifty in Fredericks's shadow at Perth, but had two mediocre games before coming good with 76 and 67 in the fifth Test at Adelaide.

Although Viv Richards dominated the successful home rubber against India in 1976, other batsmen did score some runs, including Kallicharran, who finished second in the averages to the Antiguan. The two batsmen were involved in a double-century third-wicket partnership in the first Test at Bridgetown. Mohinder Amarnath had the left-hander caught by Viswanath for 93 after he had struggled with unexpected difficulty. The onset of the shoulder ailment which curtailed his play later in the year might have affected his scoring rate. When the third Test was moved to Port of Spain because of excessive rain in Guyana he made a watchful second innings 103 not out which prompted Lloyd to declare with unfortunate results.

Kallicharran did not have a happy time in England that summer. His injury seriously restricted his stroke-play, and he toiled long to score 97 in his third-wicket stand of 303 with Richards in the first Test Match at Nottingham. Derek Underwood had him caught by David Steele: the sixth time he had been out in the nineties. Alvin did not score in either innings at Lord's, and when it was apparent that he was still not fit after the Manchester game he was excluded from the rest of the tour. Kallicharran, still out of touch in the next rubber against Pakistan, scored slowly in his only substantial innings of 72 in the third Test Match at Georgetown. Apart from the physical pain, he may have been jaded by so much continuous cricket. But within months the unprecedented schism which rent world cricket put unexpected responsibility on him.

By the mid-1970s Kallicharran was well settled into the pattern of the English county championship competition. He still plays for Warwickshire, the West Midland county which opened the way for the West Indian influx by accepting fast bowlers Shirley Griffith and

Caribbean Cricketers

Rudi Webster in the preceding two decades. Recently four West Indian Test Match players have appeared together for Warwickshire —namely, Kallicharran, Kanhai, Gibbs and Deryck Murray. By coincidence the first three are Guyanese. Seven-day-a-week cricket may have blunted the edge of Kallicharran's batting brilliance, which has lost much of its inspiration since he flayed Lillee. Perhaps like Kanhai he has just grown older. Clive Lloyd has suffered no change of approach as he matured, but his style based on power rather than touch is altogether different.

Keith Boyce was heralded as a contemporary Constantine when he burst into the 1973 series with such force. His hard-hitting batting and no-nonsense fast bowling were an attractive characteristic of Essex cricket, because, like Julien and Shepherd, Boyce was essentially a product of the English game. He swept England to defeat in the first Test at the Oval with a superb display of all-round talent. Batting at number nine, Keith struck a whirlwind 72 and took 11 wickets. It is fair to say, though, that nothing he did after that—especially as a batsman—came up to that initial promise. His vigorous methods of making runs did not come off in an increasingly technical and tactical environment. Maybe he was born too late.

Boyce made 68 in a seventh-wicket century stand with Richards at New Delhi, but he was generally batting too low to achieve anything positive. With Keith's ability, however, there was always the chance that he could come off again. Though almost squeezed out of the team by Andy Roberts and Michael Holding on the tour to Australia, he showed with 49 not out at Perth that he could not be disregarded. At last he produced his old form in the fifth Test Match at Adelaide. Coming to the crease at 110-5 with Jeff Thomson's pace too much for the earlier batsmen, he scored with such freedom that he had 95 not out when the innings closed. The Barbadian saved the follow-on almost single-handed, but even his further 69 could not stave off another heavy defeat. Boyce was lbw without scoring in his next innings at Melbourne. His meteoric international career was over. For several years after that he was still one of the most popular players in the county championship.

Bernard Julien also suffered from too much success too soon. In 1973 his impact was only slightly below that of Boyce, culminating in a tornado 121 in the third Test at Lord's which pulverized an attack already shattered by Kanhai and Sobers. With 86 not out Julien was the only batsman to stay with Kallicharran in the 7 wickets win in the

Batsmen of the Seventies

first Test at Port of Spain in 1973/74, but he did little more after that until he scored 101 in the drawn game at Karachi the following year. Bernard showed courage and excitement on the occasions when he opened the innings with Fredericks in Australia. He participated in the stand which set up the avalanche of runs and victory in the second Test at Perth.

CHAPTER SEVENTEEN
The Return of Speed

The West Indies swept through England in 1973 as if the last seven years had not happened. For the third time in a decade they totally demolished a country which was the professional home for most of them. They were supported by the large West Indian section of the crowd, which was not divided into territorial components: it was more catholic Caribbean than anywhere in Jamaica, Trinidad, Barbados or Guyana. The tourists constructed their one-sided victories in two of the three Test Matches on the traditional virtues of attractive batting and straightforward fast bowling. This time the new ball was shared by two newcomers who had learned their skills with English counties, Keith Boyce and Bernard Julien, and another, Vanburn Holder, who had improved his control and precision during his time with Worcestershire.

Boyce was the first really quick bowler since Wesley Hall. He represented all that was best in the cricket of the early 1970s and made immediate headway as soon as he joined Essex. The Barbadian was an asset in limited-over competition with his spectacular hitting and a mixture of conventional and unorthodox strokes. The public looked upon him as a brilliant batsman who could bowl a little. Stimulated by Test Match tension, Boyce took 5 wickets for 70 and 6 wickets for 77 at the Oval. In the first innings he sent the total spinning from 247–5 to 257, and again cut through the tail in the second. Keith took another 4 wickets in each innings at Lord's. For England only Keith Fletcher, his Essex team-mate, got beyond 50 at either attempt, even though the West Indies had hit up 652–8 declared.

Several reputations so newly won were lost in the return rubber at

The Return of Speed

the end of the year. Boyce started as well there as he had left off in England. He took 4 wickets for 42 in bowling the tourists out for a lowly 131 when Kanhai put them in to bat in almost English conditions at Port of Spain. The West Indies led by 261 runs. Dennis Amiss held up the bowlers with 174, including an opening partnership of 209 with Boycott, but the leeway was too great and his team went down by 7 wickets. The Warwickshire opener continued his prolific form in the second Test Match at Kingston. When England went in a second time 230 runs behind, Amiss saved the game by scoring 262 not out from the 432-9. Boyce's initial impact was blunted. His inspiration and surprise did not come back. Andy Roberts succeeded him as the spearhead of the attack in India and Pakistan, and the Antiguan was joined in partnership by Michael Holding against Australia. Boyce was back to his best as a bowler in England once more for the Prudential Cup. He took 3 wickets against Sri Lanka at Manchester, and settled the Final at Lord's with four of the five Australian wickets which fell to bowlers. His successes in his adopted country were a strong argument for his selection in 1976. However, with Roberts, Holding, Daniel and Holder available there was no room for him in the party.

Bernard Julien of Trinidad suffered from early comparisons with Gary Sobers, whom he resembled in style. He was as successful in Kent as was Boyce in Essex. Julien's vigorous hitting in the lower order was invaluable, though he was not consistent. He moved the ball well on English pitches, and several times opened the attack in preference to a faster bowler. His best international bowling was 5 wickets for 57 against England at Bridgetown in 1973/74. Julien bowled well in the preliminary rounds of the Prudential Cup. He took 4 wickets in putting Sri Lanka out for 86 in the first fixture, and dismissed 4 more batsmen in the semi-final against New Zealand at the Oval. His subsequent record did not match his potential. He failed with the bat and the ball in 1976.

Vanburn Holder took the new ball from 1969, when there was no alternative, until Boyce and the present abundance of fast bowlers came on the scene. Then he moved to first or second change and was much more effective. Holder's tight slower pace claimed many victims who misjudged the speed and movement of his deliveries after their battering by the pacemen. The quiet Barbadian could be deadly whenever the pitch deteriorated in the final stages of the game and he could still wobble the ball effectively when the wicket was green. He shot out Geoff Boycott, Brian Luckhurst and Frank Hayes in his 4 wickets for 56 at Lord's in 1973.

The 'new' Holder was startlingly evident in the second innings of the fifth Test Match at Bombay in 1974/75. It was the decisive match of the series. Although the batting of Clive Lloyd, Roy Fredericks and Alvin Kallicharran gave the tourists an early advantage, the Indians refused to concede defeat. Eknath Solkar made 102 and there were half-centuries from Gundappa Viswanath, Sunil Gavaskar and Anshuman Gaekwad. They did not get the same chance in the second innings. Holder had Solkar lbw, bowled Viswanath and finished with 6 wickets for 39. A year later he took 5 wickets for 108 against a very strong Australian batting side in the fifth Test Match at Adelaide. That game was lost by the West Indians' own shortcomings in batting. In 1976 Vanburn was used primarily as a stock bowler to keep the English batsmen penned down while Roberts, Holding and Daniel were rested. He seemed to retire from international cricket after that tour, but life holds many surprises. Holder's greatest honour was yet to come.

With the failure of all the new spin bowlers Lance Gibbs was summoned back to play against Australia in 1973. He was instantly successful, and gave the bowling greater purpose than it had shown over the two previous series. Gibbs took 4 wickets for 85 in the first Test Match at Kingston, plus 5 wickets for 102 and 4 wickets for 66 in the two games played at Port of Spain. In the first of the matches in Trinidad he attacked the principal batsmen, even to the extent of using three short-legs. Later he threw away some of the advantage by bowling defensively to the tail. There was nothing negative, however, about the 6 wickets for 108 with which he spun England to defeat in the first Test at Port of Spain in 1973/74. The visitors seemed to have extricated themselves from the worst of their trouble as Amiss, Boycott and Mike Denness steered them to 328 before the second wicket went down. Then Gibbs struck home and, as happened so often in the past, he ran right through the innings. Now he could not be left out of the team.

Lance was still a match-winner in India. He took 6 wickets for 76 in the win by an innings and 17 runs in the second Test at New Delhi. Once he had bowled Faroukh Engineer—whose burst of scoring had looked dangerous—the West Indies were on their way to victory. Gibbs had another 7 wickets for 98 in the first innings of the fifth Test at Bombay. Sunil Gavaskar and Solkar added 168 runs for the second

The Return of Speed

wicket, but the off-spinner bowled the former and dismissed Viswanath five runs short of his century. He was more incisive than any of the Indian spinners, who had given their side such a good chance of squaring the rubber. Lance was not needed in the Prudential Cup with its emphasis on fast and medium-paced bowlers, and his inclusion in the touring party to Australia was criticized.

Gibbs had his best game on his third tour of that country in the first Test at Brisbane, the scene of his successful twinning with Sobers on the previous visit. After bowling the West Indies out for 214 Australia reached 317-4, with captain Greg Chappell hitting a hundred. Gibbs had Rodney Marsh caught behind the wicket for 48, and the remaining wickets fell for less than 50 runs. He bowled badly after that, but was retained in the side in the hope that he would beat Freddie Trueman's record for the highest number of victims in international cricket. Gibbs achieved that honour by having Ian Redpath caught on the first day of the sixth Test at Melbourne. Retirement was not far away now, and there was general disappointment when torrential rain caused the third Test against India in 1976, which would have been his finale on his home ground, to be moved from Georgetown to Port of Spain.

Andy Roberts's sorrowfully languid look betrays no emotion. Sometimes when a catch goes astray off his bowling he looks upwards in resignation and silent reproach before resuming his place at his mark for the next delivery. No words, no throwing up of the hands or theatrical gestures, and no exuberance either when he takes a wicket. In his undemonstrative approach as well as his day-in, day-out accuracy he resembles Brian Statham. When he broke into an environment which considered Boyce fast Andy's own speed was electrifying. Holding and Croft have become even faster in their turn, but Roberts's sharpness and occasional bumper come as a nasty shock. Where does he stand in the pantheon of great West Indian fast bowlers? The facts speak for themselves. He invariably opens the attack, even in this age of unprecedented fast bowling talent, and he has done so almost without respite for a number of years of almost incessant international competition all over the world.

Although his performances with Hampshire had brought him swiftly to public attention, the Antiguan was only one of several young fast bowlers in contention for a team place in the 1974/75 series against India. Because of his superior speed he was given the new ball in the first Test Match at Bangalore, and responded with 3 wickets in each innings. That was a good enough start, but exploiting his hosts' known fear of pace, Roberts came close to repeating the performances of Hall and Gilchrist a generation earlier. Ironically, his best achievements were in the two games which the West Indies lost. He rocked the Indians with 5 wickets for 50 at Calcutta, having set up the triumph by getting opener Naik taken at the wicket without a run scored and dismissing the charismatic Engineer shortly afterwards.

Andy was more devastating, with 7 wickets for 64, in the fourth Test at Madras. Only little Viswanath stood up to him with 97 not out, which in this low-scoring game was sufficient to tip the scales. Roberts took another 5 wickets for 57 in the second innings. This time Anshuman Gaekwad stayed there long enough to ensure an Indian victory. When the party moved on to Pakistan the Antiguan returned 5 wickets for 66 and 4 wickets for 121 in the first Test at Lahore. That was excellent bowling on traditionally lifeless pitches. He began the game well by removing the formidable Majid Khan, Agha Zahid his unknown partner, and Zaheer Abbas, but came under fire from Mustaq Mohammad as the game developed into a draw. Roberts was now as secure and established as any West Indian fast bowler for a decade.

Although his bowling was a major drawing card in the Prudential Cup competition for spectators who wanted to compare his speed with that of Lillee and Thomson, Andy is best remembered that year for his feat with the bat in the narrow win over Pakistan at Birmingham. With their opponents scoring 266-7, the West Indies were thrown out of their stride by the intelligent use of the seam by Sarfraz Nawaz, who played for Northamptonshire in the county championship. They seemed out of the running at 166-8, and placed even more precariously with Holder's dismissal at 203. The last pair, Deryck Murray and Roberts, had to score another 64 runs against a team which many people were tipping as ultimate winners of the tournament. They kept calm while the more inexperienced Pakistanis made errors in the field. Gradually they edged nearer the target, which they reached with only two balls of the final over to spare. Roberts was 24 not out.

Andy was a fast bowler again against Australia in 1975/76. His greatest triumph was in the second Test at Perth. Even though Australia were 256 runs behind on first innings, their unusually strong batting was not expected to capitulate a second time. Roberts un-

The Return of Speed

leashed a powerful assault in which he dismissed Alan Turner and Ian Redpath—both without scoring—Rick McCosker and Ian Chappell (who had held the first innings together with 156) before the close of play on the third day. That burst ripped the heart out of the batting, and he finished with 7 wickets for 54. The West Indies won by an innings and 87 runs. Roberts and young Michael Holding bowled quite well together for the rest of the series without becoming as penetrative as their opposite numbers, Lillee and Thomson, who could rely on a greater depth of support.

The Antiguan had a comparatively modest return against India as his younger partner grabbed the headlines. With Holding feeling the effects of indisposition, Roberts bit deep into the English batting at Lord's in 1976. He dismissed Barry Wood and the stubborn David Steele in his opening overs, and finished with 5 wickets for 60. The West Indies did not bat well, giving the home country a lead of 68. When they reached 169-3 England seemed to have the tourists with their backs against a wall. Meanwhile Roberts had not deviated in either speed or accuracy, and he was soon rewarded. The main obstacle, Steele, was caught for 64, and the bowler finished with another 5 wickets for 63. It was the first time a West Indian fast bowler had taken 10 wickets in a Test Match at Lord's.

English batting sank to an all-time low in the face of the three-pronged pace attack at Manchester. Roberts took 3 wickets in the first-innings débâcle, in which England were bowled out for 71. Then veterans John Edrich and Brian Close grafted a half-century first-wicket stand as the West Indian fast bowlers seemed to waste their superiority with some intimidating deliveries which threatened the batsman rather than the stumps. Holding was the chief offender, and Roberts, more accurate and direct, reaped the harvest of wickets. He dismissed Close and Bob Woolmer with successive balls. Later in the innings he had Alan Knott and Derek Underwood out in two deliveries, only for the hat-trick chance to be dropped into the slips. His 6 wickets for 37 were an outstanding contribution to his side's victory by 425 runs.

Andy Roberts was now the senior member of a generation of fast bowlers almost too numerous to mention. The Antiguan was always there, whoever might be his bowling partner. He had new partners in Joel Garner and Colin Croft when Pakistan toured the West Indies in 1977. Roberts bowled well, but was less effective than he had been in England, Australia or India. It seemed that he reserved his best

173

performances for overseas. Although he took 4 wickets for 85 in the second Test Match at Port of Spain his effort was hardly noticed as it was overshadowed by Colin Croft's record return in only his second game. Majid Khan and Sadiq Mohammad had given the Pakistanis every chance of drawing by putting on 123 for the first wicket in the second innings, but Roberts's success confirmed the victory for the West Indies.

Michael Holding is the best fast bowler I have seen. My recollection goes back to Ray Lindwall and Keith Miller, through Frank Tyson, Freddie Trueman, Brian Statham, Wesley Hall, Roy Gilchrist, Charlie Griffith, Neil Adcock, Peter Heine, Cuan McCarthy and Alan Davidson to those of present or recent memory. The young Jamaican's talent is such that I would be prepared to back him against Harold Larwood, Ted McDonald and all the giants of yesteryear. His tall, slim physique is well proportioned, and his approach to the wicket and delivery are beautifully executed. The most exciting aspects of his bowling are the generation of sheer pace, which gets through even the most experienced batsman, and the ability to extract fire from any pitch. Once he got over his temperamental immaturity Holding became the 'greatest'.

Michael was taken to Australia on speculation rather than on any proven record. His talent was so obvious that he took the new ball with Roberts in preference to either Boyce, Julien or Holder. His captain's act of faith was rewarded with 4 wickets for 88 in the first innings at Perth. Australia had recovered from a poor start with former captain Ian Chappell's aggressive century, and were 277-5. Holding bowled Chappell and dismissed the last three batsmen in one over as Australia closed at 329. In spite of injury he continued to bowl well technically, but because of his youth he became despondent and upset when umpiring decisions went against him.

Nothing restrained the Jamaican in the next series against India. In spite of yet another fine hundred by Richards, the West Indies batted unevenly in the third Test Match at Port of Spain. The Indians lost Sunil Gavaskar lbw early on to Holding, who closed with 6 wickets for 65. He had tasted success, and bowled flat out before his own people at Kingston. Gavaskar and Gaekwad opened with 136 for the first wicket. To minimize their scoring Holding went round the wicket and kept his deliveries pitched short. Almost immediately the innings buckled under his assault of 4 wickets for 82. With Gaekwad and Patel injured from balls which rose sharply from the uneven

The Return of Speed

pitch, India declared at 306–6. The West Indies lost wickets steadily to Chandrasekhar, and owed their lead of 85 in a good part to Holding's 55. India began their second innings comfortably against the fast bowlers, but when three wickets fell with the score at 95 the innings closed. Five batsmen declared themselves 'absent hurt'. The suspicion that some of them at least had taken the easy way out for fear of Holding only added to the Jamaican's reputation.

Michael missed the first Test in England, and was not fully fit for the second. Then he burst the series apart at Manchester. Although the West Indies batted weakly, their initial total of 211 was more than England could manage in their two innings combined. The home country reached 36 before their second wicket went down. Shortly afterwards they were all out for 71. Holding struck with electric speed and such control that several of his deliveries were really unplayable. Steele, who made his twenty before the bowler had got into his rhythm, was the only batsman to reach double figures. Holding took 5 wickets for 17. Anyone who got away from him had to face Roberts or Daniel at the other end. It was no place for the faint-hearted.

The Jamaican's bowling in the fifth Test at the Oval was equally awe-inspiring, and probably better. The passive pitch gave the bowlers no help at all. As a result his record-breaking performance was one of the great examples of fast bowling in any class of cricket. The West Indians revelled in the almost tropical heat to score 687–8 declared. Dennis Amiss batted with comparative ease in making 203, over 150 more than the next man. His partners went down before Holding with consistent regularity. This was not a one-off dynamic blitz which swept the opposition aside. Holding kept plugging away with a pace and sense of direction which was hardly credible. Never once did he lose his almost poetic action. His figures of 8 wickets for 92 were especially remarkable, seeing that Roberts, Holder and Daniel were also in the side, and that they could do nothing. The procedure was repeated in the second innings, with the exception that once Holding dismissed Amiss there was no effective resistance. He had another 6 wickets for 57 as England went down by 231 runs.

Wayne Daniel, strongly built in the manner of Charlie Griffith, was the newest fast bowler in England that summer. He was enthusiastic and kept trying, but he would probably not have been chosen for the first Test Match at Nottingham if Holding had been well. The Barbadian stepped into the breach boldly with 4 wickets for 53. The success of Roberts and Holding restricted his scope in the other four games. Even so, Wayne came out of the season a better and more mature bowler. The growth of fast-bowling power, in both quality and quantity, has curtailed his international career. Although his efforts for Middlesex have made him one of the leading pacemen in England, Daniel was not selected for the side which won the Prudential Cup in 1979.

The West Indies returned to the Caribbean in September 1976 as popular world champions. It was not yet a year since they had set out for Australia with such high hopes, and met with the painful realization of defeat. Those memories had been washed away by two victorious series. However, nobody who had seen Roberts, Holding and Daniel operating so well together would have accepted that they would never do so again in an official Test Match. Daniel and Holding were both injured by the time the Pakistanis arrived in early 1977. The tall Colin Croft of Guyana and the even taller Joel Garner of Barbados came in as replacements with very little first-class experience. They were expected to hold the fort until the front-line bowlers returned, but it did not work out quite like that. Each of them took 4 wickets in an innings in the vacillating first Test at Bridgetown, which either side could have won in the dying moments.

Croft made history in the second Test at Port of Spain. In a very lively opening he forced Sadiq Mohammad to retire, and quickly sent back Haroon Rashid, Asif Iqbal and Mustaq Mohammad. Majid Khan and Wasim Raja won a brief breathing space before Colin bowled the latter on his way to 8 wickets for 29. In only his second international game, he had eclipsed Holding's best innings analysis for a West Indian fast bowler, set up so recently at the Oval. Garner, who took 4 wickets in each innings at Georgetown, and Croft bowled throughout the rubber in the best tradition of West Indian fast bowling. The selectors could in theory choose from Roberts, Holding, Daniel, Croft and Garner for the next Test Matches against Australia, a rare embarrassment of riches. But a cloud was hanging over international cricket even then, and they would have to select another two pacemen to open the bowling before the series was halfway through.

CHAPTER EIGHTEEN
Fredericks and Greenidge

Roy Fredericks had two distinct styles as a batsman, a complement rather than a contradiction which events may have forced on him. He underwent his baptism of international fire in Australia when the triumphant team of the 1960s was breaking up, and he survived into the Packer age. Roy was always there, however much his partners chopped and changed. At Birmingham in 1973 he compiled one of the most boring innings in contemporary cricket, and perhaps the most exciting at Perth just over two years later. Fredericks's more adventurous knocks came when he was sure of support at the other end. His delight in hooking, even off the first ball of a Test Match, brough him either summary dismissal or assured mastery.

The short, compact opener from Guyana was comparatively unknown when he went to Australia in 1968/69. Although the West Indies won well at Brisbane, the flaws in their batting were exposed very quickly on the first morning of the second Test Match at Melbourne. Graham McKenzie, the well-built fast-medium bowler, started the slide by having the normally secure Steve Camacho caught for a duck. It was enough to unnerve most of the other batsmen. McKenzie took 8 wickets for 71 in bowling them out for 200, of which Fredericks made 76. Roy didn't get another 50 that season, but he had shown enough fighting spirit to be taken to England in 1969.

He did not do very well at first. Within a few overs of the start of the first Test at Manchester the West Indies were 5–2 with both Fredericks and Carew out. The batsmen could have been out of practice with so much rain in the early weeks of the tour. They improved in the second innings by putting on 92, of which Fredericks made 64. Camacho went in first with him at Lord's, where they were subjected to some short-pitched bowling by John Snow, who had caused them so much trouble in the last series at home, but because of his size Roy could slip inside the line of a bumper. Their partnerships were worth 106 and 73, the most consistent batting in a variable match, and Fredericks's scores were 63 and 60. As yet he was still a useful rather than a prominent member of the team.

The following rubber against India was personally disappointing. Abid Ali bowled him first ball with a shooter in the second Test at Port of Spain. He was prepared for this in the second innings, and made the top score of 80 before he was run out. The total was 150–1, but slumped to 261 all out as Venkataraghavan bowled the Indians to their first victory in the Caribbean. None of the batsmen were troubled unduly by the New Zealand bowlers in 1972. Fredericks and Rowe drew up the blueprint with a second-wicket stand of 269 in the first Test at Kingston, in which the former made 163. The tourists, who hovered at 108–5, were let off the hook by the failure to apply sufficient pressure. Opening batsman Glenn Turner, carrying his bat for the first of his two double centuries, found a dependable partner in the wicket-keeper, the late Ken Wadsworth. Roy's half-centuries in the two matches at Port of Spain kept him in the side.

Fredericks found his real touch in 1973. Until then he had managed only one good game in each rubber. Now he welcomed the Australians with a glimpse of the consistency which would mark his future play. In the second Test at Bridgetown the left-hander matched Greg Chappell's hundred with another fine innings of his own. He was frustratingly lbw to Jeff Hammond for 98. Then the West Indies had to score 334 to win the next match at Port of Spain. Fredericks and Kallicharran batted so well that as lunchtime approached the target seemed little more than a formality. Roy was out for 76, Alvin departed to the first ball after the interval, and the whole effort collapsed. The West Indian batting had talent in abundance, but it was short on stability. Few batsmen could or would put their head down and play through a patch of trouble. The West Indies needed an anchor-man.

With that in mind Fredericks, like Hunte before him, abandoned his natural, enterprising style for the 1973 tour to England. Let Clive Lloyd, Rohan Kanhai, and Alvin Kallicharran score the runs; he would stay there. His position was made more difficult because he had no recognized partner: neither Camacho nor Geoff Greenidge had come on as well as expected, and Lawrence Rowe had difficulties with his health and temperament. The younger Headley was tried, without real success. Everything depended on Fredericks for a good start to the innings. Because of this responsibility he batted slowly through almost nine hours for 150 in the second Test at Birmingham. It was extremely dull, but ensured that the West Indies would not lose the rubber. Because of Roy's patience Rohan Kanhai, Gary Sobers and Bernard Julien could afford to strike the ball without fear at Lord's.

With Rowe temporarily back to his brilliant best, hitting hundreds with unaccustomed repetition, the West Indies were given a good start in nearly every game against England in 1973/74. Fredericks, who was 65 not out in bringing his team home by 7 wickets in the first Test at Port of Spain, and the Jamaican put on a record opening stand of 206 in the second Test at Kingston. Roy was out for 94, and came even nearer to his hundred at Georgetown, being caught and bowled by Tony Greig for 98. He made 67 in the fifth Test at Port of Spain, where only he and Rowe countered Greig's devastating off-spin. The tall South African-born all-rounder took 13 wickets in the match, after hitting centuries in the two previous games. Geoff Boycott, who made 99 and 112, was the other main contributor to England's surprising victory, by which they were able to share the series in which they were outplayed nearly all along the way. Although Rowe's health soon let him down again, Fredericks did not have to carry the burden of the initial batting alone any more. The selection of so many new batsmen for the tour to India and Pakistan unearthed a sparkling young Barbadian with whom his name would henceforth be linked. Before recording the success of that partnership I must devote a few paragraphs to the man who had all the attributes bar one for true greatness.

Twice in his life Lawrence Rowe showed a touch of genius so far above those around him that he aspired to the class of George Headley, Viv Richards and Don Bradman. His debut was unique, and he made a lot of runs in all conditions during 1973/74. The rest of his career was something of a disappointment. Rowe was troubled consistently by ill-health, and by injuries. Above all, his temperament was not as adequate as his technique. Even so, it is a clear indication of the strength of West Indian batting in the middle and late 1970s that the selectors could ignore for long stretches a man who made a double century in his first Test Match, and has recorded the second largest score ever made by a West Indian at the highest level.

Rowe made his international debut in the first Test at Kingston against New Zealand in February 1972, and immediately showed his class. He made a memorable first-innings 214 in taking the West Indies to 508–4 declared. When Turner's similar effort extinguished any possibility of a definite result Sobers let the batting continue until the young Jamaican completed his second century of the match. No other batsman has started with 314 runs for only once out. Even allowing for the modest quality of the opposing bowling, Lawrence seemed to be a star runmaker, and perhaps the most entertaining since Gary Sobers, Collie Smith and Rohan Kanhai came to the fore in the late 1950s, but he did not live up to that promise. He made only one other fifty that season, and he became dogged by injury: his best score over the next three years was 76 in the first Test at Kingston against Australia.

Lawrence Rowe plugged the first-wicket gap by going in with Fredericks against England in 1973/74. On recent form he would not have been chosen if others had been available, but in the event he had the best season of his chequered career in terms of quality and quantity, with one triple century and two single hundreds. His success underlined still further what the cricketing public missed in his fallow years. Rowe set the sequence in motion with 120 in a double-century stand with Fredericks in the second Test at Kingston—how he liked his home ground! He established another record partnership of 249 for the second wicket with Kallicharran in the next game at Bridgetown. By making an exciting and impressive 302 he stood head and shoulders above the other batsmen. This was second only to Sobers's world record 365 not out as an individual score by a West Indian in a Test Match.

The extent of his ability was made even clearer in the fifth Test at Port of Spain. Whereas he had attacked the bowling majestically at Bridgetown, Rowe was now required to defend on a turning pitch. Even Tony Greig, who was not a regular spin bowler, was dangerous here. Lawrence scored an excellent 123 in taking the total well beyond 200 before the third wicket went down. His dismissal emphasized the really difficult nature of the conditions. The remaining batsmen were out so quickly that the West Indies could not secure a sufficiently substantial lead to keep them out of trouble in the last innings. Rowe's hopes of a continuous career were shattered by further injury; Gordon Greenidge took over his position and kept it.

West Indian Spectators Spectator support in the Caribbean is spontaneous and colourful. A section of the crowd watching play in a Test Match at Queen's Park, Port of Spain *Patrick Eagar*

West Indian fast bowling is shown here at its best by action from three continents. **Wesley Hall** (*left*) exhibits a textbook correct straight arm and back at Manchester in 1963 (*Central Press*). **Andy Roberts** (*centre*) bowled with his customary intensity and accuracy at Perth in 1975 to take 7–54 (*Patrick Eagar*). **Joel Garner** (*right*) is delighted on taking a wicket against Australia at Port of Spain in 1978 (*Patrick Eagar*)

Michael Holding The poetry of pace. Holding, one of the most naturally talented fast bowlers, approaches the wicket at Lord's in 1976, his very successful year *Patrick Eagar*

Two great exponents of the hook-shot in possibly their best remembered games. **Rohan Kanhai** (*left*) made a blistering, match-winning 77 at the Oval in 1963. Ken Barrington is the fielder (*Central Press*). **Roy Fredericks** (*right*) hit a magnificent whirlwind 169 at Perth in 1975. The unfortunate bowler is Gary Gilmour (*Patrick*

A pair of unusually gifted left-handers from Guyana. **Clive Lloyd** (*left*), an outstanding batsman, fielder and captain, strikes the ball firmly on the off-side. **Alvin Kallicharran** (*right*), the gentle assassin of speed and spin, hits crisply in front of the wicket *Patrick Eagar*

Viv Richards is the greatest contemporary batsman, and a master of all strokes *Patrick Eagar*

Gordon Greenidge, a specialist in the unorthodox, hooks John Snow for a spectacular 6 at Lord's in 1976. The fielder is Tony Greig *Patrick Eagar*

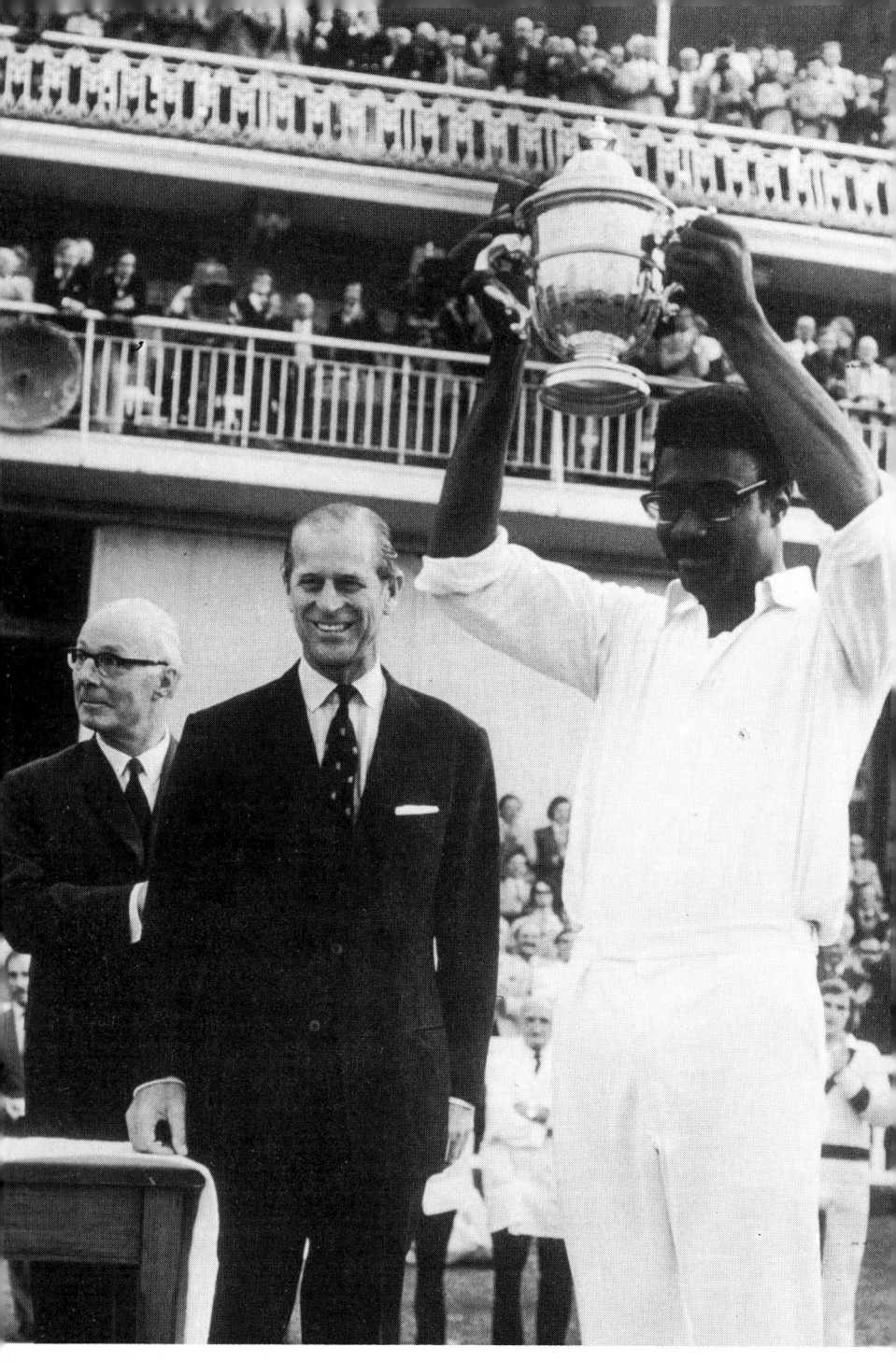

Prudential Cup Winners Champions of the world. Clive Lloyd holds up the Prudential Cup which he has just received from Prince Philip. The West Indies won the trophy in both 1975 and 1979 *Patrick Eagar*

Yet again the Jamaican battled back to fitness, and came in at number three in Australia. He showed a glimpse of his former brilliance as early as the second innings of the first Test Match at Brisbane. The West Indies were 152 runs behind, and lost 3 more quick wickets to the varied pace of Lillee, Thomson and Gilmour. It was the kind of near-hopeless situation which has often inspired heroic deeds. Rowe and Kallicharran played their favourite strokes, drives and hooks respectively, in putting on 198 for the fourth wicket. That threw the challenge right back at the Australians. Lawrence relaxed his concentration on passing his century, and was caught for 107. Straight away Clive Lloyd was dismissed for a duck and Viv Richards ran himself out. These suicides undid all the previous good work. The Chappell brothers shared an unbroken partnership of 159 as Australia won by 8 wickets. After this tour Rowe opened the innings again against India in the West Indies. He was useful, without doing enough to make the selectors take notice of him. The Jamaican did not play against England in 1976 until Kallicharran pulled out with an injury. Then he made 50 at Leeds and 70 at the Oval in the two matches available to him.

Gordon Greenidge embodies all that is characteristic and best in West Indian batting, although that may seem strange for somebody who developed his skills in England from childhood before he returned to cricket in Barbados. Greenidge always tries to score runs, and to show the bowlers and fielders that he is in command. There is a continuous movement in his strokes, whether driving, cutting or hooking, all of which he does very well. He moves his feet freely, including an instantly recognizable treading hop towards his stumps, and swings the bat through various angles, conventional and otherwise. His constant search for quick singles, which may disconcert an unsuspecting partner, breaks up any rhythm the opposition may try to attain. While he always gives the bowler a chance to take his wicket—more so than Viv Richards— Greenidge is also more likely to force the game immediately along a path advantageous to himself and his team.

Greenidge had an admirable debut at Bangalore in 1974/75 which was only slightly less satisfying than Rowe's first appearance. The Indian spinners, Chandrasekhar, Prasanna and Venkataraghavan, suffered early punishment but came back to take the last 9 wickets for 108 runs. Anxious to reach his hundred, Greenidge was run out for 93. He needn't have worried about passing this particular landmark.

Caribbean Cricketers

In the second innings Gordon scored 107 and shared a fourth-wicket stand of 207 with Lloyd which aborted any Indian hopes of survival. The West Indies won by 267 runs, and seemed destined for an even more impressive record than any of their successful predecessors. It was not as easy as that. The opening partnership was still not fully forged, being as yet a combination of two gifted individuals.

The third Test at Calcutta upset all notions that the tourists would have a straightforward passage. India batted feebly against the fast bowling of Roberts to be out for 233. That total seemed well within the range of this formidable batting side, yet when Madanlal, the medium-paced opening bowler, dismissed Greenidge and Kallicharran, and Richards was run out, the West Indies knew that they had a fight on their hands. Thanks only to Roy Fredericks's 100, they went 7 runs ahead. It was not enough for a team batting last against Bishen Bedi and Chandrasekhar, especially after little Viswanath had hit a courageous 139. The Indian slow bowlers were victorious again in the fourth Test at Madras. The dearth of good spin bowling in the Caribbean was reflected in the West Indian batsmen's own difficulty when the ball did not come through at a lively pace.

Fredericks and Greenidge gave the tourists the consistent start of which they were capable with 81 and 75 in the fifth Test at Bombay. In the first innings the more experienced Guyanese made another century, sharing in two three-figure stands, and Greenidge got his 50 in the second. Fredericks's embryonic understanding with the Barbadian seemed to be going the same way as his short-lived associations with Joey Carew, Steve Camacho and Lawrence Rowe when the patient Leonard Baichan—yet another Guyanese left-hander—replaced Greenidge for the two matches in Pakistan. He too made a hundred on his debut with 105 not out at Lahore and took the first-wicket score to 95 at Karachi before he was caught behind the wicket off leg-spinner Intikhab Alam. Baichan's success did him little good because he was not given many more opportunities, even when Greenidge failed in Australia.

Roy Fredericks made 58 against Australia at the Oval in the preliminary round of the Prudential Cup. He was at the other end when Kallicharran made his famous attack on Lillee, and took the West Indies to within sight of victory. Fredericks started the Final at Lord's in a most unusual way. He hooked the same Lillee for a spectacular six. At least, it should have been a six, but in completing the stroke Roy fell into the stumps and broke his wicket. Greenidge's best innings was 55 against New Zealand in the semi-final at the Oval. His second-wicket stand with Kallicharran put the verdict beyond all reasonable doubt.

When the West Indies went to Australia in 1975/76 they had their most experienced opening partnership since Rae and Stollmeyer. Their meeting with the fast bowlers 'down under' was equally traumatic. In the first Test Match at Brisbane the flamboyant Lillee had Greenidge lbw before he scored, and Gilmour (who was being described prematurely as a second Davidson) dismissed him for a second duck. The Barbadian had a nightmare tour, and did not reach double figures in any of his four innings. Fredericks batted unevenly, but enjoyed perhaps his greatest performance ever in the second Test at Perth. Following Australia's score of 329, Fredericks and Julien, the temporary opener, let drive a stream of unorthodox shots which took the bowlers completely by surprise. The partnership of 91 was achieved at something more than 9 runs an over. Roy's own century came up at almost a run a minute. Eventually Greg Chappell caught him off Lillee for 169. The bewildered Australians were too stunned to resist Andy Roberts's match-winning bowling. Fredericks was more defensive in the third Test at Melbourne. He made a hesitant top score of 59 as Thomson and Lillee broke through the batting on the first day.

With Greenidge out of the running Rowe was moved up the order again for the series against India. He and Fredericks combined well and crowned their partnership with a stand of 105 in the fourth Test at Kingston. Roy was run out after hitting 82 on a pitch which assisted Chandrasekhar. Rowe, who did not reach 50 that season, came very close when Kirmani stumped him off Bedi for 47. Either Gordon Greenidge, Lawrence Rowe or Viv Richards—all of whom had been tried in the position—could have joined Fredericks in England in 1976. The first-named did enough in the early games to merit preference, especially as Richards had established himself lower in the order.

Fredericks was now sure enough of himself to try out his hook shot before he was really settled. Sometimes it came off, as when he hit Lillee's second ball straight into the crowd at Perth, but in the first over of the second Test at Lord's he struck a tempting delivery from Chris Old to John Snow in the deep. Larry Gomes and Kallicharran were soon in the pavilion with him. Greenidge and Lloyd stopped the slide with 99 runs for the fourth wicket. Left-armer Derek

Underwood accounted for both of them. The Barbadian, who was hitting out fearlessly, was caught for 84. With nobody else making a worth-while contribution the tourists were 68 runs behind. The loss of the entire third day through rain and England's inexplicable batting crawl seemed to rule out any result other than a draw. Fredericks started slowly, but increased the tempo of his run-scoring until he raised the outside possibility of a win. That option ended with his dismissal to a catch at deep mid-off for 138.

He was out for another duck at Manchester in exactly the same manner as at Lord's. Mike Selvey, a moderate seamer brought in because of the large number of injuries to key players, dismissed Richards and Kallicharran as well in the same session. Greenidge should have gone also, but he was missed when the wicket-keeper and nearest fieldsman got in a tangle over a catch. He used his extra life to punish the bowling with another exciting exhibition of strokes in making 134 out of 211. None of the other 21 batsmen in the first innings came within a hundred of him, a fact which underlines the value of his performance in bad batting conditions. England made only 71. The West Indies were so far ahead that Fredericks and Greenidge could again strike out confidently. They hammered 116 before the former hit his own wicket for 50. Gordon did not stop until he reached his second hundred of the game.

The two opening batsmen scored so quickly on the first morning of the fourth Test at Leeds that they had 147 runs on the board by lunchtime. Memories of Victor Trumper and Reggie Duff in 1902! The stand ended eventually at 192. Fredericks made 109, and Greenidge 115. It was the latter's third hundred in as many innings, and more than adequate atonement for any shortcomings in Australia. He could expect to fail some time, and did so at the Oval. Bob Willis had him lbw before he had even opened his account. Fredericks scored a typical 71 in a second-wicket stand with Viv Richards. As Clive Lloyd did not enforce the follow-on Fredericks (86 not out) and Greenidge (85 not out) knocked the final nail in England's coffin with an undefeated 182 in not much over two hours.

The batting suffered a reaction from its surfeit of success, and was less steady against Pakistan in 1977. Once more it was a question of one outstanding innings compensating for several failures elsewhere in the order. Fredericks and Greenidge were the honourable exception. They dealt as firmly as ever with the new-ball bowling of Sarfraz Nawaz, Salim Altaf and Imran Khan. Roy made an important 52 in the second innings of the first Test at Bridgetown, and 120 in the next encounter at Port of Spain. At their second attempt the openers put on 97, with left-handed Fredericks scoring 57 and right-handed Greenidge 70, which was the foundation of the victory by 6 wickets. Greenidge resumed the more aggressive role with 91 in the third Test at Georgetown. The West Indies led by 254 runs, but Pakistan responded admirably to the challenge. Majid Khan batted gloriously. He made 167 in raising 219 for the first wicket with Sadiq Mohammad, who retired injured, and Zaheer Abbas. The tourists reached 540 in their drive to save the match. The West Indian openers, however, continued to play attractive cricket on the final day. Greenidge was caught by Haroon Rashid off Imran Khan for 96, his second near-century of the game. His partner made an undefeated 52 out of the runs they put on.

Pakistan levelled the rubber in winning by 266 runs at Port of Spain. Their captain, Mustaq Mohammad, had a personal triumph with 121 and 56, plus 8 wickets in all. Yet again everything hung on the fifth Test at Kingston. Greenidge gave another superlative batting demonstration by making exactly 100. Almost alone he stood up to the ordeal of fast bowler Imran Khan, who took 6 wickets for 90. Fredericks, who had announced his impending retirement from international cricket, and Greenidge went out together for the last time in the second innings. They had developed a Midas touch and would not be denied. It was a vintage occasion. The stand was not broken until they had scored 182 runs—Greenidge 82 and Fredericks 83. In spite of Asif Iqbal's century, Pakistan went under by 140 runs.

Roy Fredericks and Gordon Greenidge comprised arguably the greatest West Indian first-wicket pairing of all time. How easy would it be to find a suitable replacement?

CHAPTER NINETEEN
Viv Richards

Viv Richards in his prime looks more ominously secure than any batsman I have seen. Older writers and former opponents have written the same about George Headley. That is quite a compliment, for Rohan Kanhai, Clive Lloyd and even Gary Sobers were vulnerable in their desire to get on with the scoring. Everton Weekes was merciless when he was in the mood, and perhaps Clyde Walcott was in the same league on firm Caribbean pitches. Richards has proved his value under all conditions in four continents, and his sound technique does not inhibit his scoring rate or his entertainment value. He makes his runs all round the wicket with every stroke in the book. From the moment Viv comes down the pavilion steps a long and forceful innings seems inevitable. As an attacking batsman he has an impenetrable defence, and as a defensive batsman he is irresistible in attack. Added to that, he is probably the best close-in ground fielder in the world.

Maurice Foster of Jamaica was probably the batsman displaced by Richards in the widespread growth of middle-order batting talent during Clive Lloyd's leadership. He had every quality, but the ability to keep his place. Foster was unfortunate to play Abid Ali into his stumps with his score at 99 in the fifth Test Match at Port of Spain in 1971. That was the game in which Gavaskar's double century picked the tourists up from a 166 runs deficit. The West Indians themselves struggled on the last day, finishing almost 100 runs behind with just 2 wickets to fall. The Jamaican's best effort was 125 against Australia in the first Test Match at Kingston, which enabled the West Indies to tie on first innings in spite of some tight medium-fast bowling by Max

Walker and Jeff Hammond. Foster was the regular reserve batsman down to the series against Bobby Simpson's side in 1978.

Viv Richards and Andy Roberts were sent to England for further cricket education by the Volunteers' Cricket Committee in Antigua. They were lucky to develop at this time, as the smaller islands had been almost totally ignored by selectors and administrators until the late 1960s. While Richards joined Somerset his compatriot played for Hampshire alongside Gordon Greenidge. All three youngsters were called for service against India in 1974/75. Viv's debut was undistinguished, but he cut loose in the second Test Match at New Delhi. Bowled out for 220, India won the initial exchanges as the West Indians suffered for sending in too many nightwatchmen instead of specialist batsmen on the first evening. In spite of his inexperience, Richards dominated stands with Lloyd and Boyce with a succession of boundary shots. He was 192 not out when the innings closed with both Gibbs and Roberts being run out. The West Indies won without having to bat a second time. The Antiguan scored 50 against the triumphant Indian spinners in the fourth Test Match at Madras. Because of his youthful impatience, he failed to realize his real potential in the remaining games.

Although he did not come off with the bat, Richards the fielder was a popular attraction in the first Prudential Cup competition. He showed lightning reflexes in running out Doug Walters in the preliminary round match against Australia at the Oval, and he bowled top-scorer Ross Edwards with his occasional off-breaks. Richards's adequate slow bowling was useful in allowing his captain to dispense with a specialist spinner. He did more than anyone else to win the Final. Ian Chappell and Alan Turner retaliated strongly after the West Indies had powered their way to 291–8 in their 60 overs. Viv broke the partnership by running out Turner, who chanced a run when the fieldsman seemed to fumble, and produced a brilliant turn of speed to send back Greg Chappell. As if that wasn't enough, he made Ian Chappell his third run-out victim. The Australian captain had seemed the batsman most likely to take the title from the West Indies.

Richards began the Australian tour with a duck against Dennis Lillee at Brisbane. He didn't do much better afterwards. Clive Lloyd was in such a quandary about the brittle first-wicket position that he moved him there for the fifth Test Match at Adelaide. It was a fateful decision. The Antiguan saw Gilmour dismiss Fredericks without a run scored. He made a competent 30 himself, and then really settled down in the second innings by making 101 with a confidence he had not shown since New Delhi. Australia won at a canter as expected, but had to fight harder than in either of the two previous games. When the tourists were out for 160 in the sixth Test Match at Melbourne Viv made their only 50. Lillee with his express speed and left-armer Gilmour made the ball lift awkwardly in taking 5 wickets each. There was nothing except honour left to play for in the last innings of that disappointing season. Richards went out defiantly, caught Greg Chappell bowled Lillee 98. Now that he was not getting out through impatience, nervousness or inexperience before he got started, Viv was producing results in keeping with his promise. Even so, his most ardent supporter would not have forecast the flood of runs which flowed from his bat in the next twelve months.

The Indians came to the Caribbean cast in their traditional role of sacrificial stepping stones for the West Indies to recover confidence after failure in Australia. It had so happened in 1962, and also in 1953, when the touring bowlers could not get past Everton Weekes. This time Viv Richards was the stumbling-block. Moving down the order again, he survived a shaky start through lapses in the field to score 142 in the first Test Match at Bridgetown. True to form, the tourists were outplayed by an innings and 97 runs. The Indian batsmen improved in Trinidad, where they have usually fared better than anywhere else in the region. Sunil Gavaskar and Brijesh Patel hit centuries in establishing a lead of 161 in the second Test Match. Bishen Bedi and his bowlers held the initiative from the moment Madalal bowled Fredericks for no score. Richards struck 130 of the 239 which came from the bat. The West Indies were lucky to get off with a draw.

When the third Test was moved to Port of Spain also Richards completed his third and best century in consecutive matches. Chandrasekhar, who bowled either very well or very badly, was at his best, and Bedi's tantalizing flighted spin induced the other batsmen into error. The Antiguan remained unperturbed, and scored a near-faultless 177. Since Lloyd had sent him in first at Adelaide, he had acquired four hundreds in five games, with 98 in the other. India surprised their hosts by getting over 400 to win in the last innings. Gavaskar and Mohinder Amarnath laid the groundwork with some careful batting. Viswanath was more aggressive, and inspired his colleagues to their victory by 6 wickets. It was better than the

Viv Richards

performance of Don Bradman's Australians at Leeds in 1948. Richards concluded the series modestly with 64 at Kingston for an average of 92·66.

This superb batsman, surely the best right-hander in the post-war era, was seemingly unbowlable against England in 1976. He handled pace or speed with equal assurance. Although he favoured driving or tucking the ball round to fine-leg, Viv mastered practically every scoring shot. The first Test was played on the batsmen's paradise at Nottingham. Frank Worrell scored 261 there in 1950, and carried his bat for 191 not out seven years later. Basil Butcher made another double century in 1966. Somebody had to get runs, and this time it was Richards. He attacked while the injured Kallicharran defended in a third-wicket stand of 303 which left England sagging at the end of the first day. Although the rest of the batting caved in suddenly, Viv's mammoth 232 gave the West Indies an unshakable grip on the drawn game. He missed the second Test at Lord's through injury, making his aggregate for the rest of the summer all the more remarkable.

Bowled by Selvey before he had settled, Richards had a rare failure in the third Test at Manchester. He started his second innings with the West Indies 256 in front and Greenidge set for another hundred. The Antiguan piled on the agony. He made 135, and the battered Englishmen lost by 425 runs. The Caribbean cricket steamroller was on the road. The next match at Leeds was closer, the margin being only 55 runs, due to centuries by Tony Greig and Alan Knott and a West Indian batting slide in the second innings. England's resolute fight-back failed because the tourists had built such a commanding position on the first morning. With the two openers passing three figures, Richards weighed in with 66, bringing the total to 330–3 when he was out. The home country did much better after that, but it was too late to make any difference. The pundits argued long as to whether Greenidge or Richards was the better batsman. I have found the Barbadian the more entertaining because of his sheer brilliance and the ever-present feeling that he would do something unpredictable. Richards is far more sure and professional. Since he got over his first two international series it is difficult to imagine him doing anything stupid.

Viv's performance in the fifth Test at the Oval confirmed that impression. Greenidge went early, but the Antiguan continued on and on. He added 159 with Roy Fredericks for the second wicket, 191 with Lawrence Rowe for the third, and 174 with Clive Lloyd for the fourth. Richards gave hardly a chance. This was unbowlability par excellence. He passed Worrell's highest individual score by a West Indian in England. Gary Sobers's world record was in his sights. Having struck Greig's innocuous off-spin for six to reach 291, he faced the next ball without due concentration, and diverted it into his stumps. It was the stroke of a tired man. The West Indies amassed 687–8 declared. Dennis Amiss's own double century and a total of 435 could not save England from another humiliating defeat. Richards's record for the rubber was 829 runs at an average of 118·42 in four matches. Donald Bradman, Walter Hammond and Neil Harvey, the only batsmen to make more, played in five. He eclipsed the aggregates of Clyde Walcott against Australia in 1955, Gary Sobers against Pakistan in 1957/58, and Everton Weekes in India in 1948/49.

Without really failing, Richards went through a quiet patch against Pakistan in 1977. He registered two half-centuries, and finished seventh in the averages. The closing stages of the first Test Match at Bridgetown that year were extremely bizarre. Pakistan started their second innings a mere 14 runs ahead. When the first nine batsmen were out the West Indies could afford to celebrate. The unorthodox southpaw Wasim Raja and wicket-keeper Wasim Bari added another 133 for the last wicket, helped by a record 68 extras. Fredericks and Richards batted so soundly in their second-wicket stand of 130 that it seemed that only slow scoring could prevent them from winning. As he tried to quicken the run-rate Viv was caught by Sadiq Mohammad off Sarfraz Nawaz for 92. Now it was the turn of the Pakistani fast bowlers to take over; altogether eight wickets went down in the course of 75 runs. The last two batsmen scrambled another 34 to keep the game drawn, though 55 runs short of the required total. Whereas the West Indian bowlers delivered 28 no-balls, the Pakistanis sent down 31.

Deryck Murray's place as wicket-keeper was never challenged. He was the last survivor of Frank Worrell's team, and as vice-captain was invaluable in reasserting morale after the depressing years of transition. The Trinidadian made several useful batting contributions. This was first obvious when he made 90 in the second Test at Bridgetown in 1973. He scored 53 not out against England on the same ground the next year. Deryck showed that his run-scoring was more than a fluke by notching 91 in the fifth Test Match at Bombay in 1974/75. Until he was caught by Patel off Karsan Ghavri he put on 250 runs with Lloyd for the sixth wicket.

Murray's name will always be associated with the preliminary-round match of the Prudential Cup against Pakistan at Birmingham in 1975. Majid Khan, Wasim Raja and Mustaq Mohammad passed 50 in a total of 266–7. The West Indian reply started badly, with Sarfraz Nawaz taking 4 wickets for 44. Five wickets were down for 99, and in spite of Clive Lloyd's flurry of resistance the eighth batsman was out at 151. Although his batting was not considered highly, the wicket-keeper masterminded that narrow victory. He remained calm throughout the critical overs, encouraged Holder and then Roberts, and stuck to his post in making 61 not out. Few innings in official Test Matches have been as valuable.

The Trinidadian was more reliable than many of the specialist batsmen in Australia. He scored 66, after the first six men were out for 99, and 55 in the first Test at Brisbane, making further half-centuries at Perth and Sydney. With the rapid improvement in West Indian batting during 1976 Murray's contributions were not needed so frequently. He scored an important 71 against India at Kingston, and 52 against Pakistan at Bridgetown. Deryck Murray would not have been selected for his batting alone, but he was certainly useful. As the most regular wicket-keeper since Gerry Alexander, he has stood up to two generations of pace, from Wesley Hall and Charlie Griffith to Andy Roberts and Michael Holding.

Collis King ousted Larry Gomes in the team against England in 1976. He is a lively striker of the ball, and a medium-fast bowler to supplement the pace attack. King scored 58 when the West Indian second innings seemed to be coming apart at Leeds, and 63 in more secure circumstances at the Oval. He reminded me much of a young Seymour Nurse or Collie Smith, and I hoped that his direct approach to batting would not hinder his career by putting him in bad grace with the selectors. As it happened he missed most of the visit by the Pakistanis in 1977 due to injury. His replacement was veteran Irvine Shillingford from Dominica, who had been considered a candidate for the West Indies team since his kinsman, fast bowler Grayson Shillingford, played against England in 1969. More subdued and with better batting control than King, he scored 120 in the third Test Match at Georgetown. International recognition came to him too late.

The West Indian potential team for the forthcoming series against Australia in 1978 was indeed formidable. It is difficult to imagine any time, in any country, when so much cricket talent was readily available. With only Roy Fredericks's successor to be determined, the eventual line-up could very well have been Gordon Greenidge, Viv Richards, Alvin Kallicharran, Clive Lloyd, Collis King or Irvine Shillingford, Deryck Murray, Michael Holding, Andy Roberts, Colin Croft and Joel Garner or Wayne Daniel. They had come a long way since their defeats on the other side of the world, and were strongly favoured to avenge themselves on a touring side which though still very good may have been slightly past its best. However instead of the Test Match series becoming the confrontation which everyone so devoutly wished, one Australian who was not even in the party scuttled the entire season at a stroke.

It is now time to tell his story.

CHAPTER TWENTY
The Packer and Prudential Age

Controversy has never been far from cricket, but now it escalated swiftly, and on an international scale. One dispute seemed about to destroy the cohesion of the successful 1976 touring side to England even before it reached home. Jamaica and Guyana were threatening to take action against any cricketers who had appeared to encourage established sport in South Africa. The careers of John Shepherd and Geoff Greenidge were almost certainly affected by their involvement, and even such august personalities as Rohan Kanhai did not escape criticism. These two territories threatened to refuse to receive any visiting teams so 'contaminated', and carried out this sanction against the Young England tourists. With Australia moving nearer to closer links with South Africa, it seemed that world cricket would be divided on racial and territorial lines.

Suddenly the 'South African' challenge was swamped by a new and greater crisis. Within a remarkably short time the leading West Indians, with the support of many of the more radical anti-colonialist spokesmen, were lining up with South African players against the 'official' teams of the International Cricket Conference. The intervention of one entrepreneur, Kerry Packer, split the game on quite a different issue. The international schism cut friend from friend, administrator from administrator, and supporter from supporter. The walk-out of the leading Australian cricketers in the years leading up to the First World War was mild in comparison, and so was the dissension which affected the All England XI midway through the last century.

The dilemma began when Mr Packer was refused exclusive rights to cover official Test Matches in Australia through his television network. He responded by signing the world's leading players to participate in his own World Series Cricket tournament, where instant entertainment replaced tradition. The storm broke during the Australian tour of England in 1977. At first it seemed that only those two countries were involved, but the West Indies and Pakistan were also implicated within the year. England were most effective in rebuilding their team after the defection of former captain Tony Greig, wicket-keeper Alan Knott, Derek Underwood, Dennis Amiss and Bob Woolmer. The selectors were already revising the side after the humiliating defeat by the West Indies, and were more favourably inclined to the introduction of younger talent.

Australia was hit particularly severely in losing the recently retired Ian Chappell and Ian Redpath, current captain Greg Chappell, fast bowler Dennis Lillee, wicket-keeper Rodney Marsh, and practically all of the incumbent team and their immediate reserves. Their attempt to rebuild the side under the direction and leadership of veteran Bobby Simpson was hampered by the later departure of controversial fast bowler Jeff Thomson and almost every youngster who seemed to be making good. The Pakistanis wavered at first in their allegiance. It seemed that they were prepared to go along with the other countries in excluding any player who had signed with World Series Cricket, but they changed their minds after a one-sided defeat in England.

The situation in the West Indies was more delicate than anywhere else. By the beginning of the rubber against Australia in 1978 the established team had divided almost equally between the two codes. A rush of the younger players to join Packer before the start of the third Test at Georgetown provoked a final 'showdown', even though the selectors had tried to keep the peace initially by including members from both camps. Admittedly the Australian magnate seemed to have more to offer cricket in the Caribbean than elsewhere. He had the double trump cards of financial investment in facilities and the contracts of the players whom the public most wanted to see. West Indian spectators had been starved of much first-class cricket through so many Test Match representatives making their homes in England, away from the traditional club environment. The commercial game also promised to do more to improve standards throughout the region than the conventional authorities had achieved in decades.

The Packer and Prudential Age

Naturally, when it came the Australian challenge was weaker than at any time in that country's hundred years of international cricket. Even the 1912 side, depleted as it was by the absence of most of its leading members, could count on quality cricketers in Charlie Macartney, Charles Kelleway, Warren Bardsley and Syd Gregory. Bobby Simpson, summoned back to the captaincy after ten years in retirement, had only one player, fast bowler Jeff Thomson, who would have been sure of his place in a full national side. Of the newcomers, Gary Cosier and Graham Yallop had impressed against Clive Lloyd's touring team two years earlier, but they had done nothing since then to further their promise. Against the full might which the West Indies could muster it was obviously no true contest.

As expected, the West Indies won the first two games without really trying. The fast bowling of Andy Roberts, Colin Croft and Joel Garner was far too good for the Australians. Unless something happened the remaining matches would have developed into one-way annihilation. Something did happen, of course. There was a dispute about team-selection, concerning particularly the younger Packer players, and Clive Lloyd walked out with most of the team who were contracted to World Series Cricket. Alvin Kallicharran, the one regular member to stand out against the commercial tide, was given the task of patching together a side of recalled veterans and newcomers hardly known outside their own territory. It was not easy. Kerry Packer's organization had signed up-and-coming talent such as Richard Austin and Jim Allen, and those from the recent past like David Holford, as well as the current crop.

The last three fixtures, therefore, were contested more evenly. Each side won a victory, and Australia had the better of a disreputable draw in the fifth Test Match at Kingston. It was enough for the West Indies to win the rubber. Any hopes that the reconstituted team might come to fill the place of its predecessor disappeared during the six Test Matches against India in 1978/79. With defeat by 3 wickets at Madras, the only game brought to a definite conclusion, the West Indies lost in that country for the first time. Their defeat was made the more painful by their hosts' own drubbing at the hands of Pakistan just a few weeks beforehand. The batting could have passed muster. The bowling failed to make any impression at all. Sunil Gavaskar started the series with 205 at Bombay, registered a century in each innings at Calcutta and finished with an aggregate of 732 runs. India made their highest ever Test score with 566-8 dec at New Delhi, and beat it with 644-7 dec in the next game at Kanpur. Gavaskar and Vengsarkar put on 344 in an unbroken second-wicket stand at Calcutta. It was worse than 1971.

Alvin Kallicharran did his best to set a good example. That was the trouble: his success only showed up the lack of talent elsewhere. The little Guyanese left-hander made the top score of 127 against Australia in the first Test Match at Port of Spain before the split. He was obviously back to his very best, and it was disappointing that the new flowering of his batting should have occurred in these difficult circumstances. During the fourth Test in Trinidad he shepherded his inexperienced colleagues through a difficult crisis before he was caught by Yallop off Wayne Clark for 92. With the exception of Clem Hill, Frank Woolley and possibly Roy Fredericks, has any other batsman ended his most valuable innings so often in the nineties? Alvin hit his second century of the season at Kingston, when the West Indies had to score 369 to win. Kallicharran resisted resolutely with 126, but the young batsmen were confused by spinners Bruce Yardley and Jim Higgs. On Vanburn Holder's dismissal at 258-9 the crowd invaded the pitch, and the match was abandoned for the day. The umpires refused to extend play into a sixth morning, so that Australia were denied a certain victory.

Kallicharran continued to score heavily in India. He came close to matching Sunil Gavaskar's double century in the first Test at Bombay with his own 187. No other West Indian batsman came within a hundred of him: that was the size of the problem. Alvin picked up another 71 at Bangalore, and 55 at Calcutta. In the latter game the tourists were ahead on first innings, but, chasing 335 to win, were poised precariously at 197-9 when bad light brought the proceedings to a close. Kallicharran was out for 98, typically short of a century, at Madras. Whereas his batting place was assured in a combined West Indian eleven, he must have realized that his captaincy would be forfeit whenever the Packer players returned. Alvin has a safe pair of hands anywhere in the field; and he is an incessant chatterer in the slips.

In his first two official Test Matches before departing to commercial cricket, Desmond Haynes of Barbados proved himself a worthy successor of Roy Fredericks. His bright batting had the ring of a young Conrad Hunte. Haynes made 61 in his stand of 87 with Gordon Greenidge in the first match at Port of Spain, and top score of 66 in the first innings at Bridgetown, where Thomson took 6 wickets for 77. Greenidge and Haynes knocked up 131 with some spectacular strokes as the West Indies won in a flourish by 9 wickets. Desmond was out for 55, and his partner scored 80 not out. The ragged Australian pace bowlers would have suffered a tough test if these two openers had played throughout the series.

As it was, Alvin Greenidge of Barbados, the third of his name and island to play in the position during the decade, and Basil Williams of Jamaica went in first at Georgetown. Greenidge scored 56 while the other batsmen made little of Thomson and Clark. Williams made exactly 100 in the second innings; West Indian opening batsmen have a habit of hitting centuries on their international debut. The Jamaican played well in difficult conditions for his 87 in the fourth Test Match at Port of Spain. Later in the same game Greenidge countered another batting breakdown with 69. The West Indies won by 198 runs, and clinched the rubber. It seemed then that the World Series cricketers might not even be missed.

Alvin Greenidge lost his way and his place in India. Karsan Ghavri and Kapil Dev gave the pace bowling its sharpest edge for many years. Faoud Bacchus of Guyana, who could also have qualified to represent Canada, was the find of the tour. He scored 96 at Bangalore, and 61 in the follow-on at New Delhi. Williams's best innings was 111 at Calcutta. Young Bacchus had the last word by hitting 250 in the sixth Test at Kanpur. As Jumadeen's 56 was the next highest, he saved by himself a game in which three Indians made hundreds.

Clive Lloyd set a cracking pace with 86 against Australia in the first Test at Port of Spain. He put on 170 for the fourth wicket at an even pace with his successor, Kallicharran. His compatriot Sew Shivnarine did not have the same compelling charisma to bring to the middle batting. He had other gifts, though, and propped up a sagging first innings at Georgetown with 53, before scoring 63 in the second. Shivnarine, who was chosen primarily for his left-arm bowling, came to the rescue again at Kingston by scoring another 53 after the first five batsmen were out for 63. His 62 at Bangalore was his only half-century on a disappointing Indian tour.

Left-handed Larry Gomes was the new discovery. The young Trinidadian developed his game with Middlesex, but failed against England in 1976, perhaps because he was too inexperienced. Nevertheless, he grasped the second life which the withdrawals at Georgetown provided for him. When Basil Williams's attacking century ended in that match Larry provided a steady 101 to take the West Indies to 439. It couldn't save the match, but it made the Australians fight desperately hard. The mature Gomes, who had curbed his previous impetuosity, held the first innings together with 115 at Kingston. Larry began the series against India with three successive half-centuries, and scored 91 out of 151 in the fourth Test at Madras.

Deryck Murray had one further chance to show his batting dependability. By scoring 60 he eked out a narrow lead of 38 runs against Australia in the second Test at Bridgetown. He had already destroyed the backbone of the tourists' innings by catching Serjeant, Cosier and Simpson. For good measure he dismissed the first two in the second innings as well. He was succeeded by his namesake and understudy, David Murray of Barbados. The latter was already near to selection as a specialist batsman. He scored 84 in supporting Kallicharran at Bombay, and 66 when everyone else failed at Calcutta. Maybe that wasn't quite as much as he had hoped or expected.

Andy Roberts, Colin Croft and Joel Garner shared the attack at Port of Spain and Bridgetown, as Michael Holding still wasn't available. In remembering the tribulations of their own batsmen against Lindwall and Lillee, the West Indians could afford a wry smile at the havoc which the fast bowlers wrought against these ill-prepared Australians. On their first encounter Croft struck immediately by sending back Graeme Wood, Serjeant and Yallop in his 4 wickets for 15. Australia were routed for 90. When they went in again Roberts took 5 wickets for 56 as the score crashed from 200–6 to 209 all out. All three pacemen shared the honours in Barbados. Simpson's colts were helpless against the tornado which hit them.

Norbert Phillip from Dominica, one of the less prominent islands, and Barbadian Sylvester Clarke opened the revamped attack. At Georgetown the former was too sharp for batsmen softened up by the previous battery of speed. He took 4 wickets for 75 as Australia slipped to 142–6 before Simpson made the score more respectable. Phillip, who took over Boyce's berth in the Essex side, was one of the successes of the English domestic season in 1978, and he was looked upon as the bowler most likely to succeed in India. Unfortunately, Clarke and Norbert combined effectively only at Madras, where each took 4 wickets in a low-scoring match. The Barbadian took 5 wickets for 126 at Bangalore, but the fast bowlers were handled harshly by

The Packer and Prudential Age

Gavaskar and Chauhan. Vanburn Holder was recalled as vice-captain to Kallicharran and the third string in the pace attack. He was not finished yet. The West Indies struggled to make 292 in the fourth Test Match at Port of Spain and Australia were going well at 255-5, at which point Holder took the new ball. The innings ended 35 runs later, and he had 6 wickets for 28. Vanburn took another 4 wickets for 94 at Bombay, where he had been so devastating on the last tour.

Derek Parry of Nevis was the most promising spin bowler to develop since Lance Gibbs. He won his initial recognition before the Packer players withdrew. As nightwatchman Parry scored 51 at Georgetown, and followed with 65 at Port of Spain as the score progressed from 151-6 to 290. Australia, who had kept the game close until then, needed 293 to square the rubber. They stuttered to 72-5, and then the young off-spinner swept through the tail with 5 wickets for 15. He hit the stumps of the last four batsmen. Derek faded in India after his 55 at Bombay. Raphick Jumadeen, the Trinidad left-arm spinner, supported Parry at Port of Spain and rounded off the Australian innings at Kingston with 4 wickets for 72. Though making 56 at Kanpur, he had no success as a bowler against India.

A temporary truce was called in the summer of 1979 when the West Indies, like Pakistan, selected their team for the Prudential Cup competition from both commercial and conventional sides. The party comprised ten World Series Cricket players, and just four who had been with the official team in India, of whom only one, Alvin Kallicharran, actually appeared in the matches. Reunited under Clive Lloyd's leadership, the West Indies were so strong in batting and fast bowling that they could afford to dispense with a specialist spinner. They were strong favourites to retain the trophy which they had won four years previously.

Michael Holding and Gordon Greenidge were the stars of the victory by 9 wickets over India at Birmingham. The young fast bowler, who took 4 wickets, generated unexpected pace on a comparatively docile pitch. Only Gundappa Viswanath with 75 confronted him with any confidence. Greenidge and Haynes continued as they had left off against Australia by scoring 138 for the first wicket. The former excelled with a full repertoire of drives, hooks and cuts in his 106 not out. The scheduled game against Sri Lanka at the Oval was washed out, and the West Indies qualified for the semi-final in beating New Zealand by 32 runs at Nottingham. The match lacked real lustre. Greenidge and Lloyd, each of whom made a half-century, put the West Indians early in command, but the other batsmen were strangely out of touch. The New Zealanders did not buckle under the fast-bowling assault. They stood their ground admirably, and came closer than anyone else in the competition to dethroning the champions. On the other hand, their batsmen did not score with sufficient urgency to put the West Indies under any real pressure.

The fast bowlers came in for some unexpected punishment against Pakistan at the Oval. The West Indies batted first. In making his third consecutive half-century Greenidge batted brilliantly against possibly the best bowling the West Indians had faced since the last tour to Australia. Once again Haynes supported him well, and the middle batting pushed the score along at speed. The total of 293-7 was almost impregnable in this type of cricket. However, Zaheer Abbas and Majid Khan hit back with some delightful strokes in their stand of 166 runs for the second wicket. The faster the bowling the quicker they scored. Colin Croft found sufficient pace and variation to have Zaheer Abbas caught brilliantly by Deryck Murray and take two more wickets as the Pakistani batting suddenly collapsed. The West Indies won by 43 runs.

Lloyd's team overwhelmed England by 92 runs in the final at Lord's. The English seam bowlers restricted scoring in the morning session, but there was never any doubt about the result once Viv Richards and Collis King cut loose in the hour after lunch. While the latter threw his bat with unconventional brilliance, Richards played confidently and professionally. King was out for a whirlwind 86, and the Antiguan made an undefeated match-winning 138. The English openers, Geoff Boycott and Mike Brearley, spent so long at the crease that their successors had to take needless risks in trying to quicken the pace in the remaining overs available. Consequently the bowlers just had to aim straight and fast. The last 8 wickets went down for 11 runs in 16 balls. Joel Garner hit the stumps four times in dismissing five batsmen, and Croft took the other three. The West Indies were world champions again ... and without serious opposition.

On the eve of the competition the Australian authorities issued a statement of an agreement between themselves and Kerry Packer which promised to heal the schism. More than any other team the West Indies were prepared to let bygones be bygones, but there was still much negotiating to be done. The World Series Cricket

The Packer and Prudential Age

administrators wanted to protect the future in conventional Test Matches of the players contracted to them, and insisted on certain rescheduling of tours to Australia. These proposals were accepted by the International Cricket Conference. Hardly had this particular row apparently died down than the contentious subject of South Africa was raised yet again. It seemed a very long cry since the first West Indian tourists had fallen about laughing as Gilbert Jessop hit their bowling all over the ground. It has become a far different game, and a totally different world, since then.

CHAPTER TWENTY-ONE
Recollection and Reflection

It is appropriate and significant that this history of Caribbean cricketers has been written in England, because for half a century at least this country has been a real centre of West Indian cricket. There has been little conception of a regional entity in the Antilles themselves. The earliest players owed their first loyalty to their club and island, and later were regarded as West Indians only when they were touring overseas, while the modern international cricketer is really too cosmopolitan for local identification. Each territory is marked by its own unique style and approach to the game. Trinidad was foremost in the development of Caribbean cricket, and more recently has specialized in stylish, wispy batsmen and spin bowlers. The Barbadian contribution has depended on physically powerful batsmen and fast bowlers. The leading Guyanese are left-handed stroke-players. Jamaica has tended to rear one, or sometimes two, outstanding individual in each generation. The Windward and Leeward Islands have come into Test Match competition too late for any distinctive style to have been formulated, unless it is an aptitude for all-round excellence.

Writers have a tendency to explain the development of sport in terms of the social environment in which it has been played. Though fashionable, this approach can be misleading. In the summer of 1979 I watched the first West Indian women's touring team lose its series against England by two games to nil. The party was drawn predominantly from Jamaica and Trinidad. The performance depended almost entirely on one player, captain Patricia Whittaker. The batting, with flashes of occasional brilliance from Shirley-Ann

Recollection and Reflection

Bonaparte and Beverley Browne, was brittle, and in spite of the efforts of big pace bowler Peggy Fairweather the attack was not incisive. The running between wickets was deplorable, and the general lack of team cohesion frustrated much talented cricket. It was very much like watching a rerun of the early matches played by the West Indian men cricketers. Even so, the social conditions differed very much from the pioneer days.

I cannot pretend to explain how and why these things have happened, only to recollect and reflect on what has happened. In order to establish a common point of reference I have had to adopt criteria of terminology, especially in respect of earlier decades where written records are scarce and sometimes contradictory. Throughout this book the venue of each match has been expressed in terms of the city or town, except in London where Lord's and the Oval have been specified to avoid confusion. Every cricket ground has a local name, but in a history which encompasses play throughout the world it is difficult to differentiate between Kensington Oval in Barbados and Kennington Oval in South London. For reference, the other principal venues in the West Indies are Sabina Park in Jamica, Queen's Park in Trinidad and Bourda in Guyana, and those in England are Old Trafford at Manchester, Trent Bridge at Nottingham, and Headingley at Leeds.

In some cases there is no common agreement on a player's full name. Astill, the English all-rounder of the 1930s, is referred to as either 'Bill' or 'Ewart'. The first names of Rolph Grant and Clairmont Depeiza are spelled variously, and the initials 'K.T.' were applied to Sonny Ramadhin throughout the 1950s without any apparent reason. The great all-rounder Sobers has been known at different times in his career as Garfield, Gary and Garry. The forename of Srinivasaraghavan Venkataraghavan, the recent Indian captain, has been abbreviated in a number of different ways. The Kentish slow bowlers of the inter-war period, Freeman and Marriott, were always called 'Tich' and 'Father' respectively. Some cricketers are identified by only their initials. It would be close to sacrilege to refer to W. G. Grace as Bill, William or even Gilbert. B. S. Chandrasekhar is a modern equivalent.

The difficulty of identification is not confined to the several S. Banerjees who contended for selection to the Indian side during the 1940s. When Australian-born Sammy (S. M. J.) Woods toured the Caribbean with an English side in the last decade of the nineteenth

203

century, his visit was returned by Sam Woods with the first West Indian team. These early parties were known either by the name of their patron or that of the captain. Thus what on the surface seems to be two distinct sides could be the same one under different names. The name Cumberbatch is mentioned several times in performances against amateur English sides, nearly always with a separate initial, so that it is nearly impossible to determine just how many were playing. As late as the more orderly 1930s nearly every record book shows R. L. Hunte scoring a half-century against England at Port of Spain, but does not include him in the list of Test Match cricketers. Until further evidence is available, I have identified him with Errol Hunte, the wicket-keeper, who made 53 in the next game at Georgetown. Even when everything about the player is known it is best to state each name in full to avoid confusing C. W. Smith (Cammie Smith) with the more readily recognized O. G. Smith (Collie Smith).

In the pioneer days club competition was the backbone of cricket in all of the main territories. Spectators were more interested in how their heroes fared against rival clubs than their performance against touring teams and overseas. Trinidadians were convinced that the English system, not the players, were out of touch when Wilton St Hill and Joe Small could not settle into the unaccustomed environment. The attitude is still prevalent in respect of those players who remain in the Caribbean. Because the standard of club cricket is so high—even though a pale reflection of its former standard—Desmond Haynes and Michael Holding can step straight into the West Indian Test Match side without wasting their youth and talents in the frustrating advance through the county championship system which spoils the best years of many promising Englishmen.

The pioneers were rarely specialists. Lebrun Constantine filled in as wicket-keeper in 1900, bowled a bit six years later and was a dependable batsman throughout. The West Indian cricketer has never lost the ability to engage in the game at all levels and with all skills. Wicket-keeper Clyde Walcott opened the bowling at Manchester in 1950, and when Pakistan seemed to be running away with the Prudential Cup semi-final match at the Oval last summer Viv Richards, the best batsman in the world, took the ball and claimed 3 important wickets. I can think of no other country where general cricketing ability is more important than a division of that ability. Some observers have drawn subjective conclusions from observing

Recollection and Reflection

that the early batsmen were predominantly white and the bowlers usually black. It is no more significant than noting that English fast bowlers have been drawn from the Derbyshire and Yorkshire coalmines as much as the batsmen have come from Oxbridge Universities ... from each according to his physical ability.

Because the early matches were more localized and restricted in their geographical extent the players became 'characters' of their neighbourhood, both treated with honour and regarded as the man next door. English supporters, who are used to seeing their heroes only on television or in print, and segregated from them at the county grounds, cannot easily understand how a West Indian with little apparent knowledge of the subject can walk up to Viv Richards, Andy Roberts or Michael Holding and offer them gratuitous advice, or even begin a conversation that has nothing to do with cricket. There is a much greater personal rapport between the West Indian player and the crowd. While the islands have very little written record of the past, there is much verbal folklore which is handed down whenever men sit around and discuss the game.

Fast bowler Woods was one of the uncomplicated cricketers around whom legends are established. The technical possibilities of a long run did not interest him. Woods bowled very fast off just two or three paces, rather like Eddie Gilbert, the unconventional Australian aborigine of the 1930s. He felt so much better with just the bare earth beneath his feet that, so it is reported, he tore off the soles of his boots before bowling. George John, another fast bowler, so dominated Trinidadian cricket just after the First World War that no captain dared to take him off. John himself always said when he had had enough. This attitude of mind goes a long way to explain the complete amazement of those who saw the young Wilton St Hill treat this venerated figure with such cavalier disdain. The arrival of international cricket, with its accent on conformity, leadership and diplomacy did as much to diminish the outstanding eccentric in the Caribbean as it did Tom Emmett and Bobby Peel in England.

George Headley and Learie Constantine became more than local heroes. By the start of the 1930s they were already international celebrities. Due to the pace of events, their fame did not seep out gradually from their homeland through the rest of the Caribbean and from thence overseas, but exploded almost overnight throughout the cricketing world. Both settled ultimately in England during their professional career, though they commuted back and forth between the two focal points of their existence. Although they were away from home—and therefore by definition less personally approachable than the earlier generation—they did not cease in any way to be West Indian cricketers. Even if it had been possible, Constantine, Martin and Francis would not have become 'English' players in the manner of K. S. Ranjitsinhji or the elder Nawab of Pataudi.

Nearly every leading West Indian cricketer from the 1920s to the early 1960s spent one or more seasons in the northern leagues. The experience broadened their ability and fitted them better for playing on unaccustomed pitches. At the same time, the few who had made this transition developed much more quickly than those who were left behind, and, particularly in the 1930s, the difference between the professionals and the other members of the side became increasingly marked. Would Leslie Hylton have faded so suddenly if he had enjoyed Learie Constantine's regular competition? As it became obvious that a young cricketer would have to come to England in order to develop his game to the required international standard, so that country, rather than his home territory, became more important to his career. Frank Worrell, Everton Weekes and Clyde Walcott learned all their skills in the Caribbean before coming to the leagues because the opportunities of their youth were restricted by the war. It is surely no mere coincidence that the successful post-war side was the first one in which every member had nearly equal merit and there was no immediately obvious gap between the talented few and the others.

Travel and competition between the territories were still almost non-existent in the years leading up to the outbreak of hostilities. Trinidadians, Barbadians and Guyanese had little opportunity of seeing the great George Headley in his prime, except in the Test Matches against England in 1929/30 and 1934/35. The thousands of English spectators, including my own parents, who saw him in the various county and international games of 1933 and 1939, were able to appreciate his batting at first hand better than any West Indians outside of Jamaica. The situation was even more pronounced in respect of the bowlers, who were frequently left out of the side for matches outside their own territories. The four overseas tours were the only real basis for moulding a definite West Indian identity, and even this was made difficult by the inability of several leading players to leave their employment for such a long time. It says much for the Caribbean character that they succeeded even against these near-impossible odds.

Recollection and Reflection

The spread of radio broadcasting and newspaper reporting made the names of West Indian cricketers known in households from Antigua to Adelaide and Barbados to Bombay. Fans of all ages could follow the progress of Sonny Ramadhin and Alfred Valentine throughout England and Australia. Non-Jamaicans who had missed out on the verbal tradition and stories concerning Headley and Martin could read everything that was written about Valentine. In this way it was possible for any Test Match representative, or even leading contenders for selection, to be recognized by a much wider public than was available even ten years previously. When the West Indies took the field against India, England and Australia between 1948 and 1952 they carried the hopes and the fears of the Caribbean with them. The days were long since gone when reports of their deeds filtered back by word of mouth several weeks after they had happened. World cricket was brought inside the front door.

The personalities of this time were still larger than life. Verbal pictures of Worrell, Weekes and Walcott were more imposing than watching the same batsmen in club matches. The reports did not have time to show up their weaknesses. To that extent the cricketers of the 1940s and 1950s were more aloof than either their predecessors or their successors. The appeal which they had for the public is illustrated best in Andy Roberts and Colin Croft of the present side (who were born during that period) each having the forename 'Everton'—and neither is a Barbadian. There was also so much more cricket available by which the players could be seen by a wider section of the community. This was the heyday of five-day competition. Whenever they were on tour the West Indians were requested individually to participate in festival and charity matches. By doing so they were able to appear at venues where few Test Match cricketers had played previously. In this way I was able to see Allan Rae at Gravesend when my scant pocket-money was not enough for me to travel to Lord's or the Oval for a first-class game.

The horizons of the international sport were expanding almost yearly. Before 1939 the West Indies had visited only England and Australia, and only the former had toured the Caribbean. Within a decade of the resumption of play Test Matches had been contested in India and New Zealand as well, and the West Indies had been hosts to India, Australia and Pakistan in addition to England. Only South Africa stood outside this general expansion. More significantly from the point of view of the future, composite Commonwealth sides had

Caribbean Cricketers

made several tours to India, and, following the bad feeling after the visit by Len Hutton's England team in 1953/54, journalist E. W. 'Jim' Swanton brought a team of talented amateurs mixed with Test Match professionals to the eastern Caribbean, and the Duke of Norfolk arranged a similar tour of Jamaica. World cricket was sprouting quickly in many directions. In retrospect 1957, the year in which I was first able to follow a West Indian tour during the school-holidays and actually speak to some of the players, was the hinged doorway between the seemingly medieval and modern times. On their return home Gary Sobers and Rohan Kanhai matured into master batsmen, and Collie Smith was killed shortly afterwards. Suddenly the whole attitude towards cricket was more professional and uncompromising.

There was too much conventional cricket in the 1960s. The outstanding players moved from the leagues into the county championship, where they had three-day cricket all the season through. With the prospect of an official West Indian tour some time in those same twelve months, club competition was finally denuded of its best participants and overshadowed by other loyalties and responsibilities. At this same time cricketers lost much of their awe-inspiring reputation in the eyes of the public. The day of the 'character' was over. The players were too busy playing and being fitted into the requirements of each evolving code of the game for their personality to be fully assessed. The West Indians were not the only ones to be affected. In this decade Australia had no-one to match the temperamental Keith Miller, and England did not find anyone to compare with Freddie Trueman. The authorities tried to halt the decline in attendances by introducing 'instant cricket', tampering with the laws and traditions, and by attempting to manipulate a spectacular result. The period of maximum alteration coincided with the 'years of transition' in which all cricket, and West Indian cricket in particular, lost its sparkle, its conviction and its ability to please.

Those administrators who struggled so hard to 'bring about a result' forgot that much really exciting international play—including the Brisbane 'tie' and the drawn game at Lord's in 1963—came about without forcing one side to yield artificially to the other. The pre-war West Indian sides did not owe their popularity to any close finishes, because they lost so consistently away from home. They were attractive through the individual qualities of their representatives. Nor was it marketable 'personality' alone. The magnet which

Recollection and Reflection

attracted Sobers, Kanhai, Gibbs, Lloyd, Procter, Barry Richards, McKenzie, Bedi and Turner into the county championship destroyed the attraction of the overseas tour. The visits of George Headley and Don Bradman were awaited with increasing expectation. Each of their innings was a moment to savour, made sweeter by the knowledge that they would not be back for another several years. Such a feeling of excited expectation could not be generated after Gary Sobers's tour in 1966 because he would be back three years later, again with the Rest of the World in 1970, and in the meanwhile could be seen any summer's day playing for Nottinghamshire. His appearances became commonplace. The administrators prostituted personality by over-exposure.

The press-box reflected these same trends. When I started working for Hayter's agency in 1961 every major newspaper had its distinguished former cricketer contributor whose opinions were valued considerably by the readers. At major matches the seats were packed with these gentlemen sitting next to their respective 'ghost', who took down their words and phrased the necessary copy for them. Translation to the press-box was as much the natural progression of successful cricketers as is a place in the House of Lords of a politician. All that has changed. The present public, which takes its first-hand information from the television and radio, prefers to read comment to the point by an anonymous scribe than any amount of worthy advice by a 'name' contributor. Those former cricketers who remain in the press belong to the Len Hutton, Denis Compton and Richie Benaud generation, with hardly any recruits since then. The 'scoop interview' was very important a decade or so ago. For example, I remember the considerable attention given to the Duke of Norfolk's comments which allegedly Keith Miller had taped with a hidden microphone while they walked in conversation around his lordship's estate at Arundel. Today the emphasis is more on what has been said than on who said it.

Since the débâcle in 1957 the West Indian record in England has been much better than in the Caribbean, a clear indication that they are now more at home here than almost anywhere else. They have won four of the last five rubbers in this country. The victories in 1973 and 1976 were by landslide proportions, and the one defeat in 1969 occurred during a process of team rebuilding when they would have lost wherever they had played. Rohan Kanhai's side ended seven years of frustration, with a confidence which disappeared as soon as they got back to the West Indies. In addition to their official Test Match triumphs, the West Indians have won the two Prudential World Cup limited-over tournaments. During this same time they have been humiliated in Australia, beaten in India, and forced to struggle to share the honours in New Zealand and Pakistan.

Cricket in the Caribbean has not been neglected. The Shell Shield competition, which was initiated in the late 1960s, was the first opportunity for the four main territories to play against each other on a regular basis. It has also provided the launching-pad for taking the game into the smaller islands. Viv Richards, Andy Roberts and the Shillingfords are among the first fruits of that missionary activity. The public now has the chance to see leading players from the other territories at home and away. While the front-line West Indians may be participating overseas, the Shell Shield and other domestic competitions have stimulated successive waves of home-produced talent. Examine the swift development of fast bowlers Keith Boyce, Andy Roberts, Michael Holding and Wayne Daniel, Colin Croft and Joel Garner, Norbert Phillip and Sylvester Clarke, and Malcolm Marshall right after each other.

Competition for selection to territorial sides has encouraged a resurgence of interest in club cricket. Like a compass with its legs set on England and the Caribbean, the West Indies are now capable of fielding two, or possibly three, sides capable of extending anybody else in the world.

South Africa had become increasingly isolated from the mainstream of international cricket. The Republic's withdrawal from the Commonwealth in 1961 adversely affected its remaining sporting and social links with the other member countries, and the last official Springbok team toured England in 1965. Australia, the last cricketing country with which they enjoyed normal relations, ended that partnership by the end of the decade. Unfortunately, South African cricket was very strong at this time and spectators in many countries wanted to see Michael Procter, Barry Richards, Graeme and Peter Pollock, Eddie Barlow and Ali Bacher in competition against the best players in the world. Individual entrepreneurs tried to bypass officialdom with visits by *ad hoc* teams such as the Cavaliers. Those adminstrations which abhorred apartheid knew that the situation could not be left to solve itself, and that steps would have to be taken either to welcome South Africa back to international competition on a compromise basis or to expel the country altogether. The attitude of

Recollection and Reflection

the West Indies was vital towards a problem which has still not been solved, and, as I have described in the previous chapter, the careers of several individuals have been harmed already.

International competition reached saturation point in the 1970s. Tours were shortened so that the main countries could visit each other more frequently. Test Matches were played in all four seasons of the year. The concentration on the 'big match' led to an immediate devaluation of the three-day game, and, in fact, of the Test Matches themselves. With Viv Richards and Andy Roberts playing almost as many times in 1976 as did Manny Martindale and George Headley in their entire careers the aggregation of runs and wickets assumed an inflationary spiral. Records were broken as a matter of course. Overseas tours have been particularly affected, with additional Test Matches and knockabout one-day games replacing the middle tier of matches against county or state sides. It is now almost impossible for an outsider to build himself into a fully fledged player during the course of a tour, as Wesley Hall did in 1958/59. That series was exactly ten years after the previous West Indian visit. These same two countries have now played each other four times in the last decade.

Television exposure, unlike radio broadcasting, has finally destroyed the mystique of a cricketer's personality. Everybody knows what each player looks like, his weaknesses, his style and even his private life. Commentators analyse his approach and attitude from dawn to dusk. Cricketers are generally too accessible and too well known. The delight of exchanging a few words with Frank Worrell or Rohan Kanhai while they were practising in the nets is no longer such a thrill to the youngster, who can see Clive Lloyd and Alvin Kallicharran interviewed on the television day after day. The modern players are too packaged and too conventional to have any identifiable marks of their own. Such exposure has destroyed the value of the 'scoop' for the journalist. I obtained some personal comments from several of the West Indian team when their match against Sri Lanka at the Oval was washed out in the last Prudential Cup competition. The information was passed directly to my newspaper, but before the next edition could be out on the street the impact of the story had been lost because one of the players had repeated exactly the same words in a television interview.

This does not mean that cricket is any worse today than it was in yesteryear. Nor does it imply a *cri de cœur* for times past. Because of their regular play against the best opposition, today's batsmen and

Caribbean Cricketers

bowlers are consistently very good. Gordon Greenidge hits as many sparkling centuries in a season as—if I dare say so—our grandfathers would have seen in a lifetime of Victor Trumper or George Challenor. It is difficult to recall a favourite shot of Viv Richards or a special type of delivery from Andy Roberts because they are very good at every aspect of their art. Fielding has improved beyond recognition. Captains do not have to worry about 'hiding' bad catchers in inconspicuous positions. The fortunes of India are a good yardstick for judging the improved quality of the world game. Sunil Gavaskar and Gundappa Viswanath are among the best batsmen that country has ever produced, and the spin-bowling quartet has rarely been equalled anywhere, but at the time of writing, India is the weakest of all Test Match teams, with a record far inferior to their own achievement when they had less talent. The face of international cricket has changed but it is still very acceptable.

Because Test Matches have replaced county games as the staple spectator diet, there has been increased demand for a new level of competition for the special occasion. The Prudential Cup has become so important because it is contested only once every four years. Kerry Packer's World Series Cricket has experimented with 'super' Test Matches. By drawing their support from several national entities, commercial patrons may be able to provide that new dimension. Great interest has been aroused by the recent series between the current West Indian team and Australia's Packer players. A 'Barry Richards' XI' of Springboks might avoid the stigma attached to an official South African side. The present picture is very similar to the mid-eighteenth century when the squire picked his team from the peasants on his estate and rich patrons such as the Duke of Dorset or Earl of Tankerville enticed the leading cricketers to their own estates. The more things change, the more they stay the same.

Cricket is not the same as it was—it never has been. Club cricket gave way to inter-territorial competition, which in turn was superseded by Test Match encounters. The pace and complexity of modern life is threatening even that structure. West Indian cricket may alter beyond recognition within the next decade, and yet West Indian cricketers will surely remain essentially the same. The talent and enthusiasm which has flowed from Charles Ollivierre to Clive Lloyd or from George John to Michael Holding will surely continue in whatever form it is called upon to manifest itself.

CHAPTER TWENTY-TWO
Towards the Future

Much has happened since the West Indies won the Prudential Cup in June 1979. As part of the process of healing the breach between commercial and conventional cricket, a triangular tournament of Test Matches and limited-over fixtures was arranged in Australia in the following winter between the three leading countries. It was the first attempt to measure comparative ability since the onset of the schism in 1977, and at the same time an experiment in tour organization. The selectors of the West Indian party retained the kernel of the side which won the world one-day tournament. The fast-bowling battery survived intact, supplemented by only one spinner, Derek Parry. The biggest surprise was the recall of Lawrence Rowe—ostensibly as the third opener—in place of Faoud Bacchus, a double-centurion in India less than a year earlier. David Murray came back into the side as the second-choice wicket-keeper.

Joel Garner and Viv Richards were instrumental in Somerset's victories in the Gillette Cup and John Player League. Encouraged by his success at Lord's, the big Barbadian extracted bounce from seemingly placid pitches, and finished first in the national bowling averages. Gordon Greenidge mastered the one-day game so completely that he has now recorded the highest individual scores in all three limited-over competitions. Norbert Phillip was in the forefront of Essex's triumph in the County Championship. Sylvester Clarke, Wayne Daniel and Phillip terrorized the English county batsmen to such a degree that their victims did not understand how these three fast bowlers could not find a place in the Test Match side.

Caribbean Cricketers

On paper at least, England seem to be more doughty adversaries in 1980 than they were four years ago, even allowing for their heavy defeat in the final of the Prudential Cup. A new breed of young players has come forward, and though the batting is still suspect by the highest standards, the first-wicket positions are the only points of immediate concern. Meanwhile the West Indies have even greater all-round ability than before, and their prospects are enhanced by the side having played four international competitions in England in the last seven years . . . winning each one.

World Series Cricketers have fared comparatively better in the West Indies than elsewhere. Only the inclusion of Alvin Kallicharran prevents their total monopoly of the first team. Some observers have described the situation as the latest stage in the development of 'player power', similar in effect to the status that the Australian cricketers won earlier in the century. If Caribbean cricket is to survive as an entity it needs a focal point of power and direction.

Every team or power structure is judged ultimately by its success on the field of play. Even before the reinstatement of those players contracted to World Series Cricket, the post-Packer official West Indian and Australian teams lost their right to recognition through their defeats in Test Matches. The united West Indian side will be tested by its performance over the conventional five-day course. The demands of WSC competition in emphasizing quick scoring at the expense of caution, and eliminating spin bowling almost entirely, may not be the most appropriate training for consistency in all circumstances, especially when the flow of talent is less abundant.

The choice of a successor to Clive Lloyd as captain must be faced sooner rather than later. The genial left-hander, who has been regularly in the side for a decade and a half, has led the West Indies to unprecedented feats of achievement. Deryck Murray, his long-serving deputy, should approach the end of his own career at about the same time. There is no immediate replacement for either. Kallicharran, perhaps the strongest contender, harmed his chances of universal acceptance by his team's failure in India. He does have the experience, however. Possibly Viv Richards could emulate Donald Bradman in becoming as great a captain as he was batsman. Any other choice at this time would risk dissension.

The strength of the present side is that so many members are in the same age group. All being well, they should stay together for another

Towards the Future

five or six years, and provide the new leader with a firm foundation. That same factor, on the other hand, is also the most glaring weakness. They could all pass their peak within a few months or matches of each other: it happened to that other victorious combination in the 1960s. If such a predicament is to be avoided new players will have to be introduced on a steady basis. It is harder to say which of the regulars should be left without weakening the balance so finely established.

Some West Indian supporters fear the next downswing of the pendulum. However, I do not think that the well of ability will dry up this time—at least, not immediately. The base of participation is much wider today than it has ever been. Almost every Caribbean territory has the chance of representation. Black youngsters in England still look to the homeland of their parents, and, whatever else it may have achieved, Kerry Packer's intervention has put Australia on a par with Lord's as a pivot of international cricket. The West Indians now play as much there as anywhere. The wheel has turned full circle back to the experience of Sam Morris almost exactly a hundred years ago.

West Indians are paramount among the game's first fully fledged world professionals. Together with the itinerant South Africans who have sought absorption among the Australians, they have taken the first positive steps towards the creation of supra-national sides to supersede the present Test Match structure. As potentially the strongest team of their age, the West Indies are indicative of contemporary cricket. We are at the threshold of the next era, and generations yet to come will envy us the opportunity of witnessing what will develop this season and in the years ahead.

Statistical Appendix

Every Test Match played by the West Indies
Note: These records apply only to Test Matches, and are updated to the start of the West Indian tour to Australia in November 1979.

1928
Lord's   England won by an innings and 58 runs
England 401 (Ernest Tyldesley 122, Percy Chapman 50, Learie Constantine 4–82): West Indies 177 (Vallance Jupp 4–37) & 166 (Joe Small 52, 'Tich' Freeman 4–37)

Manchester   England won by an innings and 30 runs
West Indies 206 (Clifford Roach 50, 'Tich' Freeman 5–54) & 115 ('Tich' Freeman 5–39): England 351 (Douglas Jardine 83, Walter Hammond 63, Herbert Sutcliffe 54, Jack Hobbs 53)

Oval   England won by an innings and 71 runs
West Indies 238 (Clifford Roach 53, Maurice Tate 4–59) & 129 ('Tich' Freeman 4–47): England 438 (Jack Hobbs 159, Herbert Sutcliffe 63, Ernest Tyldesley 73, Maurice Tate 54, Herman Griffith 6–103, George Francis 4–112)

1929/30
Bridgetown   Match drawn
West Indies 369 (Clifford Roach 122, Frank De Caires 80, Derek Sealy 58, Greville Stevens 5–105) & 384 (George Headley 176, Clifford Roach 77, Frank De Caires 70, Greville Stevens 5–90): England 467 (Andy Sandham 152, Patsy Hendren 80) & 167–3 (Andy Sandham 51)

Statistical Appendix

Port of Spain   England won by 167 runs
England 208 (Patsy Hendren 77, Herman Griffith 5-63) & 425-8 dec (Patsy Hendren 205 n.o., Leslie Ames 105, Learie Constantine 4-165): West Indies 254 (Errol Hunte 58, Learie Constantine 58, Ewart Astill 4-58, Bill Voce 4-79) & 212 (Bill Voce 7-70)

Georgetown   West Indies won by 289 runs
West Indies 471 (Clifford Roach 209, George Headley 114, Errol Hunte 53) & 290 (George Headley 112, 'Snuffy' Browne 70 n.o., Ewart Astill 4-70): England 145 (Patsy Hendren 56, Learie Constantine 4-35, George Francis 4-40) & 327 (Patsy Hendren 123, Learie Constantine 5-87)

Kingston   Match drawn
England 849 (Andy Sandham 325, Leslie Ames 149, George Gunn 85, Patsy Hendren 61, Bob Wyatt 58, Jack O'Connor 51, Tommy Scott 5-266) & 272-9 dec (Patsy Hendren 55, Andy Sandham 50, Tommy Scott 4-108): West Indies 286 (Karl Nunes 66) & 408-5 (George Headley 223, Karl Nunes 92)

1930/31
Adelaide   Australia won by 10 wickets
West Indies 296 (Edward Bartlett 84, Clifford Roach 56, Jackie Grant 53 n.o., Clarrie Grimmett 7-87) & 249 (Jackie Grant 71 n.o., Lionel Birkett 64, A. Hurwood 4-86, Clarrie Grimmett 4-96): Australia 376 (Alan Kippax 146, Stan McCabe 90, Tommy Scott 4-83) & 172-0 (Bill Ponsford 92 n.o., Archie Jackson 70 n.o.)

Sydney   Australia won by an innings and 172 runs
Australia 369 (Bill Ponsford 183, Bill Woodfull 58, Tommy Scott 4-66): West Indies 107 (Clarrie Grimmett 4-54) & 90 (A. Hurwood 4-22)

Brisbane   Australia won by an innings and 217 runs
Australia 558 (Don Bradman 223, Bill Ponsford 109, Alan Kippax 84, Herman Griffith 4-133): West Indies 193 (George Headley 102 n.o., Ron Oxenham 4-39, Clarrie Grimmett 4-95) & 148 (Clarrie Grimmett 5-49)

Melbourne   Australia won by an innings and 122 runs
West Indies 99 (Herbert Ironmonger 7-23) & 107 (Alan Fairfax 4-31, Herbert Ironmonger 4-56): Australia 328-8 dec (Don Bradman 152, Billy Woodfull 83)

Sydney   West Indies won by 30 runs
West Indies 350-6 dec (Frank Martin 123 n.o., George Headley 105, Jackie Grant 62) & 124-5 dec: Australia 224 (Alan Fairfax 54, George Francis 4-48) & 220 (Alan Fairfax 60 n.o., Herman Griffith 4-50)

Caribbean Cricketers

1933

Lord's   England won by an innings and 27 runs
England 296 (Leslie Ames 83 n.o., Cyril Walters 51, Manny Martindale 4–85): West Indians 97 (Walter Robins 6–32) & 172 (George Headley 50, Hedley Verity 4–45, George Macaulay 4–57)

Manchester   Match drawn
West Indies 375 (George Headley 169 n.o., Ivan Barrow 105, Nobby Clark 4–99) & 225 (Clifford Roach 64, Learie Constantine 64, James Langridge 7–56): England 374 (Douglas Jardine 127, Walter Robins 55, Manny Martindale 5–73)

Oval   England won by an innings and 17 runs
England 312 (Alfred Bakewell 107, Charlie Barnett 52, Manny Martindale 5–93): West Indies 100 ('Father' Marriott 5–37) & 195 (Clifford Roach 56, 'Father' Marriott 6–59)

1934/35

Bridgetown   England won by 4 wickets
West Indies 102 (Ken Farnes 4–40) & 51–6 dec (Jim Smith 5–15): England 81–7 dec & 75–6 (Manny Martindale 5–22)

Port of Spain   West Indies won by 217 runs
West Indies 302 (Derek Sealy 92, Learie Constantine 90, Jim Smith 4–100) & 280–6 dec (George Headley 93): England 258 (Errol Holmes 85 n.o., Jack Iddon 73) & 107

Georgetown   Match drawn
England 226 (Leslie Hylton 4–27) & 160–6 dec (Bob Wyatt 71): West Indies 184 (George Headley 53, Ken Wishart 52, Eric Hollies 7–50) & 104–5

Kingston   West Indies won by an innings and 161 runs
West Indies 535–7 dec (George Headley 270 n.o., Derek Sealy 91, Rolph Grant 77, George Paine 5–168): England 271 (Leslie Ames 126, Jack Iddon 54) & 103 (Manny Martindale 4–28)

1939

Lord's   England won by 8 wickets
West Indies 277 (George Headley 106, Jeff Stollmeyer 59, Bill Copson 5–85) & 225 (George Headley 107, Bill Copson 4–67): England 404–5 dec (Len Hutton 196, Denis Compton 120) & 100–2

Manchester   Match drawn
England 164–7 dec (Joe Hardstaff 76) & 128–6 dec (Learie Constantine 4–42): West Indies 133 (George Headley 51, Bill Bowes 6–33) & 43–4

Statistical Appendix

Oval   Match drawn
England 352 (Joe Hardstaff 94, Norman Oldfield 80, Len Hutton 73, Learie Constantine 5–75) & 366–3 (Len Hutton 165 n.o., Walter Hammond 138): West Indies 498 (Kenny Weekes 137, Victor Stollmeyer 96, Learie Constantine 79, George Headley 65, Jeff Stollmeyer 59, Reg Perks 5–156)

1947/48
Bridgetown   Match drawn
West Indies 296 (Gerry Gomez 86, Jeff Stollmeyer 78, Jim Laker 7–103) & 351–9 dec (Robert Christiani 99, Edward Williams 72, Wilfred Ferguson 56 n.o., Dick Howorth 6–124): England 253 (Joe Hardstaff 98, Jack Robertson 80, Prior Jones 4–54) & 86–4 (Jack Robertson 51 n.o.)

Port of Spain   Match drawn
England 362 (Billy Griffith 140, Jim Laker 55, Wilfred Ferguson 5–137) & 275 (Jack Robertson 133, Wilfred Ferguson 6–92): West Indies 497 (Andy Ganteaume 112, George Carew 107, Frank Worrell 97, Gerry Gomez 62) & 72–3

Georgetown   West Indies won by 7 wickets
West Indies 297–8 dec (Frank Worrell 131 n.o., Robert Christiani 51, Ken Cranston 4–78) & 78–3: England 111 (John Goddard 5–31) & 263 (Joe Hardstaff 63, Wilfred Ferguson 5–116)

Kingston   West Indies won by 10 wickets
England 227 (Jack Robertson 64, Len Hutton 56, Hines Johnson 5–41) & 336 (Winston Place 107, Joe Hardstaff 64, Len Hutton 60, Hines Johnson 5–55): West Indies 490 (Everton Weekes 141, Wilfred Ferguson 75, Ken Rickards 67) & 76–0

1948/49
New Delhi   Match drawn
West Indies 631 (Clyde Walcott 152, Everton Weekes 128, Robert Christiani 107, Gerry Gomez 101, C. R. Rangachari 5–107): India 454 (Hemu Adhikari 114 n.o., K. C. Ibrahim 85, Rusi Modi 63, Lala Amarnath 62) & 220–6

Bombay   Match drawn
West Indies 629–6 dec (Everton Weekes 194, Allan Rae 104, Jimmy Cameron 75 n.o., Robert Christiani 74, Clyde Walcott 68, Jeff Stollmeyer 66): India 273 (Dattu Phadkar 74, Wilfred Ferguson 4–126) & 333–3 (Vijay Hazare 134 n.o., Rusi Modi 112, Lala Amarnath 58 n.o.)

Calcutta   Match drawn
West Indies 366 (Everton Weekes 162, Clyde Walcott 54, Ghulam Ahmed

Caribbean Cricketers

4–94, Sunil Banerjee 4–120) & 336–9 dec (Clyde Walcott 108, Everton Weekes 101): India 272 (Rusi Modi 80, Vijay Hazare 59, Mustaq Ali 54) & 325–3 (Mustaq Ali 106, Rusi Modi 87, Vijay Hazare 58 n.o.)

Madras   West Indies won by an innings and 193 runs
West Indies 582 (Jeff Stollmeyer 160, Allan Rae 109, Everton Weekes 90, Gerry Gomez 50, Dattu Phadkar 7–159): India 245 (Rusi Modi 56, John Trim 4–48) & 144 (Vijay Hazare 52, Prior Jones 4–30)

Bombay   Match drawn
West Indies 286 (Jeff Stollmeyer 85, Everton Weekes 56, Dattu Phadkar 4–74) & 267 (Allan Rae 97, S. N. Banerjee 4–54): India 193 & 355–8 (Vijay Hazare 122, Rusi Modi 86, Prior Jones 5–85)

1950
Manchester   England won by 202 runs
England 312 (Godfrey Evans 104, Trevor Bailey 82 n.o., Alfred Valentine 8–104) & 288 (Bill Edrich 71): West Indies 215 (Everton Weekes 52, Bob Berry 5–63) & 183 (Jeff Stollmeyer 78, Eric Hollies 5–63, Bob Berry 4–53)

Lord's   West Indies won by 326 runs
West Indies 326 (Allan Rae 106, Everton Weekes 63, Frank Worrell 52, Roly Jenkins 5–116) & 425–6 dec (Clyde Walcott 168 n.o., Gerry Gomez 70, Everton Weekes 63, Roly Jenkins 4–174): England 151 (Sonny Ramadhin 5–66, Alfred Valentine 4–48) & 274 (Cyril Washbrook 114, Sonny Ramadhin 6–86)

Nottingham   West Indies won by 10 wickets
England 223 & 436 (Cyril Washbrook 102, Reg Simpson 94, Gilbert Parkhouse 69, John Dewes 67, Godfrey Evans 63, Sonny Ramadhin 5–135): West Indies 558 (Frank Worrell 261, Everton Weekes 129, Allan Rae 68, Alec Bedser 5–127) & 103–0 (Jeff Stollmeyer 52 n.o.)

Oval   West Indies won by an innings and 56 runs
West Indies 503 (Frank Worrell 138, Allan Rae 109, Gerry Gomez 74, John Goddard 58 n.o., Doug Wright 5–141): England 344 (Len Hutton 202 n.o., John Goddard 4–25, Alfred Valentine 4–121) & 103 (Alfred Valentine 6–39)

1951/52
Brisbane   Australia won by 3 wickets
West Indies 216 (Ray Lindwall 4–62) & 245 (Everton Weekes 70, Gerry Gomez 55, Doug Ring 6–80): Australia 226 (Ray Lindwall 61, Alfred Valentine 5–99) & 236–7 (Sonny Ramadhin 5–90)

Statistical Appendix

Sydney   Australia won by 7 wickets
West Indies 362 (Robert Christiani 76, Frank Worrell 64, Clyde Walcott 60, Gerry Gomez 54, Ray Lindwall 4–66) & 290 (John Goddard 57 n.o., Everton Weekes 56): Australia 517 (Lindsay Hassett 132, Keith Miller 129, Doug Ring 65, Alfred Valentine 4–111) & 137–3

Adelaide   West Indies won by 6 wickets
Australia 82 (Frank Worrell 6–38) & 255 (Doug Ring 67, Alfred Valentine 6–102): West Indies 105 (Bill Johnston 6–62) & 233–4

Melbourne   Australia won by 1 wicket
West Indies 272 (Frank Worrell 108, Keith Miller 5–60) & 203 (Jeff Stollmeyer 54, Gerry Gomez 52): Australia 216 (Neil Harvey 83, John Trim 5–34) & 260–9 (Lindsay Hassett 102, Alfred Valentine 5–88)

Sydney   Australia won by 202 runs
Australia 116 (Gerry Gomez 7–55) & 377 (Keith Miller 69, Lindsay Hassett 64, Colin McDonald 62, Graeme Hole 62, Frank Worrell 4–95): West Indies 78 (Keith Miller 5–26) & 213 (Jeff Stollmeyer 104, Ray Lindwall 5–52)

1952
Christchurch   West Indies won by 5 wickets
New Zealand 236 (Sonny Ramadhin 5–86) & 189 (Sonny Ramadhin 4–39): West Indies 287 (Frank Worrell 71, Clyde Walcott 65, Sammy Guillen 54, Tom Burtt 5–69) & 142–5 (Frank Worrell 62 n.o.)

Auckland   Match drawn
West Indies 546–6 dec (Jeff Stollmeyer 152, Clyde Walcott 115, Frank Worrell 100): New Zealand 160 (Vernon Scott 84) & 17–1

1953
Port of Spain   Match drawn
India 417 (Polly Umrigar 130, Madhav Apte 64, G. S. Ramchand 61) & 294 (Polly Umrigar 69, Dattu Phadkar 65, Madhav Apte 52): West Indies 438 (Everton Weekes 207, Bruce Pairaudeau 115, Subhash Gupte 7–162) & 142–0 (Jeff Stollmeyer 76 n.o., Allan Rae 63 n.o.)

Bridgetown   West Indies won by 142 runs
West Indies 296 (Clyde Walcott 98) & 228 (Jeff Stollmeyer 54, Dattu Phadkar 5–64): India 253 (Madhav Apte 64, Vijay Hazare 63, Polly Umrigar 56, Alfred Valentine 4–58) & 129 (Sonny Ramadhin 5–26)

Port of Spain   Match drawn
India 279 (G. S. Ramchand 62, Polly Umrigar 61, Frank King 5–74) & 362–7

Caribbean Cricketers

dec (Madhav Apte 163 n.o., Vinoo Mankad 96, Polly Umrigar 67): West Indies 315 (Everton Weekes 161, Subhash Gupte 5-107) & 192-2 (Jeff Stollmeyer 104 n.o., Everton Weekes 55 n.o.)

Georgetown Match drawn
India 262 (Vinoo Mankad 66, C. V. Gadkari 50 n.o., Alfred Valentine 5-127) & 190-5: West Indies 364 (Clyde Walcott 125, Everton Weekes 86, Frank Worrell 56, Subhash Gupte 4-122)

Kingston Match drawn
India 312 (Polly Umrigar 117, Pankaj Roy 85, Alfred Valentine 5-64) & 444 (Pankaj Roy 150, Vijay Manjrekar 118, Gerry Gomez 4-72, Alfred Valentine 4-149): West Indies 576 (Frank Worrell 237, Clyde Walcott 118, Everton Weekes 109, Bruce Pairaudeau 58, Subhash Gupte 5-180, Vinoo Mankad 5-228) & 92-4

1953/54
Kingston West Indies won by 140 runs
West Indies 417 (John Holt 94, Clyde Walcott 65, Jeff Stollmeyer 60, Everton Weekes 55, Cliff McWatt 54, Brian Statham 4-90) & 209-6 dec (Everton Weekes 90 n.o.): England 170 (Sonny Ramadhin 4-65) & 316 (Willie Watson 116, Peter May 69, Len Hutton 56, Esmond Kentish 5-49)

Bridgetown West Indies won by 181 runs
West Indies 383 (Clyde Walcott 220, Bruce Pairaudeau 71, Denis Atkinson 53, Jim Laker 4-81) & 292-2 dec (John Holt 166, Frank Worrell 76 n.o.): England 181 (Len Hutton 72, Sonny Ramadhin 4-50) & 313 (Denis Compton 93, Len Hutton 77, Tom Graveney 64 n.o., Peter May 62)

Georgetown England won by 9 wickets
England 435 (Len Hutton 169, Denis Compton 64, Sonny Ramadhin 6-113) & 75-1: West Indies 251 (Everton Weekes 94, Cliff McWatt 54, Brian Statham 4-64) & 256 (John Holt 64)

Port of Spain Match drawn
West Indies 681-8 dec (Everton Weekes 206, Frank Worrell 167, Clyde Walcott 124, Denis Atkinson 74) & 212-4 dec (Frank Worrell 56, Denis Atkinson 53 n.o., Clyde Walcott 51 n.o.): England 537 (Peter May 135, Denis Compton 133, Tom Graveney 92) & 98-3

Kingston England won by 9 wickets
West Indies 139 (Clyde Walcott 50, Trevor Bailey 7-34) & 346 (Clyde Walcott 116, Jeff Stollmeyer 64, Jim Laker 4-71): England 414 (Len Hutton 205, Johnny Wardle 66, Gary Sobers 4-75) & 72-1

Statistical Appendix

1955

Kingston   Australia won by 9 wickets
Australia 515-9 dec (Keith Miller 147, Neil Harvey 133, Arthur Morris 65, Colin McDonald 50) & 20-1: West Indies 259 (Clyde Walcott 108, Ray Lindwall 4-61) & 275 (Collie Smith 104, John Holt 60)

Port of Spain   Match drawn
West Indies 382 (Everton Weekes 139, Clyde Walcott 126, Ray Lindwall 6-95) & 273-4 (Clyde Walcott 110, Everton Weekes 87 n.o.): Australia 600-9 dec (Neil Harvey 133, Arthur Morris 111, Colin McDonald 110, Ron Archer 84, Ian Johnson 66)

Georgetown   Australia won by 8 wickets
West Indies 182 (Everton Weekes 81, Richie Benaud 4-15) & 207 (Clyde Walcott 73, Frank Worrell 56, Ian Johnson 7-44): Australia 257 (Richie Benaud 68, Colin McDonald 61) & 133-2

Bridgetown   Match drawn
Australia 668 (Keith Miller 137, Ray Lindwall 118, Ron Archer 98, Neil Harvey 74, Les Favell 72, Gil Langley 53, Tom Dewdney 4-125) & 249 (Ian Johnson 57, Les Favell 53, Denis Atkinson 5-56): West Indies 510 (Denis Atkinson 219, Clairmont Depeiza 122) & 234-6 (Clyde Walcott 83)

Kingston   Australia won by an innings and 82 runs
West Indies 357 (Clyde Walcott 155, Frank Worrell 61, Everton Weekes 56, Keith Miller 6-107) & 319 (Clyde Walcott 110, Gary Sobers 64): Australia 758-8 dec (Neil Harvey 204, Ron Archer 128, Colin McDonald 127, Richie Benaud 121, Keith Miller 109)

1956

Dunedin   West Indies won by an innings and 71 runs
New Zealand 74 (Sonny Ramadhin 6-23) & 208 (John Beck 66): West Indies 353 (Everton Weekes 123, Collie Smith 64, Bob Blair 4-90)

Christchurch   West Indies won by an innings and 64 runs
West Indies 386 (Everton Weekes 103, Denis Atkinson 85, John Goddard 83 n.o.): New Zealand 158 (Sonny Ramadhin 5-46) & 164 (Alfred Valentine 5-32, Collie Smith 4-75)

Wellington   West Indies won by 9 wickets
West Indies 404 (Everton Weekes 156, Bruce Pairaudeau 68, Denis Atkinson 60) & 13-1: New Zealand 208 (John Beck 55) & 208 (D. D. Taylor 77, Denis Atkinson 5-66)

Caribbean Cricketers

Auckland   New Zealand won by 190 runs
New Zealand 255 (John Reid 84, Tom Dewdney 5–21) & 157–9 dec (Denis Atkinson 7–53): West Indies 145 (Hammond Furlonge 64, Harry Cave 4–22, Tony MacGibbon 4–44) & 77 (Harry Cave 4–21)

1957

Birmingham   Match drawn
England 186 (Sonny Ramadhin 7–49) & 583–4 dec (Peter May 285 n.o., Colin Cowdrey 154): West Indies 474 (Collie Smith 161, Clyde Walcott 90, Frank Worrell 81, Gary Sobers 53, Jim Laker 4–119) & 72–7

Lord's   England won by an innings and 36 runs
West Indies 127 (Trevor Bailey 7–44) & 261 (Everton Weekes 90, Gary Sobers 66, Trevor Bailey 4–54): England 424 (Colin Cowdrey 152, Godfrey Evans 82, Peter Richardson 76, Roy Gilchrist 4–115)

Nottingham   Match drawn
England 619–6 dec (Tom Graveney 258, Peter Richardson 126, Peter May 104, Colin Cowdrey 55) & 64–1: West Indies 372 (Frank Worrell 191 n.o., Freddie Trueman 5–63) & 367 (Collie Smith 168, John Goddard 61, Brian Statham 5–118, Freddie Trueman 4–80)

Leeds   England won by an innings and 5 runs
West Indies 142 (Peter Loader 6–36) & 132: England 279 (Peter May 69, Colin Cowdrey 68, David Sheppard 68, Frank Worrell 7–70)

Oval   England won by an innings and 237 runs
England 412 (Tom Graveney 164, Peter Richardson 107, Sonny Ramadhin 4–107): West Indies 89 (Tony Lock 5–28) & 86 (Tony Lock 6–20)

1957/58

Bridgetown   Match drawn
West Indies 579–9 dec (Everton Weekes 197, Conrad Hunte 142, Collie Smith 78, Gary Sobers 52, Mahmood Hussain 4–153) & 28–0: Pakistan 106 (Roy Gilchrist 4–32) & 657–8 dec (Hanif Mohammad 337, Imtiaz Ahmed 91, Saeed Ahmed 65)

Port of Spain   West Indies won by 120 runs
West Indies 325 (Rohan Kanhai 96, Everton Weekes 78, Gary Sobers 52) & 312 (Gary Sobers 80, Gerry Alexander 57, Collie Smith 51, Fazal Mahmood 4–89): Pakistan 282 (Wallis Mathias 73, Fazal Mahmood 60, Collie Smith 4–71) & 235 (Hanif Mohammad 81, Saeed Ahmed 64, Roy Gilchrist 4–61)

Statistical Appendix

Kingston   West Indies won by an innings and 174 runs
Pakistan 328 (Imtiaz Ahmed 122, Wallis Mathias 77, Saeed Ahmed 52, Eric Atkinson 5-42) & 288 (Wazir Mohammad 106, A. H. Kardar 57): West Indies 790-3 dec (Gary Sobers 365 n.o., Conrad Hunte 260, Clyde Walcott 88 n.o.)

Georgetown   West Indies won by 8 wickets
Pakistan 408 (Saeed Ahmed 150, Hanif Mohammad 79, Roy Gilchrist 4-102) & 318 (Wazir Mohammad 97 n.o., A. H. Kardar 56, Lance Gibbs 5-80): West Indies 410 (Clyde Walcott 145, Gary Sobers 125, Nasimul Ghani 5-116) & 317-2 (Conrad Hunte 114, Gary Sobers 109 n.o., Rohan Kanhai 62)

Port of Spain   Pakistan won by an innings and 1 run
West Indies 268 (Collie Smith 86, Everton Weekes 51, Fazal Mahmood 6-83) & 227 (Clyde Walcott 62, Nasimul Ghani 6-67): Pakistan 496 (Wazir Mohammad 189, Saeed Ahmed 97, Hanif Mohammad 54, Jaswick Taylor 5-109, Lance Gibbs 4-108)

1958/59
Bombay   Match drawn
West Indies 227 (Rohan Kanhai 66, Collie Smith 63, Subhash Gupte 4-86) & 323-4 dec (Gary Sobers 142 n.o., Basil Butcher 64 n.o., Collie Smith 58): India 152 (Polly Umrigar 55, Roy Gilchrist 4-39) & 289-5 (Pankaj Roy 90, G. S. Ramchand 67 n.o.)

Kanpur   West Indies won by 203 runs
West Indies 222 (Gerry Alexander 70, Subhash Gupte 9-102) & 443-7 dec (Gary Sobers 198, Joe Solomon 86, Basil Butcher 60): India 222 (Polly Umrigar 57, Wesley Hall 6-50) & 240 (Nariman Contractor 50, Wesley Hall 5-76)

Calcutta   West Indies won by an innings and 336 runs
West Indies 614-5 dec (Rohan Kanhai 256, Gary Sobers 106 n.o., Basil Butcher 103, Joe Solomon 69 n.o.): India 124 & 154 (Vijay Manjrekar 58 n.o., Roy Gilchrist 6-55)

Madras   West Indies won by 295 runs
West Indies 500 (Basil Butcher 142, Rohan Kanhai 99, John Holt 63, Vinoo Mankad 4-95) & 168-5 dec (John Holt 81 n.o., Subhash Gupte 4-78): India 222 (Kripal Singh 53, Gary Sobers 4-26) & 151 (Chandrakant Borde 56)

New Delhi   Match drawn
India 415 (Chandrakant Borde 109, Nariman Contractor 92, Polly Umrigar

Caribbean Cricketers

76, Hemu Adhikari 63, Wesley Hall 4–66) & 275 (Chandrakant Borde 96, Pankaj Roy 58, Dattu Gaekwad 52, Collie Smith 5–90): West Indies 644–8 dec (John Holt 123, Collie Smith 100, Joe Solomon 100 n.o., Conrad Hunte 92, Basil Butcher 71, Ramakant Desai 4–169)

1959

Karachi   Pakistan won by 10 wickets
West Indies 146 (Fazal Mahmood 4–35, Nasimul Ghani 4–35) & 245 (Joe Solomon 66, Basil Butcher 61): Pakistan 304 (Hanif Mohammad 103, Saeed Ahmed 78) & 88–0

Dacca   Pakistan won by 41 runs
Pakistan 145 (Wallis Mathias 64, Wesley Hall 4–28) & 144 (Eric Atkinson 4–42, Wesley Hall 4–49): West Indies 76 (Fazal Mahmood 6–34) & 172 (Fazal Mahmood 6–66, Mahmood Hussain 4–48)

Lahore   West Indies won by an innings and 156 runs
West Indies 469 (Rohan Kanhai 217, Gary Sobers 72, Joe Solomon 56): Pakistan 209 (Wesley Hall 5–87) & 104 (Sonny Ramadhin 4–25)

1959/60

Bridgetown   Match drawn
England 482 (Ted Dexter 136 n.o., Ken Barrington 128, Geoff Pullar 65) & 71–0: West Indies 563–8 dec (Gary Sobers 226, Frank Worrell 197 n.o., Freddie Trueman 4–93)

Port of Spain   England won by 256 runs
England 382 (Ken Barrington 121, Mike Smith 108, Ted Dexter 77) & 230–9 dec: West Indies 112 (Freddie Trueman 5–35) & 244 (Rohan Kanhai 110)

Kingston   Match drawn
England 277 (Colin Cowdrey 114, Wesley Hall 7–69) & 305 (Colin Cowdrey 97, Geoff Pullar 66, Chester Watson 4–62): West Indies 353 (Gary Sobers 147, Easton McMorris 73, Seymour Nurse 70) & 175–6 (Rohan Kanhai 57, Freddie Trueman 4–54)

Georgetown   Match drawn
England 295 (Colin Cowdrey 65, David Allen 55, Wesley Hall 6–90) & 334–8 (Ted Dexter 110, Raman Subba Row 100, Frank Worrell 4–49): West Indies 402–8 dec (Gary Sobers 145, Rohan Kanhai 55)

Port of Spain   Match drawn
England 393 (Colin Cowdrey 119, Ted Dexter 76, Ken Barrington 69, Sonny

Ramadhin 4-73) & 350-7 dec (Jim Parks 101 n.o., Mike Smith 96, Geoff Pullar 54): West Indies 338-8 dec (Gary Sobers 92, Conrad Hunte 72 n.o., Clyde Walcott 53) & 209-5 (Frank Worrell 61)

1960/61
Brisbane Tie
West Indies 453 (Gary Sobers 132, Frank Worrell 65, Joe Solomon 65, Gerry Alexander 60, Wesley Hall 50, Alan Davidson 5-135) & 284 (Frank Worrell 65, Rohan Kanhai 54, Alan Davidson 6-87): Australia 505 (Norman O'Neill 181, Bobby Simpson 92, Colin McDonald 57, Wesley Hall 4-140) & 232 (Alan Davidson 80, Richie Benaud 52, Wesley Hall 5-63)

Melbourne Australia won by 7 wickets
Australia 348 (Ken Mackay 74, John Martin 55, Les Favell 51, Wesley Hall 4-51) & 70-3: West Indies 181 (Rohan Kanhai 84, Seymour Nurse 70, Alan Davidson 6-53) & 233 (Conrad Hunte 110, Gerry Alexander 72)

Sydney West Indies won by 222 runs
West Indies 339 (Gary Sobers 168, Alan Davidson 5-80, Richie Benaud 4-86) & 326 (Gerry Alexander 108, Frank Worrell 82, Cameron Smith 55, Richie Benaud 4-113): Australia 202 (Norman O'Neill 71, Alfred Valentine 4-67) & 241 (Neil Harvey 85, Norman O'Neill 70, Lance Gibbs 5-66, Alfred Valentine 4-86)

Adelaide Match drawn
West Indies 393 (Rohan Kanhai 117, Frank Worrell 71, Gerry Alexander 63 n.o., Richie Benaud 5-96) & 432-6 dec (Rohan Kanhai 115, Gerry Alexander 87 n.o., Conrad Hunte 79, Frank Worrell 53): Australia 366 (Bobby Simpson 85, Richie Benaud 77, Colin McDonald 71, Lance Gibbs 5-97) & 273-9 (Norman O'Neill 65, Ken Mackay 62 n.o.)

Melbourne Australia won by 2 wickets
West Indies 292 (Gary Sobers 64, Frank Misson 4-58) & 321 (Gerry Alexander 73, Conrad Hunte 52, Alan Davidson 5-84): Australia 356 (Colin McDonald 91, Bobby Simpson 75, Peter Burge 68, Gary Sobers 5-120, Lance Gibbs 4-74) & 258-8 (Bobby Simpson 92, Peter Burge |53)|

1962
Port of Spain West Indies won by 10 wickets
India 203 (Rusi Surti 57, Salim Durani 56) & 98 (Gary Sobers 4-22): West Indies 289 (Jackie Hendriks 64, Conrad Hunte 58, Salim Durani 4-82) & 15-0

Caribbean Cricketers

Kingston   West Indies won by an innings and 18 runs
India 395 (Chandrakant Borde 93, Raghunath Nadkarni 78 n.o., Faroukh Engineer 53, Polly Umrigar 50, Gary Sobers 4–75) & 218 (Wesley Hall 6–49): West Indies 631–8 dec (Gary Sobers 153, Rohan Kanhai 138, Easton McMorris 125, Ivor Mendonca 78, Frank Worrell 58)

Bridgetown   West Indies won by an innings and 30 runs
India 258 & 187 (Dilip Sardesai 60, Vijay Manjrekar 51, Lance Gibbs 8–38): West Indies 475 (Joe Solomon 96, Rohan Kanhai 89, Frank Worrell 77, Conrad Hunte 59)

Port of Spain   West Indies won by 7 wickets
West Indies 444–9 dec (Rohan Kanhai 139, Frank Worrell 73 n.o., Easton McMorris 50, Willie Rodriguez 50, Wesley Hall 50 n.o., Polly Umrigar 5–107) & 176–3 dec (Easton McMorris 56): India 197 (Polly Umrigar 56, Wesley Hall 5–20) & 422 (Polly Umrigar 172 n.o., Salim Durani 104, Vijay Mehra 62, Lance Gibbs 4–112)

Kingston   West Indies won by 123 runs
West Indies 253 (Gary Sobers 104, V. B. Ranjane 4–72) & 283 (Frank Worrell 98 n.o., Gary Sobers 50): India 178 (Raghunath Nadkarni 61, Lester King 5–46) & 235 (Polly Umrigar 60, Gary Sobers 5–63)

1963
Manchester   West Indies won by 10 wickets
West Indies 501–6 dec (Conrad Hunte 182, Rohan Kanhai 90, Frank Worrell 74 n.o., Gary Sobers 64) & 1–0: England 205 (Ted Dexter 73, Lance Gibbs 5–59) & 296 (Micky Stewart 87, Lance Gibbs 6–98)

Lord's   Match drawn
West Indies 301 (Rohan Kanhai 73, Joe Solomon 56, Freddie Trueman 6–100) & 229 (Basil Butcher 133, Freddie Trueman 5–52, Derek Shackleton 4–72): England 297 (Ken Barrington 80, Ted Dexter 70, Freddie Titmus 52 n.o., Charlie Griffith 5–91) & 228–9 (Brian Close 70, Ken Barrington 60, Wesley Hall 4–93)

Birmingham   England won by 217 runs
England 216 (Brian Close 55, Gary Sobers 5–60) & 278–9 dec (Phil Sharpe 85 n.o., Ted Dexter 57, Tony Lock 56, Lance Gibbs 4–49): West Indies 186 (Freddie Trueman 5–75, Ted Dexter 4–38) & 91 (Freddie Trueman 7–44)

Leeds   West Indies won by 221 runs
West Indies 397 (Gary Sobers 102, Rohan Kanhai 92, Joe Solomon 62,

Statistical Appendix

Freddie Trueman 4–117) & 229 (Basil Butcher 78, Gary Sobers 52, Freddie Titmus 4–44): England 174 (Tony Lock 53, Charlie Griffith 6–36) & 231 (Jim Parks 57, Brian Close 56, Lance Gibbs 4–76)

Oval   West Indies won by 8 wickets
England 275 (Phil Sharpe 63, Charlie Griffith 6–71) & 223 (Phil Sharpe 83, Wesley Hall 4–39): West Indies 246 (Conrad Hunte 80, Basil Butcher 53) & 255–2 (Conrad Hunte 108 n.o., Rohan Kanhai 77)

1965
Kingston   West Indies won by 179 runs
West Indians 239 (Tony White 57 n.o., Laurie Mayne 4–43) & 373 (Conrad Hunte 81, Joe Solomon 76, Basil Butcher 71, Laurie Mayne 4–56, Peter Philpott 4–109): Australia 217 (Wesley Hall 5–60) & 216 (Brian Booth 56, Wesley Hall 4–45)

Port of Spain   Match drawn
West Indies 429 (Basil Butcher 117, Conrad Hunte 89, Gary Sobers 69, Bryan Davis 54, Norman O'Neill 4–41) & 386 (Bryan Davis 58, Conrad Hunte 53, Rohan Kanhai 53): Australia 516 (Bob Cowper 143, Brian Booth 117, Graham Thomas 61)

Georgetown   West Indies won by 212 runs
West Indies 355 (Rohan Kanhai 89, Neil Hawke 6–72) & 180 (Peter Philpott 4–49, Neil Hawke 4–43): Australia 179 & 144 (Lance Gibbs 6–29)

Bridgetown   Match drawn
Australia 650–6 dec (Bill Lawry 210, Bobby Simpson 201, Bob Cowper 102, Norman O'Neill 51) & 175–4 dec (Norman O'Neill 74 n.o., Bill Lawry 58): West Indies 573 (Seymour Nurse 201, Rohan Kanhai 129, Conrad Hunte 75, Gary Sobers 55, Charlie Griffith 54, Graham McKenzie 4–114) & 242–5 (Conrad Hunte 81, Bryan Davis 68)

Port of Spain   Australia won by 10 wickets
West Indies 224 (Rohan Kanhai 121) & 131 (Conrad Hunte 60 n.o., Graham McKenzie 5–33): Australia 294 (Bobby Simpson 72, Bob Cowper 69, Charlie Griffith 6–46) & 63–0

1966
Manchester   West Indies won by an innings and 40 runs
West Indies 484 (Gary Sobers 161, Conrad Hunte 135, Freddie Titmus 5–83): England 167 (Lance Gibbs 5–37) & 277 (Colin Milburn 94, Colin Cowdrey 69, Lance Gibbs 5–69)

Caribbean Cricketers

Lord's Match drawn
West Indies 269 (Seymour Nurse 64, Ken Higgs 6–91) & 369–5 dec (Gary Sobers 163 n.o., David Holford 105 n.o.): England 355 (Tom Graveney 96, Jim Parks 91, Geoff Boycott 60, Wesley Hall 4–106) & 197–4 (Colin Milburn 126 n.o.)

Nottingham West Indies won by 139 runs
West Indies 235 (Seymour Nurse 93, John Snow 4–82, Ken Higgs 4–71) & 482–5 dec (Basil Butcher 209 n.o., Gary Sobers 94, Rohan Kanhai 63, Seymour Nurse 53): England 325 (Tom Graveney 109, Colin Cowdrey 96, Basil D'Oliveira 76, Gary Sobers 4–90, Wesley Hall 4–105) & 253 (Geoff Boycott 71, Basil D'Oliveira 54, Charlie Griffith 4–34)

Leeds West Indies won by an innings and 55 runs
West Indies 500–9 dec (Gary Sobers 174, Seymour Nurse 137, Ken Higgs 4–94): England 240 (Basil D'Oliveira 88, Gary Sobers 5–41) & 205 (Bob Barber 55, Lance Gibbs 6–39)

Oval England won by an innings and 34 runs
West Indies 268 (Rohan Kanhai 104, Gary Sobers 81) & 225 (Seymour Nurse 70, Basil Butcher 60): England 527 (Tom Graveney 165, John Murray 112, Ken Higgs 63, John Snow 59 n.o.)

1966/67

Bombay West Indies won by 6 wickets
India 296 (Chandrakant Borde 121, Salim Durani 55) & 316 (Budhisagar Kunderan 79, Nawab of Pataudi 51, Lance Gibbs 4–67): West Indies 421 (Conrad Hunte 101, Clive Lloyd 82, David Holford 80, Gary Sobers 50, B. S. Chandrasekhar 7–157) & 192–4 (Clive Lloyd 78 n.o., Gary Sobers 53 n.o., B. S. Chandrasekhar 4–78)

Calcutta West Indies won by an innings and 45 runs
West Indies 390 (Rohan Kanhai 90, Gary Sobers 70, Seymour Nurse 56): India 167 (Lance Gibbs 5–51) & 178 (Gary Sobers 4–56)

Madras Match drawn
India 404 (Chandrakant Borde 125, Faroukh Engineer 109, Rusi Surti 50 n.o.) & 323 (Ajit Wadekar 67, Venkatraman Subramanya 61, Hanumant Singh 50, Charlie Griffith 4–61, Lance Gibbs 4–96): West Indies 406 (Gary Sobers 95, Rohan Kanhai 77, B. S. Chandrasekhar 4–130) & 270–7 (Gary Sobers 74 n.o., Bishen Bedi 4–81)

Statistical Appendix

1967/68
Port of Spain   Match drawn
England 568 (Ken Barrington 143, Tom Graveney 118, Colin Cowdrey 72, Geoff Boycott 68, Charlie Griffith 5–69): West Indies 363 (Clive Lloyd 118, Rohan Kanhai 85) & 243–8 (Basil Butcher 52)

Kingston   Match drawn
England 376 (Colin Cowdrey 101, John Edrich 96, Ken Barrington 63, Wesley Hall 4–63) & 68–8: West Indies 143 (John Snow 7–49) & 391–9 dec (Gary Sobers 113 n.o., Seymour Nurse 73)

Bridgetown   Match drawn
West Indies 349 (Basil Butcher 86, Gary Sobers 68, Steve Camacho 57, John Snow 5–86) & 284–6 (Clive Lloyd 113 n.o., Basil Butcher 60): England 449 (John Edrich 146, Geoff Boycott 90, Tom Graveney 55, Basil D'Oliveira 51)

Port of Spain   England won by 7 wickets
West Indies 526–7 dec (Rohan Kanhai 153, Seymour Nurse 136, Steve Camacho 87) & 92–2 dec: England 404 (Colin Cowdrey 148, Alan Knott 69 n.o., Geoff Boycott 62, Basil Butcher 5–34) & 215–3 (Geoff Boycott 80 n.o., Colin Cowdrey 71)

Georgetown   Match drawn
West Indies 414 (Gary Sobers 152, Rohan Kanhai 150, John Snow 4–82) & 264 (Gary Sobers 95 n.o., John Snow 6–60): England 371 (Geoff Boycott 116, Tony Lock 89, Colin Cowdrey 59) & 206–9 (Colin Cowdrey 82, Alan Knott 73 n.o., Lance Gibbs 6–60)

1968/69
Brisbane   West Indies won by 125 runs
West Indies 296 (Rohan Kanhai 94, Joey Carew 83, Alan Connolly 4–60) & 353 (Clive Lloyd 129, Joey Carew 71 n.o., Johnny Gleeson 5–122): Australia 284 (Ian Chappell 117, Bill Lawry 105, Lance Gibbs 5–88) & 240 (Ian Chappell 50, Gary Sobers 6–73)

Melbourne   Australia won by an innings and 30 runs
West Indies 200 (Roy Fredericks 76, Graham McKenzie 8–71) & 280 (Seymour Nurse 74, Gary Sobers 67, Johnny Gleeson 5–61): Australia 510 (Bill Lawry 205, Ian Chappell 165, Doug Walters 76, Gary Sobers 4–97, Lance Gibbs 4–139)

Sydney   Australia won by 10 wickets
West Indies 264 (Clive Lloyd 50, Graham McKenzie 4–85) & 324 (Basil

Caribbean Cricketers

Butcher 101, Rohan Kanhai 69, Johnny Gleeson 4–91): Australia 547 (Doug Walters 118, Ian Redpath 80, Eric Freeman 76, Keith Stackpole 58) & 42–0

Adelaide   Match drawn
West Indies 276 (Gary Sobers 110, Basil Butcher 52, Eric Freeman 4–52) & 616 (Basil Butcher 118, Joey Carew 90, Rohan Kanhai 80, David Holford 80, Gary Sobers 52, Alan Connolly 5–122): Australia 533 (Doug Walters 110, Ian Chappell 76, Bill Lawry 62, Keith Stackpole 62, Graham McKenzie 59, Paul Sheahan 51, Lance Gibbs 4–145) & 339–9 (Ian Chappell 96, Bill Lawry 89, Keith Stackpole 50, Doug Walters 50)

Sydney   Australia won by 382 runs
Australia 619 (Doug Walters 242, Bill Lawry 151, Eric Freeman 56) & 394–8 dec (Ian Redpath 132, Doug Walters 103): West Indies 279 (Joey Carew 64, Clive Lloyd 53, Alan Connolly 4–61) & 352 (Seymour Nurse 137, Gary Sobers 113)

1969
Auckland   West Indies won by 5 wickets
New Zealand 323 (Bruce Taylor 124, Bevan Congdon 85) & 297–8 dec (Graham Dowling 71, Vic Pollard 51 n.o.): West Indies 276 (Joey Carew 109, Seymour Nurse 95) & 348–5 (Seymour Nurse 168, Basil Butcher 78 n.o.)

Wellington   New Zealand won by 6 wickets
West Indies 297 (Jackie Hendriks 54 n.o., Basil Butcher 50, Dick Motz 6–69) & 148 (Basil Butcher 59): New Zealand 282 (Glenn Turner 74, Bevan Congdon 52, Richard Edwards 5–84) & 166–4 (Brian Hastings 62 n.o.)

Christchurch   Match drawn
West Indies 417 (Seymour Nurse 258, Joey Carew 91, Dick Motz 5–113): New Zealand 217 (David Holford 4–66) & 367–6 (Brian Hastings 117 n.o., Graham Dowling 76)

1969
Manchester   England won by 10 wickets
England 413 (Geoff Boycott 128, Tom Graveney 75, John Edrich 58, Basil D'Oliveira 57, John Shepherd 5–104) & 12–0: West Indies 147 (David Brown 4–39, John Snow 4–54) & 275 (Roy Fredericks 64)

Lord's   Match drawn
West Indies 380 (Charlie Davis 103, Steve Camacho 67, Roy Fredericks 63, John Snow 5–114) & 295–9 dec (Clive Lloyd 70, Roy Fredericks 60, Gary Sobers 50 n.o.): England 344 (Ray Illingworth 113, John Hampshire 107, Alan Knott 53) & 295–7 (Geoff Boycott 106, Phil Sharpe 86)

Statistical Appendix

Leeds   England won by 30 runs
England 223 (John Edrich 79, Vanburn Holder 4-48) & 240 (Gary Sobers 5-42): West Indies 161 (Barry Knight 4-63) & 272 (Basil Butcher 91, Steve Camacho 71, Derek Underwood 4-55)

1971

Kingston   Match drawn
India 387 (Dilip Sardesai 212, Eknath Solkar 61, Vanburn Holder 4-60): West Indies 217 (Rohan Kanhai 56, Erapalli Prasanna 4-65) & 385-5 (Rohan Kanhai 158 n.o., Gary Sobers 93, Clive Lloyd 57)

Port of Spain   India won by 7 wickets
West Indies 214 (Charlie Davis 71 n.o., Erapalli Prasanna 4-54) & 261 (Roy Fredericks 80, Charlie Davis 74 n.o., Srinivas Venkataraghavan 5-95): India 352 (Dilip Sardesai 112, Sunil Gavaskar 65, Eknath Solkar 55, Jack Noreiga 9-95) & 125-3 (Sunil Gavaskar 67 n.o.)

Georgetown   Match drawn
West Indies 363 (Desmond Lewis 81 n.o., Clive Lloyd 60) & 307-3 dec (Charlie Davis 125 n.o., Gary Sobers 108 n.o.): India 376 (Sunil Gavaskar 116, Gundappa Viswanath 50, Abid Ali 50 n.o.) & 123-0 (Sunil Gavaskar 64 n.o., Ashok Mankad 53 n.o.)

Bridgetown   Match drawn
West Indies 501-5 dec (Gary Sobers 178 n.o., Desmond Lewis 88, Rohan Kanhai 85, Charlie Davis 79) & 180-6 dec: India 347 (Dilip Sardesai 150, Eknath Solkar 65, Uton Dowe 4-69) & 221-5 (Sunil Gavaskar 117 n.o.)

Port of Spain   Match drawn
India 360 (Sunil Gavaskar 124, Dilip Sardesai 75, Srinivas Venkataraghavan 51) & 427 (Sunil Gavaskar 220, Ajit Wadekar 54, Jack Noreiga 5-129): West Indies 526 (Gary Sobers 132, Charlie Davis 105, Maurice Foster 99, Desmond Lewis 72, Srinivas Venkataraghavan 4-100) & 165-8 (Clive Lloyd 64)

1972

Kingston   Match drawn
West Indies 508-4 dec (Lawrence Rowe 214, Roy Fredericks 163) & 218-3 dec (Lawrence Rowe 100 n.o.): New Zealand 386 (Glenn Turner 223 n.o., Ken Wadsworth 78) & 236-6 (Mark Burgess 101, David Holford 4-55)

Port of Spain   Match drawn
New Zealand 348 (Bevan Congdon 166 n.o., Bob Cunis 51, Vanburn Holder

Caribbean Cricketers

4–60) & 288–3 dec (Glenn Turner 95, Bevan Congdon 82, Mark Burgess 62 n.o.): West Indies 341 (Charlie Davis 90, Roy Fredericks 69, Bruce Taylor 4–41) & 121–5

Bridgetown   Match drawn
West Indies 133 (Bruce Taylor 7–74) & 564–8 (Charlie Davis 183, Gary Sobers 142, Lawrence Rowe 51, David Holford 50): New Zealand 422 (Bevan Congdon 126, Brian Hastings 105, Gary Sobers 4–64)

Georgetown   Match drawn
West Indies 365–7 dec (Alvin Kallicharran 100 n.o., Geoff Greenidge 50) & 86–0: New Zealand 543–3 dec (Glenn Turner 259, Terry Jarvis 182, Bevan Congdon 61 n.o.)

Port of Spain   Match drawn
West Indies 368 (Alvin Kallicharran 101, Roy Fredericks 60) & 194 (Bruce Taylor 5–41): New Zealand 162 (Inshan Ali 5–59) & 253–7 (Bevan Congdon 58, Glenn Turner 50, Vanburn Holder 4–41)

1973
Kingston   Match drawn
Australia 428–7 dec (Rodney Marsh 97, Doug Walters 72, Ross Edwards 63, Lance Gibbs 4–85) & 260–2 dec (Keith Stackpole 142, Ian Redpath 60): West Indies 428 (Maurice Foster 125, Rohan Kanhai 84, Lawrence Rowe 76, Alvin Kallicharran 50, Max Walker 6–114, Jeff Hammond 4–79) & 67–3

Bridgetown   Match drawn
Australia 324 (Greg Chappell 106, Rodney Marsh 78, Ian Chappell 72) & 300–2 dec (Ian Chappell 106 n.o., Doug Walters 102 n.o., Keith Stackpole 53): West Indies 391 (Rohan Kanhai 105, Roy Fredericks 98, Deryck Murray 90, Max Walker 5–97) & 36–0

Port of Spain   Australia won by 44 runs
Australia 332 (Doug Walters 112, Ian Redpath 66, Greg Chappell 56) & 281 (Ian Chappell 97, Lance Gibbs 5–102): West Indies 280 (Rohan Kanhai 56, Alvin Kallicharran 53, Terry Jenner 4–98) & 289 (Alvin Kallicharran 91, Roy Fredericks 76, Kerry O'Keeffe 4–57)

Georgetown   Australia won by 10 wickets
West Indies 366 (Clive Lloyd 178, Rohan Kanhai 57, Doug Walters 5–66) & 109 (Jeff Hammond 4–38, Max Walker 4–45): Australia 341 (Ian Chappell 109, Doug Walters 81, Greg Chappell 51) & 135–0 (Keith Stackpole 76 n.o., Ian Redpath 57 n.o.)

Statistical Appendix

Port of Spain   Match drawn
Australia 419–8 dec (Ross Edwards 74, Doug Walters 70, Ian Chappell 56, Rodney Marsh 56) & 218–7 dec (Lance Gibbs 4–66): West Indies 319 (Roy Fredericks 73, Clive Lloyd 59, Max Walker 5–75, Terry Jenner 5–90) & 135–5

1973

Oval   West Indies won by 158 runs
West Indies 415 (Clive Lloyd 132, Alvin Kallicharran 80, Keith Boyce 72, Geoff Arnold 5–113) & 255 (Alvin Kallicharran 80, Gary Sobers 51): England 257 (Geoff Boycott 97, Keith Boyce 5–70) & 255 (Frank Hayes 106 n.o., Keith Boyce 6–77)

Birmingham   Match drawn
West Indies 327 (Roy Fredericks 150, Bernard Julien 54) & 302 (Clive Lloyd 94, Gary Sobers 74, Rohan Kanhai 54, Geoff Arnold 4–43): England 305 (Geoff Boycott 56, Dennis Amiss 56, Keith Fletcher 52) & 182–2 (Dennis Amiss 86 n.o.)

Lord's   West Indies won by an innings and 226 runs
West Indies 652–8 dec (Rohan Kanhai 157, Gary Sobers 150 n.o., Bernard Julien 121, Clive Lloyd 63, Roy Fredericks 51, Bob Willis 4–118): England 233 (Keith Fletcher 68, Keith Boyce 4–50, Vanburn Holder 4–56) & 193 (Keith Fletcher 86 n.o., Keith Boyce 4–49)

1973/74

Port of Spain   West Indies won by 7 wickets
England 131 (Keith Boyce 4–42) & 392 (Dennis Amiss 174, Geoff Boycott 93, Lance Gibbs 6–108): West Indies 392 (Alvin Kallicharran 158, Bernard Julien 86 n.o., Pat Pocock 5–110) & 132–3 (Roy Fredericks 65 n.o.)

Kingston   Match drawn
England 353 (Geoff Boycott 68, Mike Denness 67) & 432–9 (Dennis Amiss 262 n.o.): West Indies 583–9 dec (Lawrence Rowe 120, Roy Fredericks 94, Alvin Kallicharran 93, Bernard Julien 66, Gary Sobers 57)

Bridgetown   Match drawn
England 395 (Tony Greig 148, Alan Knott 87, Bernard Julien 5–57) & 277–7 (Keith Fletcher 129 n.o., Alan Knott 67): West Indies 596–8 dec (Lawrence Rowe 302, Alvin Kallicharran 119, Deryck Murray 53 n.o., Tony Greig 6–164)

Georgetown   Match drawn
England 448 (Tony Greig 121, Dennis Amiss 118, Alan Knott 61): West Indies 198–4 (Roy Fredericks 98)

Caribbean Cricketers

Port of Spain   England won by 26 runs
England 267 (Geoff Boycott 99) & 263 (Geoff Boycott 112): West Indies 305 (Lawrence Rowe 123, Roy Fredericks 67, Clive Lloyd 52, Tony Greig 8–86) & 199 (Tony Greig 5–70)

1974/75
Bangalore   West Indies won by 267 runs
West Indies 289 (Alvin Kallicharran 124, Gordon Greenidge 93, Srinivas Venkataraghavan 4–75, B. S. Chandrasekhar 4–112) & 356–6 dec (Clive Lloyd 163, Gordon Greenidge 107): India 260 (H. S. Kanitkar 65) & 118

New Delhi   West Indies won by an innings and 17 runs
India 220 (P. S. Sharma 54) & 256 (Faroukh Engineer 75, Lance Gibbs 6–76): West Indies 493 (Viv Richards 192 n.o., Clive Lloyd 71, Keith Boyce 68, Erapalli Prasanna 4–147)

Calcutta   India won by 85 runs
India 233 (Gundappa Viswanath 52, Andy Roberts 5–50) & 316 (Gundappa Viswanath 139, Faroukh Engineer 61): West Indies 240 (Roy Fredericks 100, Madanlal 4–22) & 224 (Alvin Kallicharran 57, Bishen Bedi 4–52)

Madras   India won by 100 runs
India 190 (Gundappa Viswanath 97 n.o., Andy Roberts 7–64) & 256 (Anshuman Gaekwad 80, Andy Roberts 5–57): West Indies 192 (Viv Richards 50, Erapalli Prasanna 5–70) & 154 (Alvin Kallicharran 51, Erapalli Prasanna 4–41)

Bombay   West Indies won by 201 runs
West Indies 604–6 dec (Clive Lloyd 242 n.o., Roy Fredericks 104, Alvin Kallicharran 98, Deryck Murray 91, Karsan Ghavri 4–140) & 205–3 dec (Gordon Greenidge 54): India 406 (Eknath Solkar 102, Gundappa Viswanath 95, Sunil Gavaskar 86, Anshuman Gaekwad 51, Lance Gibbs 7–98) & 202 (Brijesh Patel 73 n.o., Vanburn Holder 6–39)

1975
Lahore   Match drawn
Pakistan 199 (Andy Roberts 5–66) & 373–7 dec (Mustaq Mohammad 123, Aftab Baloch 60 n.o., Asif Iqbal 52, Andy Roberts 4–121): West Indies 214 (Alvin Kallicharran 92 n.o., Sarfraz Nawaz 6–89) & 258–4 (Len Baichan 105 n.o., Clive Lloyd 83)

Statistical Appendix

Karachi   Match drawn
Pakistan 406–8 dec (Wasim Raja 107 n.o., Majid Khan 100, Wasim Bari 58) & 256 (Sadiq Mohammad 98 n.o., Asif Iqbal 77): West Indies 493 (Alvin Kallicharran 115, Bernard Julien 101, Roy Fredericks 77, Clive Lloyd 73) & 1–0

1975 (Prudential Cup)
Manchester   West Indies won by 9 wickets
Sri Lanka 86 (Bernard Julien 4–20): West Indies 87–1

Birmingham   West Indies won by 1 wicket
Pakistan 266–7 (Majid Khan 60, Wasim Raja 58, Mustaq Mohammad 55): West Indies 267–9 (Deryck Murray 61 n.o., Clive Lloyd 53, Sarfraz Nawaz 4–44)

Oval   West Indies won by 7 wickets
Australia 192 (Ross Edwards 58, Rodney Marsh 52 n.o.): West Indies 195–3 (Alvin Kallicharran 78, Roy Fredericks 58)

Oval   West Indies won by 5 wickets
New Zealand 158 (Geoff Howarth 51, Bernard Julien 4–27): West Indies 159–5 (Alvin Kallicharran 72, Gordon Greenidge 55)

Lord's   West Indies won by 17 runs
West Indies 291–8 (Clive Lloyd 102, Rohan Kanhai 55, Gary Gilmour 5–48): Australia 274 (Ian Chappell 62, Keith Boyce 4–50)

1975/76
Brisbane   Australia won by 8 wickets
West Indies 214 (Deryck Murray 66, Gary Gilmour 4–42) & 370 (Lawrence Rowe 107, Alvin Kallicharran 101, Deryck Murray 55): Australia 366 (Greg Chappell 123, Alan Turner 81, Lance Gibbs 5–102) & 219–2 (Greg Chappell 109 n.o., Ian Chappell 74 n.o.)

Perth   West Indies won by an innings and 87 runs
Australia 329 (Ian Chappell 156, Michael Holding 4–88) & 169 (Andy Roberts 7–54): West Indies 585 (Roy Fredericks 169, Clive Lloyd 149, Deryck Murray 63, Alvin Kallicharran 57)

Melbourne   Australia won by 8 wickets
West Indies 224 (Roy Fredericks 59, Jeff Thompson 5–62, Denis Lillee 4–56) & 312 (Clive Lloyd 102): Australia 485 (Gary Cosier 109, Ian Redpath 102, Rodney Marsh 56, Greg Chappell 52, Andy Roberts 4–126) & 55–2

Caribbean Cricketers

Sydney   Australia won by 7 wickets
West Indies 355 (Lawrence Rowe 67, Clive Lloyd 51, Max Walker 4-70) & 128 (Deryck Murray 50, Jeff Thomson 6-50): Australia 405 (Greg Chappell 182 n.o., Alan Turner 53) & 82-3

Adelaide   Australia won by 190 runs
Australia 418 (Ian Redpath 103, Gary Gilmour 95, Vanburn Holder 5-108) & 345-7 dec (Alan Turner 136, Ian Redpath 65): West Indies 274 (Keith Boyce 95 n.o., Alvin Kallicharran 76, Jeff Thomson 4-68) & 299 (Viv Richards 101, Keith Boyce 69, Alvin Kallicharran 67)

Melbourne   Australia won by 165 runs
Australia 351 (Ian Redpath 101, Greg Chappell 68, Graham Yallop 57) & 300-3 dec (Rick McCosker 109 n.o., Ian Redpath 70, Greg Chappell 54 n.o.): West Indies 160 (Viv Richards 50, Gary Gilmour 5-34, Denis Lillee 5-63) & 326 (Viv Richards 98, Clive Lloyd 91 n.o., Jeff Thomson 4-80)

1976

Bridgetown   West Indies won by an innings and 97 runs
India 177 (David Holford 5-23) & 214 (Gundappa Viswanath 62, Madanlal 55 n.o.): West Indies 488-9 dec (Viv Richards 142, Clive Lloyd 102, Alvin Kallicharran 93, Roy Fredericks 54, B. S. Chandrasekhar 4-163)

Port of Spain   Match drawn
West Indies 241 (Viv Richards 130, Bishen Bedi 5-82) & 215-8 (Clive Lloyd 70): India 402-5 dec (Sunil Gavaskar 156, Brijesh Patel 115 n.o.)

Port of Spain   India won by 6 wickets
West Indies 359 (Viv Richards 177, Clive Lloyd 68, B. S. Chandrasekhar 6-120, Bishen Bedi 4-73) & 271-6 dec (Alvin Kallicharran 103 n.o.): India 228 (Michael Holding 6-65) & 406-4 (Gundappa Viswanath 112, Sunil Gavaskar 102, Mohinder Amarnath 85)

Kingston   West Indies won by 10 wickets
India 306-6 dec (Anshuman Gaekwad 81 r.h., Sunil Gavaskar 66, Michael Holding 4-82) & 97 (Mohinder Amarnath 59): West Indies 391 (Roy Fredericks 82, Deryck Murray 71, Viv Richards 64, Michael Holding 55, B. S. Chandrasekhar 5-153) & 13-0

1976

Nottingham   Match drawn
West Indies 494 (Viv Richards 232, Alvin Kallicharran 97, Derek Underwood 4-82) & 176-5 dec (Viv Richards 63, John Snow 4-53): England

Statistical Appendix

332 (David Steele 106, Bob Woolmer 82, Wayne Daniel 4–53) & 156–2 (John Edrich 76 n.o.)

Lord's Match drawn
England 250 (Brian Close 60, Andy Roberts 5–60) & 254 (David Steele 64, Andy Roberts 5–63): West Indies 182 (Gordon Greenidge 84, Clive Lloyd 50, Derek Underwood 5–39, John Snow 4–68) & 241–6 (Roy Fredericks 138)

Manchester West Indies won by 425 runs
West Indies 211 (Gordon Greenidge 134, Mike Selvey 4–41) & 411–5 dec (Viv Richards 135, Gordon Greenidge 101, Roy Fredericks 50): England 71 (Michael Holding 5–17) & 126 (Andy Roberts 6–37)

Leeds West Indies won by 55 runs
West Indies 450 (Gordon Greenidge 115, Roy Fredericks 109, Viv Richards 66, Lawrence Rowe 50, John Snow 4–77) & 196 (Collis King 58, Bob Willis 5–42): England 387 (Tony Greig 116, Alan Knott 116) & 204 (Tony Greig 76 n.o.)

Oval West Indies won by 231 runs
West Indies 687–8 dec (Viv Richards 291, Clive Lloyd 84, Roy Fredericks 71, Lawrence Rowe 70, Collis King 63) & 182–0 dec (Roy Fredericks 86 n.o., Gordon Greenidge 85 n.o.): England 435 (Dennis Amiss 203, Alan Knott 50, Michael Holding 8–92) & 203 (Alan Knott 57, Michael Holding 6–57)

1977
Bridgetown Match drawn
Pakistan 435 (Wasim Raja 117 n.o., Majid Khan 88, Joel Garner 4–130) & 291 (Wasim Raja 71, Wasim Bari 60 n.o., Colin Croft 4–47): West Indies 421 (Clive Lloyd 157, Deryck Murray 52) & 251–9 (Viv Richards 92, Roy Fredericks 52, Sarfraz Nawaz 4–79)

Port of Spain West Indies won by 6 wickets
Pakistan 180 (Wasim Raja 65, Colin Croft 8–29) & 340 (Wasim Raja 84, Sadiq Mohammad 81, Majid Khan 54, Andy Roberts 4–85): West Indies 316 (Roy Fredericks 120, Mustaq Mohammad 4–50) & 206–4 (Gordon Greenidge 70, Roy Fredericks 57)

Georgetown Match drawn
Pakistan 194 (Joel Garner 4–48) & 540 (Majid Khan 167, Zaheer Abbas 80, Haroon Rashid 60, Joel Garner 4–100): West Indies 448 (Irvine Shillingford 120, Gordon Greenidge 91, Alvin Kallicharran 72, Viv Richards 50, Majid Khan 4–45) & 154–1 (Gordon Greenidge 96, Roy Fredericks 52 n.o.)

Caribbean Cricketers

Port of Spain   Pakistan won by 266 runs
Pakistan 341 (Mustaq Mohammad 121, Majid Khan 92) & 301-9 dec (Wasim Raja 70, Mustaq Mohammad 56, Sarfraz Nawaz 51): West Indies 154 (Mustaq Mohammad 5-28, Imran Khan 4-64) & 222

Kingston   West Indies won by 140 runs
West Indies 280 (Gordon Greenidge 100, Imran Khan 6-90) & 359 (Roy Fredericks 83, Gordon Greenidge 82): Pakistan 198 (Haroon Rashid 72, Colin Croft 4-49) & 301 (Asif Iqbal 135, Wasim Raja 64)

1978
Port of Spain   West Indies won by an innings and 106 runs
Australia 90 (Colin Croft 4-15) & 209 (Graham Yallop 81, Andy Roberts 5-56): West Indies 405 (Alvin Kallicharran 127, Clive Lloyd 86, Desmond Haynes 61, Jim Higgs 4-91)

Bridgetown   West Indies won by 9 wickets
Australia 250 (Bruce Yardley 74, Graeme Wood 69, Colin Croft 4-47, Joel Garner 4-65) & 178 (Graeme Wood 56, Andy Roberts 4-50, Joel Garner 4-56): West Indies 288 (Desmond Haynes 66, Deryck Murray 60, Jeff Thomson 6-77) & 141-1 (Gordon Greenidge 80 n.o., Desmond Haynes 55)

Georgetown   Australia won by 3 wickets
West Indies 205 (Alvin Greenidge 56, Sew Shivnarine 53, Jeff Thomson 4-57, Wayne Clark 4-64) & 439 (Larry Gomes 101, Basil Williams 100, Sew Shivnarine 63, Derek Parry 51, Wayne Clark 4-124): Australia 286 (Bobby Simpson 67, Steve Rixon 54, Graeme Wood 50, Norbert Phillip 4-75) & 362-7 (Graeme Wood 126, Craig Serjeant 124)

Port of Spain   West Indies won by 198 runs
West Indies 292 (Alvin Kallicharran 92, Basil Williams 87) & 290 (Alvin Greenidge 69, Derek Parry 65, Bruce Yardley 4-40): Australia 290 (Graham Yallop 75, Vanburn Holder 6-28) & 94 (Derek Parry 5-15)

Kingston   Match drawn
Australia 343 (Peter Toohey 122, Graham Yallop 57, Raphick Jumadeen 4-72) & 305-3 dec (Peter Toohey 97, Graeme Wood 90): West Indies 280 (Larry Gomes 115, Sew Shivnarine 53, Trevor Laughlin 5-101) & 258-9 (Alvin Kallicharran 126, Bruce Yardley 4-35)

Statistical Appendix

1978/79

Bombay   Match drawn
India 424 (Sunil Gavaskar 205, Chetan Chauhan 52, Gundappa Viswanath 52, Vanburn Holder 4–94, Sylvester Clarke 4–98) & 224–2 (Chetan Chauhan 84, Sunil Gavaskar 73): West Indies 493 (Alvin Kallicharran 187, David Murray 84, Larry Gomes 63, Derek Parry 55, B. S. Chandrasekhar 5–166)

Bangalore   Match drawn
West Indies 437 (Faoud Bacchus 96, Alvin Kallicharran 71, Sew Shivnarine 62, Larry Gomes 51) & 200–8 (Larry Gomes 82, Karsan Ghavri 5–51): India 371 (Anshuman Gaekwad 87, Dilip Vengsarkar 73, Gundappa Viswanath 70, Sylvester Clarke 5–126)

Calcutta   Match drawn
India 300 (Sunil Gavaskar 107, Kapil Dev 61, Norbert Phillip 4–64) & 361–1 dec (Sunil Gavaskar 182 n.o., Dilip Vengsarkar 157 n.o.): West Indies 327 (Basil Williams 111, Alvin Kallicharran 55, Srinivas Venkataraghavan 4–55) & 197–9 (David Murray 66, Karsan Ghavri 4–46)

Madras   India won by 3 wickets
West Indies 228 (Alvin Kallicharran 98, Kapil Dev 4–38) & 151 (Larry Gomes 91, Srinivas Venkataraghavan 4–43): India 255 (Gundappa Viswanath 124, Norbert Phillip 4–48, Sylvester Clarke 4–75) & 125–7

New Delhi   Match drawn
India 566–8 dec (Kapil Dev 126 n.o., Sunil Gavaskar 120, Dilip Vengsarkar 109, Chetan Chauhan 60): West Indies 172 & 179–3 (Faoud Bacchus 61)

Kanpur   Match drawn
India 644–7 dec (Gundappa Viswanath 179, Anshuman Gaekwad 102, Mohinder Amarnath 101 n.o., Chetan Chauhan 79, Kapil Dev 62): West Indies 452–8 (Faoud Bacchus 250, Raphick Jumadeen 56, Karsan Ghavri 4–118)

1979 (Prudential Cup)

Birmingham   West Indies won by 9 wickets
India 190 (Gundappa Viswanath 75, Michael Holding 4–33): West Indies 194–1 (Gordon Greenidge 106 n.o.)

Oval   Match v Sri Lanka abandoned without a ball bowled
Nottingham   West Indies won by 32 runs
West Indies 244–7 (Clive Lloyd 73 n.o., Gordon Greenidge 65): New Zealand 212–9

Caribbean Cricketers

Oval   West Indies won by 43 runs
West Indies 293-6 (Gordon Greenidge 73, Desmond Haynes 65, Asif Iqbal 4-56): Pakistan 250 (Zaheer Abbas 93, Majid Khan 81)

Lord's   West Indies won by 92 runs
West Indies 286-9 (Viv Richards 138 n.o., Collis King 86): England 194 (Mike Brearley 64, Geoff Boycott 57, Joel Garner 5-38)

Every cricketer who has played in a Test Match for the West Indies
N.B. *A dash after an initial date indicates that the cricketer is still playing, or likely to play again.*

Name	Territory	Duration of Career
Ellis 'Puss' Achong	Trinidad	1929 to 1935
F. C. M. 'Gerry' Alexander	Jamaica	1957 to 1961
Imtiaz Ali	Trinidad	1976
Inshan Ali	Trinidad	1971 to 1977
David Allan	Barbados	1962 to 1966
Nyron Asgarali	Trinidad	1957
Denis Atkinson	Barbados	1948 to 1957
Eric Atkinson	Barbados	1957 to 1959
Richard Austin	Jamaica	1978
Faoud Bacchus	Guyana	1978-
Leonard Baichan	Guyana	1974 to 1976
Arthur Barrett	Jamaica	1971 to 1975
Ivan Barrow	Jamaica	1929 to 1939
Edward Lawson Bartlett	Barbados	1928 to 1931
Nelson Betancourt	Trinidad	1929
Alfie Binns	Jamaica	1953 to 1956
Lionel Birkett	various	1930
Keith Boyce	Barbados	1971 to 1976
Cyril 'Snuffy' Browne	Guyana	1928 to 1930
Basil Butcher	Guyana	1958 to 1969
Lennox 'Bunny' Butler	Trinidad	1955
M. Robin Bynoe	Barbados	1959 to 1966
G. Stephen Camacho	Guyana	1967 to 1971

Statistical Appendix

Name	Territory	Duration of Career
Francis 'Jimmy' Cameron	Jamaica	1948
John Cameron	Jamaica	1939
George Carew	Barbados	1934 to 1939
M. C. 'Joey' Carew	Trinidad	1963 to 1972
George Challenor	Barbados	1928
Herbert Chang	Jamaica	1978
Cyril Christiani	Guyana	1934
Robert Christiani	Guyana	1947 to 1954
C. B. 'Bertie' Clarke	Barbados	1939
Sylvester Clarke	Barbados	1978
Learie Constantine	Trinidad	1928 to 1939
Colin Croft	Guyana	1977–
Oscar Da Costa	Jamaica	1929 to 1935
Wayne Daniel	Barbados	1976
Bryan Davis	Trinidad	1965
Charlie Davis	Trinidad	1968 to 1973
Frank De Caires	Guyana	1929
Clairmont Depeiza	Barbados	1955 to 1956
Tom Dewdney	Jamaica	1955 to 1958
Uton Dowe	Jamaica	1971 to 1973
Richard Edwards	Barbados	1968 to 1969
Wilfred Ferguson	Trinidad	1947 to 1954
M. P. 'Maurice' Fernandes	Guyana	1928 to 1930
T. Michael Findlay	Saint Vincent	1969 to 1973
Maurice Foster	Jamaica	1969 to 1978
George Francis	Barbados	1928 to 1933
Michael Frederick	Jamaica	1953
Roy Fredericks	Guyana	1968 to 1978
Richard Fuller	Jamaica	1934
Hammond Furlonge	Trinidad	1955 to 1956
Andy Ganteaume	Trinidad	1947
Joel Garner	Barbados	1977–
Berkeley Gaskin	Guyana	1947
Glendon Gibbs	Guyana	1955
Lance Gibbs	Guyana	1957 to 1976
Roy Gilchrist	Jamaica	1957 to 1959
George Gladstone	Jamaica	1929
John Goddard	Barbados	1947 to 1957
H. A. 'Larry' Gomes	Trinidad	1976–
Gerry Gomez	Trinidad	1939 to 1954
G. C. 'Jackie' Grant	Trinidad	1930 to 1935

Caribbean Cricketers

Name	Territory	Duration of Career
Rolph Grant	Trinidad	1934 to 1939
Alvin Greenidge	Barbados	1978
C. Gordon Greenidge	Barbados	1974–
Geoff Greenidge	Barbados	1972 to 1973
Mervyn Grell	Trinidad	1929
Charlie Griffith	Barbados	1959 to 1969
Herman Griffith	Barbados	1928 to 1933
S. C. 'Sammy' Guillen	Trinidad	1951 to 1952
Wesley Hall	Barbados	1958 to 1969
Desmond Haynes	Barbados	1978–
George Headley	Jamaica	1929 to 1954
Ron Headley	Jamaica	1973
Jackie Hendriks	Jamaica	1962 to 1969
Teddy Hoad	Barbados	1928 to 1933
Vanburn Holder	Barbados	1969 to 1979
Michael Holding	Jamaica	1975–
David Holford	Barbados	1966 to 1976
John Holt	Jamaica	1953 to 1959
Tony Howard	Barbados	1972
Conrad Hunte	Barbados	1957 to 1967
Errol Hunte	Guyana	1929
Leslie Hylton	Jamaica	1934 to 1939
Hines Johnson	Jamaica	1947 to 1950
Tyrell Johnson	Trinidad	1939
Charles Jones	Guyana	1929 to 1935
Prior Jones	Trinidad	1947 to 1952
Bernard Julien	Trinidad	1973 to 1977
Raphick Jumadeen	Trinidad	1972
Alvin Kallicharran	Guyana	1972
Rohan Kanhai	Guyana	1957 to 1974
Esmond Kentish	Jamaica	1947 to 1954
Collis King	Barbados	1976–
Frank King	Barbados	1953 to 1956
Lester King	Jamaica	1962 to 1968
Peter Lashley	Barbados	1960 to 1966
Ralph Legall	Trinidad	1953
Desmond Lewis	Jamaica	1971
Clive Lloyd	Guyana	1966–
Easton McMorris	Jamaica	1957 to 1966
Clifford McWatt	Guyana	1953 to 1955
Ivan Madray	Guyana	1957
Malcolm Marshall	Barbados	1979–

Statistical Appendix

Name	Territory	Duration of Career
Norman Marshall	Barbados	1955
Roy Marshall	Barbados	1951 to 1952
Frank Martin	Jamaica	1928 to 1931
E. A. 'Manny' Martindale	Barbados	1933 to 1939
Ivor Mendonca	Guyana	1962
Cyril Merry	Trinidad	1933
Roy Miller	Jamaica	1953
George Moodie	Jamaica	1934
David Murray	Barbados	1978–
Deryck Murray	Trinidad	1963–
James Neblett	Barbados/ Guyana	1934
Jack Noreiga	Trinidad	1971
R. Karl Nunes	Jamaica	1928 to 1930
Seymour Nurse	Barbados	1959 to 1969
Albert Padmore	Barbados	1974
Bruce Pairaudeau	Guyana	1953 to 1957
Derek Parry	Nevis	1978–
Clarence Passailaigue	Jamaica	1929
Norbert Phillip	Dominica	1978
Lance Pierre	Trinidad	1947
Allan Rae	Jamaica	1948 to 1953
Sonny Ramadhin	Trinidad	1950 to 1961
Viv Richards	Antigua	1974–
Ken Rickards	Jamaica	1947 to 1952
Clifford Roach	Trinidad	1928 to 1935
Alph Roberts	Saint Vincent	1956
Andy Roberts	Antigua	1974–
Willie Rodriguez	Trinidad	1962 to 1968
Lawrence Rowe	Jamaica	1972 to 1976
Edwin St Hill	Trinidad	1929
Wilton St Hill	Trinidad	1929 to 1930
Reg Scarlett	Jamaica	1959
Alfred Scott	Jamaica	1952
O. C. 'Tommy' Scott	Jamaica	1928 to 1931
Ben Sealey	Trinidad	1931
J. E. Derek Sealy	Barbados	1929 to 1939
John Shepherd	Barbados	1969 to 1971
Grayson Shillingford	Dominica	1969 to 1972
Irvine Shillingford	Dominica	1977 to 1978
Sew Shivnarine	Guyana	1978
Charran Singh	Trinidad	1959

Caribbean Cricketers

Name	Territory	Duration of Career
Joe Small	Trinidad	1928 to 1930
Cameron Smith	Barbados	1960 to 1962
O. G. 'Collie' Smith	Jamaica	1955 to 1959
Gary Sobers	Barbados	1953 to 1974
Joe Solomon	Guyana	1958 to 1965
S. C. 'Charlie' Stayers	Guyana	1962
Jeff Stollmeyer	Trinidad	1939 to 1955
Victor Stollmeyer	Trinidad	1939
Jaswick Taylor	Trinidad	1957 to 1959
John Trim	Guyana	1947 to 1952
Alfred Valentine	Jamaica	1950 to 1962
Vincent Valentine	Jamaica	1933
Clyde Walcott	Barbados	1947 to 1960
Leslie Walcott	Barbados	1929
Chester Watson	Jamaica	1959 to 1962
Everton Weekes	Barbados	1947 to 1958
Kenny Weekes	Jamaica	1939
W. Tony White	Barbados	1965
Claude Wight	Guyana	1928 to 1930
Leslie Wight	Guyana	1953
C. Archie Wiles	Barbados/Trinidad	1933
Elquemedo Willett	Nevis	1973 to 1975
A. Basil Williams	Jamaica	1978
E. A. V. 'Foffie' Williams	Barbados	1939 to 1948
Ken Wishart	Guyana	1934
Frank Worrell	Jamaica	1947 to 1963

Highest partnerships for each wicket

First wicket
239 by Jeff Stollmeyer and Allan Rae v India at Madras, 1948/49

Second wicket
446 by Conrad Hunte and Gary Sobers v Pakistan at Kingston, 1957/58

Third wicket
338 by Everton Weekes and Frank Worrell v England at Port of Spain, 1953/54

Fourth wicket
399 by Gary Sobers and Frank Worrell v England at Bridgetown, 1959/60

Fifth wicket
265 by Seymour Nurse and Gary Sobers v England at Leeds, 1966

Sixth wicket
274 (unbroken) by Gary Sobers and David Holford v England at Lord's, 1966

Seventh wicket
347 by Denis Atkinson and Clairmont Depeiza v Australia at Bridgetown, 1955

Eighth wicket
124 by Viv Richards and Keith Boyce v India at New Delhi, 1974/75

Ninth wicket
122 by David Holford and Jackie Hendriks v Australia at Adelaide, 1968/69

Tenth wicket
98 (unbroken) by Frank Worrell and Wesley Hall v India at Port of Spain, 1962

Individual scores of over two hundred

365 n.o. by Gary Sobers v Pakistan at Kingston, 1957/58

302 by Lawrence Rowe v England at Bridgetown, 1973/74

291 by Viv Richards v England at the Oval, 1976

270 n.o. by George Headley v England at Kingston, 1934/35

261 by Frank Worrell v England at Nottingham, 1950

260 by Conrad Hunte v Pakistan at Kingston, 1957/58

258 by Seymour Nurse v New Zealand at Christchurch, 1969

256 by Rohan Kanhai v India at Calcutta, 1958/59

250 by Faoud Bacchus v India at Kanpur, 1978/79

242 n.o. by Clive Lloyd v India at Bombay, 1974/75

237 by Frank Worrell v India at Kingston, 1953

232 by Viv Richards v England at Nottingham, 1976

226 by Gary Sobers v England at Bridgetown, 1959/60

223 by George Headley v England at Kingston, 1929/30

220 by Clyde Walcott v England at Bridgetown, 1953/54

Caribbean Cricketers

219 by Denis Atkinson v Australia at Bridgetown, 1955
217 by Rohan Kanhai v Pakistan at Lahore, 1959
214 by Lawrence Rowe v New Zealand at Kingston, 1972
209 n.o. by Basil Butcher v England at Nottingham, 1966
209 by Clifford Roach v England at Georgetown, 1929/30
207 by Everton Weekes v India at Port of Spain, 1953
206 by Everton Weekes v England at Port of Spain, 1953/54
201 by Seymour Nurse v Australia at Bridgetown, 1965

Century on debut

176 by George Headley v England at Bridgetown in 1929/30
112 by Andy Ganteaume v England at Port of Spain in 1947/48
115 by Bruce Pairaudeau v India at Port of Spain in 1953
104 by Collie Smith v Australia at Kingston in 1955
142 by Conrad Hunte v Pakistan at Bridgetown in 1957/58
214 and 100 n.o. by Lawrence Rowe v New Zealand at Kingston in 1972
100 n.o. by Alvin Kallicharran v New Zealand at Georgetown in 1972
107 by Gordon Greenidge v India at Bangalore in 1974/75
105 n.o. by Len Baichan v Pakistan at Lahore in 1975
100 by Basil Williams v Australia at Georgetown in 1978

Two separate hundreds in the same match

Clyde Walcott v Australia at Port of Spain in 1955
Clyde Walcott v Australia at Kingston in 1955 (=twice in the same series)
George Headley v England at Georgetown in 1929/30
George Headley v England at Lord's in 1939
Everton Weekes v India at Calcutta in 1948/49
Gary Sobers v Pakistan at Georgetown in 1957/58

Statistical Appendix

Rohan Kanhai v Australia at Adelaide in 1960/61

Lawrence Rowe v New Zealand at Kingston in 1972

Gordon Greenidge v England at Manchester in 1976

Carrying bat through innings

191 n.o. by Frank Worrell v England at Nottingham in 1957

60 n.o. by Conrad Hunte v Australia at Port of Spain in 1965

Most runs in a series

829 by Viv Richards v England in 1976

827 by Clyde Walcott v Australia in 1955

824 by Gary Sobers v Pakistan in 1957/58

Fastest fifty

30 minutes by E. A. V. Williams v England at Bridgetown in 1947/48 (only 2 minutes outside the world record)

Slow scoring

197 n.o. in 682 minutes by Frank Worrell v England at Bridgetown in 1959/60

Century, and five wickets in an innings, in the same match

219 and 5–56 by Denis Atkinson v Australia at Bridgetown in 1955

100 and 5–90 by Collie Smith v India at New Delhi in 1958/59

104 and 5–63 by Gary Sobers v India at Kingston in 1962

174 and 5–41 by Gary Sobers v England at Leeds in 1966

Caribbean Cricketers

Most wickets in a match

14-149 by Michael Holding v England at the Oval in 1976

Most wickets in an innings

9-95 by Jack Noreiga v India at Port of Spain in 1971
8-29 by Colin Croft v Pakistan at Port of Spain in 1977
8-38 by Lance Gibbs v India at Bridgetown in 1962
8-92 by Michael Holding v England at the Oval in 1976
8-104 by Alfred Valentine v England at Manchester in 1950

Hat-tricks

Wesley Hall v Pakistan at Lahore in 1959
Lance Gibbs v Australia at Adelaide in 1960/61

Most balls bowled in a match

774 by Sonny Ramadhin v England at Birmingham in 1957

Most wicket-keeping dismissals in a career

158 by Deryck Murray (at commencement of the recent tour to Australia and New Zealand)

Most dismissals in a series

24 by Deryck Murray v England in 1963
23 by Gerry Alexander v England in 1959/60

Most dismissals in an innings

5 by Gerry Alexander v England at Bridgetown in 1959/60

Statistical Appendix

5 by Deryck Murray v England at Leeds in 1976
5 by Deryck Murray v Pakistan at Georgetown in 1977

Most catches in a career (not wicket-keeper)

110 by Gary Sobers

Youngest players

17 years and 122 days by Derek Sealy v England at Bridgetown in 1929/30
17 years and 245 days by Gary Sobers v England at Kingston in 1953/54
18 years and 32 days by Robin Bynoe v Pakistan at Lahore in 1959
18 years and 105 days by Jeff Stollmeyer v England at Lord's in 1939
18 years and 173 days by Alph Roberts v New Zealand at Auckland in 1956

Oldest player on debut

40 years and 345 days by Archibald Wiles v England at Manchester in 1933

Oldest player

44 days and 236 days by George Headley v England at Kingston in 1953/54

Highest totals (for)

790–3 dec v Pakistan at Kingston in 1957/58
687–8 dec v England at the Oval in 1976
681–8 dec v England at Port of Spain in 1953/54
652–8 dec v England at Lord's in 1973

Highest totals (against)

849 by England at Kingston in 1929/30

Caribbean Cricketers

758–8 dec by Australia in Kingston in 1955
668 by Australia at Bridgetown in 1955
657–8 by Pakistan at Bridgetown in 1957/58
650–6 dec by Australia at Bridgetown in 1965

Lowest completed totals (for)

76 v Pakistan at Dacca in 1959
77 v New Zealand at Auckland in 1956
78 v Australia at Sydney in 1951/52
86 v England at the Oval in 1957
89 v England at the Oval in 1957

Lowest completed totals (against)

71 by England at Manchester in 1976
74 by New Zealand at Dunedin in 1956
82 by Australia at Adelaide in 1951/52
90 by Australia at Port of Spain in 1978

Captain in most matches

39 by Gary Sobers
29 by Clive Lloyd
22 by John Goddard
18 by Gerry Alexander
15 by Frank Worrell
14 by Jeff Stollmeyer
13 by Rohan Kanhai
12 by Jackie Grant
9 by Alvin Kallicharran
7 by Denis Atkinson

Index of Names

ABID ALI (India) 178, 186
Achong, E. (Trinidad) 22, 64
Adcock, N. A. T. (South Africa) 174
Adhikari, H. R. (India) 81, 135
Agha Zahid (Pakistan) 172
Alexander, F. C. M. 'Gerry' (Jamaica) 63, 73, 83, 83–93, 101, 102, 109, 119–21, 143, 155, 160, 191
Alim-ud-din (Pakistan) 117
Allan, D. W. (Barbados) 131, 143, 144
Allen, D. (England) 96, 101
Allen, G. O. 'Gubby' (England) 47, 64, 65
Allen, J. C. (Montserrat) 195
Amar Singh (India) 58
Amarnath, L. (India) 75, 76, 78
Amarnath, M. (India) 165, 188
Ames, L. E. G. (England) 15, 20, 21, 29
Amiss, D. L. (England) 169, 170, 175, 190, 194
Archer, K. (Australia) 68
Archer, R. G. (Australia) 43, 52, 79
Armstrong, W. W. (Australia) 8
Asgarali, N. (Trinidad) 63
Asif Iqbal (Pakistan) 176, 185
Astill, W. E. (England) 10, 12, 203
Atkinson, D. (Barbados) 43, 76, 80, 82, 83, 86, 144
Atkinson, E. (Barbados) 83, 119, 144
Austin, H. B. G. (Barbados) 3, 5, 6, 8, 9, 11
Austin, R. A. (Jamaica) 195

BACCHUS, S. F. A. (Guyana) 197, 213
Bacher, A. (South Africa) 210
Baichan, L. (Guyana) 160, 182
Bailey, T. E. (England) 40, 44, 52, 54, 67, 80, 83, 84, 107, 110, 114, 122
Bakewell, A. H. (England) 21
Banerjee, S. N. (India) 78, 203
Banerjee, Sunil (India) 48, 76, 203
Barber, R. W. (England) 32, 131
Bardsley, W. (Australia) 195
Barlow, E. J. (South Africa) 210
Barnes, S. G. (Australia) 41
Barnett, C. J. (England) 21
Barrington, K. E. (England) 95, 100
Barrow, I. (Jamaica) 29, 30, 34, 57, 87, 155
Bartlett, E. L. (Barbados) 35
Bedi, B. S. (India) 106, 161, 164, 182, 183, 188, 209
Bedser, A. V. (England) 40, 59, 68
Benaud, R. (Australia) 43, 52, 72, 73, 90–2, 101, 102, 112, 121, 128, 129, 141, 209
Bennett, R. A. (patron) 6
Berry, R. (England) 50, 59
Binns, A. P. (Jamaica) 79, 83, 87, 155
Birkett, L. S. (various) 35
Bland, C. (South Africa) 157
Bonaparte, Shirley-Ann (Trinidad) 203
Booth, B. C. (Australia) 131, 139
Borde, C. G. (India) 81, 97, 119
Bowes, W. E. (England) 30
Boyce, K. D. (Barbados) 166, 168, 169, 171, 174, 187, 198, 210
Boycott, G. (England) 32, 114, 132, 147, 169, 170, 179, 200
Brackley, Lord (patron) 6

253

Caribbean Cricketers

Bradman, D. G. (Australia) 8, 19, 20, 23–5, 27–9, 46, 69, 89, 95, 103, 111, 152, 179, 189, 190, 209, 214
Brearley, J. M. (England) 200
Brookes, D. B. (England) 77
Browne, Beverley (Trinidad) 203
Browne, C. R. 'Snuffy' (Guyana) 10–12, 27, 33
Burge, P. J. (Australia) 73, 93
Burke, J. W. (Australia) 41
Burton, W. J. (Guyana) 6
Butcher, B. F. (Guyana) 2, 55, 95, 96, 103, 104, 108, 109, 114, 132, 134, 136, 138–42, 146–8, 153, 189
Butler, H. J. (England) 65
Bynoe, M. R. (Barbados) 63, 109

CALTHORPE, F. S. G. (England) 10, 15, 18, 27
Camacho, G. S. (Guyana) 153, 154, 177, 178, 182
Carew, G. A. (Barbados) 29, 39, 57, 58
Carew, M. C. 'Joey' (Trinidad) 137, 143, 151, 153, 154, 177, 182
Challenor, G. (Barbados) 6–13, 27, 32, 56, 149, 212
Chandrasekhar, B. S. (India) 97, 106, 126, 133, 137, 157, 161, 164, 175, 181–3, 188, 203
Chapman, A. P. F. (England) 10, 15, 19
Chappell, G. S. (Australia) 160, 171, 178, 181, 183, 187, 188, 194
Chappell, I. M. (Australia) 133, 148, 150, 153, 159, 160, 173, 174, 181, 187, 194
Chauhan, C. P. (India) 199
Chowdhury, N. (India) 75
Christiani, C. M. (Guyana) 22, 30, 34, 76, 87
Christiani, R. J. (Guyana) 39, 76
Cipriani, A. (Trinidad) 11
Clark, E. W. 'Nobby' (England) 16, 21, 29
Clark, W. (Australia) 196, 197
Clarke, C. B. (Barbados) 23
Clarke, S. T. (Barbados) 198, 210, 213
Close, D. B. (England) 95, 105, 107, 123, 173
Compton, D. C. S. (England) 68, 109, 209
Connolly, A. N. (Australia) 153
Constantine, L. N. (Trinidad) 2, 6, 10, 12–19, 21, 26, 29, 33, 38, 39, 49, 50, 77, 79, 105, 119, 159, 166, 205, 206
Constantine, L. S. (Trinidad) 5–7, 12, 14, 204

Contractor, N. J. (India) 118, 122
Copson, W. H. (England) 30
Cosier, G. J. (Australia) 195, 198
Cowdrey, M. C. (England) 43–4, 72, 89, 94–7, 100, 101, 104, 105, 114, 119, 120, 123, 132, 139, 147
Cowper, R. M. (Australia) 124, 131
Cox, G. B. Y. (Barbados) 3
Cox, P. J. (Barbados) 4, 5
Cranston, K. (England) 39, 64, 76
Croft, C. E. (Guyana) 2, 171, 173, 174, 176, 192, 195, 198, 200, 207, 210
Cumberbatch, B. A. (Trinidad) 6, 204

DANIEL, W. W. (Barbados) 123, 169, 170, 175, 176, 192, 210, 213
Davidson, A. K. (Australia) 72, 90–3, 101, 102, 111, 121, 136, 141, 174, 183
Davis, B. A. (Trinidad) 137, 142
Davis, C. A. (Trinidad) 150, 154
De Caires, F. I. (Guyana) 27, 35
Denness, M. H. (England) 170
Denton, D. (Yorkshire) 8
Depeiza, C. (Barbados) 79, 82, 83, 87, 203
Dewdney, T. (Jamaica) 84, 100, 120
Dewes, J. G. (England) 40, 68
Dewhurst, G. (Trinidad) 11, 34
Dexter, E. R. (England) 95, 100, 101, 122
Doggart, G. H. G. (England) 67
D'Oliveira, B. L. (England) 114, 139
Dollery, H. E. 'Tom' (England) 67
Dooland, B. (Nottinghamshire) 149
Dorset, Duke of (patron) 13, 212
Douglas, J. W. H. T. (Essex) 10
Dowe, U. (Jamaica) 155
Duff, R. A. (Australia) 184

EDRICH, J. H. (England) 132, 173
Edrich, W. J. (England) 49, **59, 67**
Edwards, R. M. (Barbados) 155
Edwards, R. (Australia) 187
Elliott, G. (pioneer) 3
Emmett, T. (Yorkshire) 205
Engineer, F. M. (India) 97, 170, 172
Evans, T. G. (England) 39, 67, 68, 78, 108

FAGG, A. E. (umpire) 152
Fairfax, A. G. (Australia) 20
Fairweather, E. 'Peggy' (Jamaica) 203
Farnes, K. (England) 24, 29
Favell, L. E. (Australia) 78, 121, 128
Fazal Mahmood (Pakistan) 81, 88, 98, 109, 110, 113, 119

Index of Names

Fender, P. G. H. (Surrey) 10
Ferguson, W. (Trinidad) 39, 64, 65, 76, 77, 129
Fernandes, M. P. (Guyana) 9, 12, 16, 25, 150
Ferris, J. J. (Australia) 5
Findlay, T. M. (Saint Vincent) 155
Fletcher, K. W. R. (England) 168
Forbes, C. (Nottinghamshire) 149
Foster, M. L. C. (Jamaica) 186, 187
Francis, G. N. (Barbados) 2, 8-12, 14-16, 18-21, 66, 206
Frederick, M. (Jamaica) 62
Fredericks, R. C. (Guyana) 2, 32, 55, 56, 138, 146, 153, 154, 161, 162, 164, 165, 167, 170, 177-80, 182-5, 187-90, 192, 196
Freeman, A. P. 'Tich' (England) 15, 20, 32, 203
Furlonge, H. (Trinidad) 62, 63

GAEKWAD, A. (India) 170, 172, 174
Gaekwad, D. K. (India) 81
Ganteaume, A. (Trinidad) 39, 57, 63
Garner, J. (Barbados) 173, 176, 192, 195, 198, 200, 210, 213
Gavaskar, S. M. (India) 149, 156, 161, 170, 174, 186, 188, 195, 196, 199, 212
Ghavri, K. (India) 164, 190, 197
Ghulam Ahmed (India) 48, 75, 76
Gibbs, L. R. (Guyana) 2, 72, 73, 86, 92-4, 96, 97, 103, 121, 126-34, 140, 148, 161, 166, 170, 171, 187, 199, 209
Gilbert, E. (Queensland) 205
Gilchrist, R. (Jamaica) 72, 86-91, 107, 108, 117-20, 125, 126, 144, 172, 174
Gilmour, G. J. (Australia) 160, 161, 165, 181, 183, 188
Gleeson, J. W. (Australia) 126, 133, 143, 151, 158
Goddard, J. D. C. (Barbados) 31, 37-9, 41, 55, 57, 58, 60, 65, 66, 68, 69, 74-6, 80, 82, 83, 86, 88, 160
Goddard, T. W. (England) 36
Gomes, H. A. 'Larry' (Trinidad) 183, 191, 197, 198
Gomez, G. E. (Trinidad) 41, 48, 49, 60, 65, 67, 68, 71, 75, 76
Goodman, P. (Barbados) 5-7
Grace, W. G. (London County) 1, 4, 6, 25, 203
Grant, G. C. 'Jackie' (Trinidad) 17, 19-21, 30, 34, 35, 87
Grant, R. S. (Trinidad) 30, 35, 203

Graveney, T. W. (England) 44, 78, 104, 105, 114, 131, 132
Greenidge, A. T. (Barbados) 197
Greenidge, C. G. (Barbados) 2, 32, 56, 159, 162, 164, 165, 180-5, 187, 189, 192, 196, 197, 199, 200, 212, 213
Greenidge, G. A. (Barbados) 154, 178, 193
Gregory, J. M. (Australia) 9, 15, 122
Gregory, S. E. (Australia) 195
Greig, A. W. (England) 163, 179, 180, 189, 190, 194
Griffith, C. C. (Barbados) 2, 94, 95, 99, 103, 117, 120, 122-6, 130, 131, 134, 148, 155, 174, 175, 191
Griffith, H. C. (Barbados) 2, 11, 14, 15, 18-21, 33, 66
Griffith, S. (Warwickshire) 165
Griffith, S. C. 'Billy' (England) 57, 65, 75
Grimmett, C. V. (Australia) 28
Grout, A. T. W. (Australia) 73, 91, 93, 120, 121, 128, 129
Guillen, S. C. (Trinidad/New Zealand) 60, 80, 83, 87
Gunn, G. (England) 19, 27
Gupte, S. P. (India) 42, 69, 81, 88, 93, 99, 108, 109
Guy, J. W. (New Zealand) 80

HALL, W. W. (Barbados) 2, 72, 86, 88-91, 94, 96, 99, 100-2, 108, 112, 116-26, 129-31, 134, 144, 148, 155, 168, 172, 174, 191, 211
Hallows, C. (England) 15
Hammond, J. R. (Australia) 178, 187
Hammond, W. R. (England) 10, 11, 12, 15, 19, 21, 22, 29, 36, 190
Hampshire, J. H. (England) 148
Hanif Mohammad (Pakistan) 54, 81, 88, 89, 117
Hardstaff, J. (England) 65, 77
Haroon Rashid (Pakistan) 176, 185
Harris, Lord (Kent) 6
Harvey, R. N. (Australia) 52, 69, 79, 84, 102, 111, 120, 121, 128, 190
Hassett, A. L. (Australia) 41, 68, 69
Hastings, B. F. (New Zealand) 153
Hawke, N. J. N. (Australia) 96, 113, 137
Hawke, Lord (patron) 3, 5
Hayes, F. C. (England) 170
Haynes, D. L. (Barbados) 196, 197, 199, 200, 204
Hazare, V. S. (India) 70, 78
Headley, G. A. (Jamaica) 1, 17, 19, 21, 22,

255

Caribbean Cricketers

24–31, 33, 34, 36, 39, 46, 47, 75, 109, 179, 186, 205–7, 209, 211
Headley, R. G. A. (Jamaica/Worcestershire) 31, 32, 179
Heine, P. (South Africa) 174
Hendren, E. 'Patsy' (England) 13, 17, 19, 20, 22, 29
Hendriks, J. L. (Jamaica) 83, 87, 112, 131, 143, 144, 155
Higgs, J. (Australia) 196
Higgs, K. (England) 104, 105, 137, 142
Hill, C. (Australia) 24, 196
Hilton, M. J. (England) 68
Hoad, E. L. G. (Barbados) 27
Hobbs, J. B. (England) 8, 10, 15, 18, 23, 56, 66
Holder, V. A. (Barbados) 2, 155, 161, 168–70, 172, 174, 175, 191, 196, 199
Holding, M. A. (Jamaica) 2, 123, 149, 166, 169–71, 173–6, 191, 192, 198, 199, 204, 205, 210, 212
Holford, D. A. J. (Barbados) 96, 104, 144, 145, 195
Hollies, W. E. (England) 50, 59
Holmes, E. R. T. (England) 22
Holmes, P. (Yorkshire) 10, 12
Holt, J. K. (Jamaica) 43, 61–3, 79, 81, 84, 99, 109, 118, 135, 136
Hordern, H. V. (Philadelphia) 3
Howorth, R. (England) 65
Hunte, C. C. (Barbados) 2, 56, 63, 81, 86, 87, 89, 91, 92, 95–9, 103, 110–14, 134–9, 142, 154, 158, 178, 196
Hunte, E. A. C. (Guyana) 27, 33, 34, 204
Hutton, L. (England) 36, 47, 49, 54, 65–8, 71, 77, 78, 98, 135, 208, 209
Hylton, L. G. (Jamaica) 21, 22, 206

IKIN, J. T. (England) 64, 65
Illingworth, R. (England) 114, 148
Imran Khan (Pakistan) 184, 185
Imtiaz Ahmed (Pakistan) 81, 98, 117, 128
Ince, H. (Barbados) 9
Inshan Ali (Trinidad) 156, 163
Insole, D. J. (England) 68, 72
Intikhab Alam (Pakistan) 182
Iverson, J. (Australia) 126

JACKSON, A. A. (Australia) 19
Jahangir Khan (India) 58
Jaisimha, M. L. (India) 132
Jameson, J. A. (Warwickshire) 152
Jardine, D. R. (England) 16, 21

Jarvis, T. W. (New Zealand) 163
Jenkins, R. O. (England) 67
Jenner, T. J. (Australia) 163
Jessop, G. L. (Gloucestershire) 4, 95, 201
John, G. (Trinidad) 9, 10, 12, 205, 212
Johnson, H. H. (Jamaica) 40, 65, 77, 78
Johnson, H. L. (Derbyshire) 149
Johnson, I. W. (Australia) 43, 60, 69, 82
Johnston, W. A. (Australia) 41–3, 69
Jones, C. M. (Guyana) 29
Jones, I. J. (England) 133
Jones, P. E. (Trinidad) 65, 75, 77, 78
Julien, B. D. (Trinidad) 166–9, 174, 179, 183
Jumadeen, R. (Trinidad) 197, 199

KALLICHARRAN, A. I. (Guyana) 2, 55, 113, 146, 159, 161–6, 170, 178, 180–4, 189, 192, 195–9, 211, 214
Kanhai, R. B. (Guyana) 2, 26, 32, 35, 55, 63, 74, 81, 84–8, 90, 92, 98, 99, 102, 103, 105, 107–15, 121, 129, 134–6, 138, 139, 141–3, 146, 147, 150–3, 158–60, 166, 169, 178–80, 186, 193, 208, 209, 211
Kapil Dev (India) 197
Kardar, A. H. (Pakistan) 128
Kelleway, C. (Australia) 195
Kentish, E. S. M. (Jamaica) 78
Kilner, R. (Yorkshire) 10, 12
King, C. L. (Barbados) 191, 192, 200
King, F. H. (Barbados) 78, 84
King, L. A. (Jamaica) 117, 122
Kippax, A. F. (Australia) 19
Kirmani, S. M. H. (India) 183
Kline, L. (Australia) 90, 92, 120, 141
Knight, B. R. (England) 140, 148
Knott, A. P. E. (England) 132, 140, 163, 173, 189, 194
Kunderan, B. K. (India) 132

LAKER, J. C. (England) 44, 51, 59, 64, 67, 80, 108, 123, 126, 128
Langridge, James (England) 33
Larwood, H. (England) 24, 29, 32, 174
Lashley, P. D. (Barbados) 114
Latchman, H. (Middlesex) 149
Lawry, W. M. (Australia) 96, 124, 131, 133, 142, 148
Layne, O. H. 6, 7
Legall, R. (Trinidad) 87
Lewis, D. (Jamaica) 154, 155
Leyland, M. (England) 17, 19, 22, 29
Lillee, D. K. (Australia) 113, 160, 161,

Index of Names

164–6, 172–4, 181–3, 187, 188, 194, 198
Lindwall, R. R. (Australia) 41, 42, 52, 59, 60, 69, 75, 79, 88, 101, 118, 122, 198
Livingstone, A. D. (Hampshire) 149
Lloyd, C. H. (Guyana) 2, 26, 55, 105, 106, 130, 133, 137, 146, 152, 155, 157–62, 164–6, 170, 178, 181–4, 186–92, 195, 197, 199, 200, 209, 211, 212, 214
Loader, P. J. (England) 44, 80
Lock, G. A. R. (England) 31, 51, 71, 78, 80, 84, 110, 123
Lucas, R. Slade (patron), 3
Luckhurst, B. W. (England) 170

MACARTNEY, C. G. (Australia) 8, 195
MacGibbon, A. R. (New Zealand) 83
Mackay, K. (Australia) 73, 90, 92, 112, 128, 129
McCabe, S. J. (Australia) 19
McCarthy, C. (South Africa) 174
McCool, C. L. (Somerset) 149
McCosker, R. B. (Australia) 173
McDonald, C. C. (Australia) 52, 72, 90, 91, 93, 102, 120, 121
McDonald, E. A. (Australia) 9, 15, 122, 174
McGregor, S. N. (New Zealand) 83, 84
McKenzie, G. D. (Australia) 96, 113, 131, 137, 143, 148, 151, 177, 209
McMorris, E. A. D. (Jamaica) 100, 136, 141
McWatt, C. A. (Guyana) 62, 79, 83, 87
Madanlal (India) 164, 182, 188
Mahmood Hussain (Pakistan) 98, 108
Mailey, A. A. (Australia) 129
Majid Khan (Pakistan) 58, 164, 174, 176, 185, 191, 200
Maka, E. S. (India) 78
Manjrekar, V. L. (India) 42, 70, 118, 130
Mankad, V. (India) 42, 58, 69, 70, 77, 78, 81
Marriott, C. S. 'Father' (England) 16, 17, 21, 33, 203
Marsh, R. W. (Australia) 171, 194
Marshall, M. D. (Barbados) 210
Marshall, R. E. (Barbados/Hampshire) 60, 76, 149
Martin, F. R. (Jamaica) 12, 19, 28, 32, 34, 206, 207
Martin, J. W. (Australia) 128
Martindale, E. A. (Barbados) 2, 14, 16, 17, 20–2, 50, 66, 77, 119, 149, 211
May, P. B. H. (England) 43, 44, 72, 78, 103, 110
Mayne, L. (Australia) 144

Meckiff, I. (Australia) 91, 101, 141
Mendonca, I. (Guyana) 112, 143
Merchant, V. M. (India) 56
Milburn, C. (England) 104, 131
Miller, K. R. (Australia) 41–3, 52, 59, 60, 68, 75, 78, 79, 84, 88, 101, 118, 122, 126, 174, 208, 209
Miller, L. S. M. (New Zealand) 83
Misson, F. M. (Australia) 93, 129
Modi, R. (India) 58, 75
Mohammad Nissar (India) 58
Morales, C. A. (Jamaica) 12
Morris, A. R. (Australia) 41, 69, 78, 84
Morris, S. (Jamaica/Australia) 3, 215
Moss, A. E. (England) 101
Murdoch, W. L. (Australia) 8
Murray, D. A. (Barbados) 198, 213
Murray, D. L. (Trinidad) 2, 134, 143, 144, 155, 160–2, 166, 172, 190–2, 198, 200, 214
Murray, J. T. (England) 105
Mustaq Ali (India) 56, 78
Mustaq Mohammad (Pakistan) 119, 172, 176, 185, 191
Mynn, A. (Kent) 116

NAIK, S. (India) 172
Nash, M. (Glamorgan) 150
Nasimul Ghani (Pakistan) 54, 88, 99, 119
Nichols, M. S. (England) 21
Noreiga, J. (Trinidad) 156
Norfolk, Duke of (patron) 208, 209
Nunes, R. K. (Jamaica) 9, 12, 32, 155
Nurse, S. M. (Barbados) 92, 96, 100, 103, 104, 111, 113, 134, 139, 141–3, 146, 150, 153, 158, 191

O'KEEFE, K. (Australia) 163
Old, C. M. (England) 183
Ollivierre, C. A. (Saint Vincent) 4–6, 8, 12, 13, 56, 59, 149, 155, 212
Ollivierre, R. C. (Saint Vincent) 6, 8
O'Neill, N. C. (Australia) 91, 92, 120, 121, 128, 131

PACKER, K. (patron) 61, 146, 177, 193–6, 199, 200, 212, 214, 215
Paine, G. (England) 22, 30
Pairaudeau, B. H. (Guyana) 50, 61–3, 153
Palairet, R. C. N. (Somerset) 3
Parkhouse, W. G. A. (England) 67, 68, 77
Parks, J. M. (England) 89, 101, 132
Parry, D. R. (Nevis) 199, 213

Caribbean Cricketers

Pascall, V. (Trinidad) 10, 14
Passailaigue, C. C. (Jamaica) 26
Pataudi, Nawab of, Snr (England) 206
Pataudi, Nawab of, Jnr (India) 115
Patel, B. (India) 161, 174, 188, 190
Peel, R. (Yorkshire) 126, 205
Perrin, P. A. (Essex) 4
Phadkar, D. (India) 48, 51, 58, 77, 109
Phillip, N. (Dominica) 198, 210, 213
Philpott, P. (Australia) 131
Place, W. (England) 65, 77
Pocock, P. I. (England) 133, 163
Pollock, P. M. (South Africa) 210
Pollock, R. G. (South Africa) 210
Ponsford, W. H. (Australia) 19, 28, 56, 111, 152
Prasanna, E. A. S. (India) 97, 106, 149, 154, 164, 181
Priestley, A. (patron) 3
Procter, M. J. (South Africa) 209, 210
Pullar, G. (England) 94, 100

RAE, A. F. (Jamaica) 2, 40, 46, 49, 56–63, 67, 74, 134, 153, 183, 207
Rae, E. A. (Jamaica) 12
Ramadhin, S. (Trinidad) 2; 43–5, 49, 50, 64–74, 80, 83, 85, 87, 106, 110, 118, 126–8, 139, 203, 207
Ramchand, G. S. (India) 70, 109, 118
Rangachari, C. R. (India) 48
Ranjane, V. (India) 102
Ranjitsinhji, K. S. (England) 5, 24, 206
Redmond, R. E. (New Zealand) 57
Redpath, I. R. (Australia) 133, 148, 151, 171, 173, 194
Reid, J. R. (New Zealand) 80, 83, 84
Rhodes, W. (England) 10, 27
Richards, B. A. (South Africa) 209, 210, 212
Richards, I. V. A. (Antigua) 2, 26, 40, 159–62, 165, 166, 174, 179, 181–4, 186–90, 192, 200, 204, 205, 210–14
Richardson, P. E. (England) 44, 72, 117
Richardson, T. (Surrey) 4
Rickards, K. (Jamaica) 77
Ring, D. (Australia) 42, 69
Roach, C. A. (Trinidad) 19, 27, 29, 32, 33, 56, 57, 108
Roberts, A. M. E. (Antigua) 2, 123, 159, 161, 166, 169–76, 182, 183, 187, 191, 192, 195, 198, 205, 207, 210–12
Robertson, J. (England) 39, 64, 65, 77
Rodriguez, W. V. (Trinidad) 113, 136, 144

Root, C. F. (Worcestershire) 10
Rowe, L. G. (Jamaica) 2, 32, 146, 163, 165, 178–83, 189, 213
Roy, P. (India) 42, 70, 81, 118

SADIQ MOHAMMAD (Pakistan) 160, 174, 176, 185, 190
Saeed Ahmed (Pakistan) 81, 99
St Hill, W. (Trinidad) 11, 12, 204, 205
Salim Altaf (Pakistan) 184
Sandham, A. (England) 15, 16, 20, 23
Sardesai, D. N. (India) 129, 150, 151, 155
Sarfraz Nawaz (Pakistan) 160, 164, 172, 184, 190, 191
Scarlett, R. (Jamaica) 128
Scott, O. C. 'Tommy' (Jamaica) 22, 64
Scott, V. J. (New Zealand) 69
Sealy, J. E. D. (Barbados) 29, 30, 34, 47, 87
Selvey, M. M. (England) 184, 189
Sen, P. (India) 48
Serjeant, C. S. (Australia) 198
Shackleton, D. (England) 40, 95, 96, 122, 138
Sharpe, P. J. (England) 123
Shepherd, J. N. (Barbados) 155, 166, 193
Sheppard, D. (England) 44, 45
Shillingford, G. C. (Dominica) 191, 210
Shillingford, I. T. (Dominica) 191, 192, 210
Shivnarine, S. (Guyana) 197
Shuja-ud-din (Pakistan) 110
Simpson, R. T. (England) 67, 68, 77
Simpson, R. B. (Australia) 91, 93, 96, 102, 105, 120, 124, 129, 142, 187, 194, 195, 198
Small, J. A. (Trinidad) 9, 33, 204
Smith, C. W. (Barbados) 136, 137, 204
Smith, C. I. J. (England) 22
Smith, D. V. (England) 44
Smith, H. (England) 15
Smith, M. J. K. (England) 32, 61, 89, 101, 104, 119, 120
Smith, O. G. 'Collie' (Jamaica) 43, 44, 53, 63, 71, 74, 75, 79–83, 85–7, 100, 108, 110, 127, 180, 191, 204, 208
Smith, S. G. (Trinidad) 6–7, 12, 13
Smithson, G. A. (England) 65
Snow, J. A. (England) 105, 142, 147, 158, 178, 183
Sobers, G. S. (Barbados) 2, 6, 26, 30, 31, 38, 44, 52, 54, 63, 70, 71, 73, 74, 81, 84–94, 96–106, 108, 109, 111, 112, 114,

Index of Names

124, 125, 127–44, 146–52, 154, 157, 158, 161, 163, 166, 169, 171, 178–80, 186, 190, 203, 208, 209
Solkar, E. D. (India) 170
Solomon, J. (Guyana) 55, 63, 81, 91, 92, 100, 128, 134, 140, 141
Spofforth, F. R. (Australia) 14
Sproston, S. W. (Guyana) 5
Stackpole, K. R. (Australia) 151, 155
Statham, J. B. (England) 31, 44, 51, 54, 62, 79, 80, 107, 110, 171, 174
Steele, D. S. (England) 165, 173, 175
Stevens, G. T. S. (England) 20
Stoddart, A. E. (Middlesex) 3
Stollmeyer, J. B. (Trinidad) 2, 31, 36, 46, 56–63, 74, 75, 82, 83, 86, 153, 183
Stollmeyer, V. H. (Trinidad) 31, 36
Subba Row, R. (England) 101
Surendranath, R. (India) 109
Surti, R. F. (India) 115
Sutcliffe, B. (New Zealand) 69, 71, 80
Sutcliffe, H. (England) 15, 18, 21, 56
Swanton, E. W. 'Jim' (patron) 208
Swetman, R. (England) 119

TAMHANE, N. S. (India) 81
Tankerville, Earl of (patron) 208
Tarilton, P. H. 'Tim' (Barbados) 9, 10
Tate, M. W. (England) 32
Tayfield, H. J. (South Africa) 126
Taylor, B. R. (New Zealand) 143, 154
Taylor, D. D. (New Zealand) 83
Taylor, H. W. (South Africa) 8
Taylor, J. (Trinidad) 88, 117–19, 144
Tennyson, L. H. (Hampshire) 10, 11, 26
Thoms, G. (Australia) 76
Thomson, J. R. (Australia) 160, 161, 165, 166, 172, 173, 181, 183, 194–7
Titmus, F. J. (England) 95, 104, 131, 132
Townsend, D. C. H. (England) 17, 22
Tremlett, M. F. (England) 77
Trestrail, K. B. (Trinidad) 76
Tribe, G. E. (Northamptonshire) 149
Trim, J. (Guyana) 65, 69, 75, 77, 78
Trueman, F. S. (England) 31, 44, 45, 51, 54, 62, 78, 80, 81, 89, 95, 100, 102, 104, 107, 108, 110, 112, 113, 118, 126, 135, 136, 171, 174, 208
Trumble, H. (Australia) 129
Trumper, V. T. (Australia) 4, 8, 9, 24, 26, 184, 212
Turner, A. (Australia) 173, 187

Turner, G. M. (New Zealand) 162, 178, 180, 209
Tyldesley, E. (England) 10, 15, 18, 19
Tyson, F. H. (England) 174

UMRIGAR, P. R. (India) 70, 93, 112, 118, 122
Underwood, D. L. (England) 140, 165, 173, 184, 194

VALENTINE, A. L. (Jamaica) 2, 46, 49, 50, 64–75, 83–5, 87, 92, 101, 120, 121, 127–9, 133, 207
Vengsarkar, D. (India) 196
Venkataraghavan, S. (India) 149, 154, 178, 181, 203
Verity, H. (England) 30
Viswanath, G. R. (India) 161, 164, 165, 170–2, 182, 188, 199, 212
Voce, W. (England) 19, 20, 24, 33

WADSWORTH, K. J. (New Zealand) 178
Walcott, C. L. (Barbados) 2, 26, 38, 40, 42, 43, 46–55, 62, 74–7, 79, 80, 82, 84–7, 98, 99, 108, 109, 138, 142, 155, 186, 190, 204, 206, 207
Walker, M. H. N. (Australia) 163, 165, 187
Wallis Mathias (Pakistan) 108
Walters, C. F. (England) 21
Walters, K. D. (Australia) 133, 143, 148, 151, 159, 187
Wardle, J. H. (England) 67
Warner, P. F. (Trinidad) 4, 5, 12, 40, 59
Warner, R. S. A. (Trinidad) 4, 5, 12, 87
Washbrook, C. (England) 40, 49, 67, 159
Wasim Bari (Pakistan) 190
Wasim Raja (Pakistan) 164, 176, 190, 191
Watson, C. (Jamaica) 91, 101, 117, 120, 121
Watson, W. (Australia) 82
Watson, W. (England) 78
Wazir Mohammad (Pakistan) 88, 128
Webster, R. V. (Warwickshire) 149, 166
Weekes, E. D. (Barbados) 2, 26, 38, 40, 42, 43, 46–54, 59, 74, 79, 80, 82, 83, 85–7, 109, 138, 186, 188, 190, 206
Weekes, K. H. (Jamaica) 36
White, W. A. (Barbados) 144
Whittaker, Patricia (Barbados) 202
Wight, C. V. (Guyana) 11
Wight, P. B. (Somerset) 149
Williams, A. B. (Jamaica) 197
Williams, E. A. V. (Barbados) 77
Willis, R. G. D. (England) 184

Caribbean Cricketers

Wishart, K. L. (Guyana) 35
Wood, A. (England) 17
Wood, B. (England) 173
Wood, G. (Australia) 198
Woodfull, W. M. (Australia) 19, 24, 56
Woods, J. 'Sammy' (Trinidad) 6, 204, 205
Woods, S. M. J. (Somerset) 3, 203
Woolley, F. E. (Kent) 196
Woolmer, R. A. (England) 173, 194
Worrell, F. M. (Jamaica) 2, 26, 35, 37–50, 56, 59, 62, 63, 71, 74–6, 80, 84–7, 89–96, 100, 103–5, 107, 109–11, 114, 116, 120, 121, 128, 130, 134, 136, 138, 141, 157, 189, 190, 206, 207, 211
Wright, D. V. P. (England) 30, 40, 41
Wright, E. F. (Guyana) 3
Wyatt, R. E. S. (England) 16, 21, 22, 29

YALLOP, G. N. (Australia) 195, 196, 198
Yardley, B. J. (Australia) 196
Yardley, N. W. D. (England) 67, 68

ZAHEER ABBAS (Pakistan) 172, 185, 200